THERE'S LOTS TO SEE IN GEORGIA

THERE'S LOTS TO SEE IN GEORGIA

A Guide to Georgia's State Historic Sites

Edited by Jennifer W. Dickey

The University of Georgia Press
Athens

Athens, Georgia 30602
www.ugapress.org

Designed by Erin Kirk
Illustrations by Anna Forrester
Set in Miller Text
Printed and bound by Sheridan Books

The paper in this book meets the guidelines for permanence and durability of the Committee on Production Guidelines for Book Longevity of the Council on Library Resources.

Most University of Georgia Press titles are available from popular e-book vendors.

Printed in the United States of America
29 28 27 26 25 P 5 4 3 2 1

EU Authorized Representative
Easy Access System Europe—Mustamäe tee 50, 10621 Tallinn, Estonia, gpsr.requests@easproject.com

Library of Congress Cataloging-in-Publication Data

Names: Dickey, Jennifer W., editor.
Title: There's lots to see in Georgia : a guide to Georgia's state historic sites / edited by Jennifer W. Dickey.
Other titles: There is lots to see in Georgia
Description: Athens : The University of Georgia Press, [2025] | "Illustrations by Anna Forrester"—T.p. verso. | Includes bibliographical references and index.
Identifiers: LCCN 2025000611 | ISBN 9780820374024 (hardback ; acid-free paper) | ISBN 9780820374031 (paperback ; acid-free paper) | ISBN 9780820374048 (epub) | ISBN 9780820374055 (pdf)
Subjects: LCSH: Historic sites—Georgia—Guidebooks. | Heritage tourism—Georgia. | Culture and tourism—Georgia.
Classification: LCC F287 .T44 2025 | DDC 975.8—dc23/eng/20250207
LC record available at https://lccn.loc.gov/2025000611

Contents

Acknowledgments

This book, like all such projects, is the work of many hands. The genesis of this project was a request by my mother around 2015 for me to take her to visit all the state historic sites in Georgia. We began slowly, visiting sites that were easy day trips, such as the Chief Vann House, New Echota, Etowah Indian Mounds, the Little White House, and Dahlonega. Sadly, my mother passed away before we could complete our tour. I was shipwrecked by the loss of my mother, who was always a guiding light for me. After a pandemic pause, however, I decided to continue the statewide expedition, along with my partner in crime, Kathy Knapp, who cheerfully accompanies me on all my public history adventures. Somewhere along the way I realized that there was no comprehensive guidebook to the state historic site system, and I decided that I would write one.

Almost simultaneously, our special projects team in the Kennesaw State University Department of Museums, Archives and Rare Books (MARB) negotiated a contract with the Georgia Department of Natural Resources (DNR) to create brochures for the sixteen historic sites that are managed directly by the Georgia State Parks and Historic Sites Division (GSPHSD). James Newberry led the brochure project, and Kelly Hoomes conducted research on each of the sites. Both of them shared materials with me throughout the project. I was the team member designated to visit all the sites to gather information and take photographs, which I began doing in 2022.

As I traveled across the state, I contemplated how I might involve my students in my book project, and my associate chair, David Parker, suggested that I teach a research seminar in which each student would focus on a single site for the duration of the semester. I followed David's advice, and in the fall of 2022, Allison Allen, Izzabella Barrett, Deiah Brue, Hannah Eslinger, Kathryn Graham, Katelyn Gregory, James Mitchum, Nathaniel Perkins, Kari Ramos-Suarez, Seth Rodie, and Donovan Schumpert joined the project as students in my research seminar. Each student "adopted" a site for the semester and took responsibility for researching and writing a draft of what would become a chapter in this book.

Throughout this process, staff at GSPHSD, both in the headquarters office and at the sites, have provided me and my students with a wealth of information. The students, and sometimes I, interviewed interpretive rangers and site managers throughout the system to get an insider's perspective of the sites. To a person, each of these individuals (acknowledged in the footnotes for their interviews and email correspondence) was helpful and generous with their time. The staff at the Georgia Archives were equally helpful. They directed me to useful resources, provided a workshop for my students on how to do archival research, and were generally helpful and cheerful all along the way. Staff at the Zach S. Henderson Library Special Collections at Georgia Southern University were also extremely helpful, providing access to materials related to the Georgia Heritage Trust.

My department chair at Kennesaw State University (KSU), Bryan McGovern, was especially supportive. He encouraged me to apply to the Center for Excellence in Teaching and Learning (CETL) Tenured Faculty Enhancement Program, which allowed me to take a semester's leave from teaching to complete the book manuscript. I am grateful to Bryan, CETL, and the dean of the Radow College of Humanities and Social Sciences for their support through this program.

My dear friends and colleagues Catherine Lewis and David Parker read various iterations of the manuscript and offered helpful suggestions to improve the flow. They also pointed out mistakes, factual or otherwise. I am forever grateful to them for their friendship as well as their interest in and support of this project. Jahni Phillip, my graduate research assistant in fall 2023, researched historical images for the book and compiled spreadsheets of those images. He was a cheerful and enthusiastic presence throughout the project.

Historian Tiya Miles provided great inspiration to me as I embarked on this project. Not only has her work on the Chief Vann House and slavery in the Cherokee Nation been especially illuminating, but she also encouraged

me to say no to outside commitments and to claim my writing time, a process that was necessary for me to complete this book. Anthropologist Thomas Pluckhahn generously agreed to read the chapter on Kolomoki Mounds and provide comments, which were helpful given my thin knowledge of the prehistoric period.

Staff at the University of Georgia Press, especially Nate Holly and Elizabeth Adams, were enthusiastic about this book and encouraged me along the way. They were infinitely patient with the complications that ensued with trying to track down all the student contributors, even after most of those students were long gone from KSU.

My beloved cat, Boomerang, who fancied herself as my research assistant, provided me with no help whatsoever on this book, although she did offer great comfort to me, as pets are inclined to do. She frequently slept atop my research materials in between walks across my keyboard. I was heartbroken by her death in January 2024, although at nineteen years old, she did have a lot of good innings.

Unless otherwise noted, the photographs in this book were taken by me. Kathy Knapp provided the maps.

This book is dedicated to my mother, who first prodded me to embark on this quest to visit all the state historic sites. She remains my inspiration.

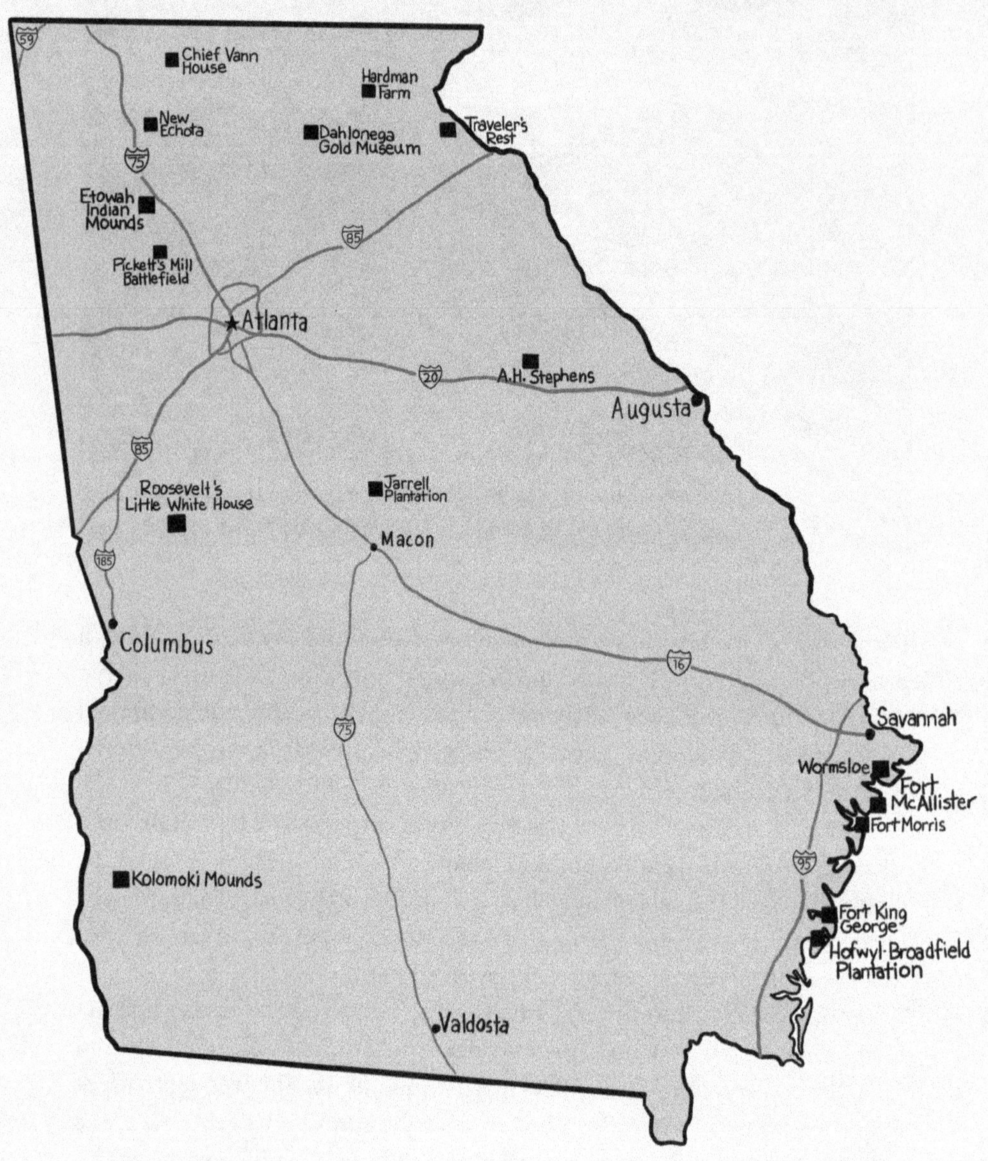

59
Chief Vann House
Hardman Farm
New Echota
Dahlonega Gold Museum
Traveler's Rest
75
Etowah Indian Mounds
85
Pickett's Mill Battlefield
Atlanta
20
A.H. Stephens
Augusta
85
Roosevelt's Little White House
Jarrell Plantation
Macon
185
Columbus
16
75
Savannah
Wormsloe
Fort McAllister
Fort Morris
95
Kolomoki Mounds
Fort King George
Hofwyl-Broadfield Plantation
Valdosta

THERE'S LOTS TO SEE IN GEORGIA

Advertisement from the *Atlanta Constitution* from August 22, 1949.

Introduction

The August 22, 1949, issue of the *Atlanta Constitution* featured on page 13 a full-page advertisement, sponsored by Rich's Department Store, promoting historic sites across the state. "There's Lots to See in Georgia," proclaimed the ad, which described Georgia as "a sightseers paradise . . . [where the] illustrious past is brought to mind by historic ruins and landmarks on every side." Thirty-three sites were highlighted across the state, from the ruins of colonial Fort Frederica in the southeast corner on the coast to the Civil War battlefield at Chickamauga in the northwest corner of the state. Among the sites listed were four locations that were under the auspices of the National Park Service (Chickamauga & Chattanooga National Military Park, Kennesaw Mountain National Battlefield Park, Ocmulgee Mounds National Monument, and Fort Frederica National Monument), three state parks (Providence Canyon, Amicalola Falls, and Indian Springs), and three sites that would become state historic sites (Alexander H. Stephens Memorial, Kolomoki Mounds, and Roosevelt's Little White House).[1]

The advertisement heralding Georgia's cultural and natural wonders appeared two years before Georgia's General Assembly created the Georgia Historical Commission, a state agency charged with "promoting understanding of the history of the state from prehistory to the present, permanently preserving and marking historic sites, publicizing Georgia's history, coordinating the commissions efforts with other agencies—both state and federal—and advising local entities on historical matters."[2] This mission was quite broad and sweeping for an agency with no budget that was made up of five volunteers. The budget question was resolved a year later, when the General Assembly designated funding for the agency, and over the next two decades the Georgia Historical Commission became a "significant state agency" and "gained national recognition as a pioneer in state historic preservation."[3]

The Historical Commission acquired ten historic sites over the next ten years, half of which are still part of the state historic site system. Those sites—Etowah Indian Mounds, Chief Vann House, Traveler's Rest, New Echota, and Fort McAllister—represent a broad swath of history from the tenth century to the nineteenth century.

Although the commission members fervently believed in the value of their work, support from the governor's office for the efforts of the commission was not always guaranteed. A little more than a decade into its existence, commission chairman Joseph B. Cumming wrote to Governor Carl Sanders bemoaning the lack of support provided to the commission and its work by the Department of Industry and Trade, noting that surveys conducted by the Department of Commerce indicated that two out of three tourists coming to Georgia preferred to see "historic sites rather than the other tourist attractions" in the state. The commission viewed "with some alarm what we speak of as the 'Rock City Syndrome' based on the belief that tourists are basically fun-seekers, not serious citizens wishing to gain information and inspiration from the country's past." The state promoted itself as a "sportsman's paradise, a place of natural wonders, mountains and seashore, a 'Fun-land' or 'Vacation-Land,'" wrote Cumming, so that it was "down-graded in its appeal for the tourist dollar so as to appear as a super Disneyland, a place for fun and frolic, not a State which has more history and background of great events and great men than any State in the Union except Virginia." Cumming wanted the "image of Georgia to be rather that of Virginia than that of Florida," noting that the visitors to the state preferred to see historical sites such as those owned and operated by the Historical Commission.[4]

This lack of state support notwithstanding, the Historical Commission acquired seven more sites, three of which—Fort King George, Dahlonega, and Fort Morris—are still owned and operated by the state, before it was disbanded under Governor Jimmy Carter's reorganization of state government plan in the early 1970s.[5] The functions of the commission moved under the Department of Natural Resources in 1973, where they were divided into the Historic Preservation Section, the state agency that carries out the federally mandated functions of the State Historic Preservation Office, and the Parks and Historic Sites Division, the agency responsible for maintenance of the state's parks and historic sites.[6] The State Parks Division had existed since 1931, when it was created to manage the state's first two state parks, Vogel in Blairsville and Indian Springs in Flovilla.[7] As part of his reorganization, Governor Carter created a new entity, the Georgia Heritage Trust, which was charged with "identifying, acquiring, and protecting those valuable, vanishing pockets of the state's heritage."[8]

By the early 1980s, the Heritage Trust had identified "some seventy Hallmark Status Sites," which were sites that had "been determined to have statewide significance, and [were] within the area of interest for State acquisition."[9] Funding for the Heritage Trust Program, which existed for about a decade, peaked at $12.6 million in 1974 and dropped dramatically thereafter. In 1974 the Heritage Trust acquired several sites that would become part of the state historic site system, including Pickett's Mill Battlefield, Jarrell Plantation, Hofwyl-Broadfield Plantation, and Wormsloe.[10] By 1979, as support for heritage preservation and the excitement of the nation's bicentennial celebration began to wane, funding for the program from both the state and federal governments dried up.[11]

The State Historic Preservation Office is now a division of the Department of Community Affairs (DCA), while the state's parks and historic sites remain under the Department of Natural Resources (DNR) in the Georgia State Parks and Historic Sites Division (GSPHSD). GSPHSD manages sixty-three state parks and historic sites on almost 85,000 acres that are open to the public. Those parks and sites received over eleven million visitors in 2022.[12] The state operates sixteen historic sites, three of which—Kolomoki Mounds in Blakely, Fort McAllister in Richmond Hill, and Alexander H. Stephens in Crawfordville—are located in state parks. GSPHSD is responsible for the preservation and interpretation of the cultural and natural resources within these sixteen sites.

All of the sites in this book are listed in the National Register of Historic Places, "the Nation's official list of historic places worthy of preservation."[13] Six of the sites (New Echota, Etowah Indian Mounds, Traveler's Rest, A. H. Stephens State Park, Roosevelt's Little White House, and Kolomoki Mounds) have been designated as National Historic Landmarks—a designation that indicates the site "represents an outstanding aspect of American history and culture."[14]

Some of the sites developed by the Georgia Historical Commission have been handed off to local entities. Among those are three sites that were once part of the state system—the Robert Toombs House in Washington, the Lapham-Patterson House in Thomasville, and the Jefferson Davis Memorial in Fitzgerald. These sites are still included on the GSPHSD website but are not included in this guidebook. The focus of this book is on sites that are owned and operated by the state as part of its state historic site system.

The system provides good coverage of broad swaths of the state's history from the prehistoric period to the mid-twentieth century. The history of human habitation in the area that is today Georgia dates to the Paleoindian period (12000–8000 BCE) toward the end of the last ice age.[15] During the Archaic period (8000–1000 BCE), sedentism increased, as did populations in the region. By the Woodland period (1000 BCE–1000 CE), modern climatic conditions prevailed, and permanently occupied residential and ceremonial sites were developed.[16] This period is interpreted at Kolomoki Mounds in Early County. The subsequent Mississippian period (c. 900–1700 CE), which saw the peak of temple mound construction and the rise of sophisticated political chiefdoms and "large, sedentary population centers," is represented at Etowah Indian Mounds in Bartow County and Hardman Farm in White County.[17]

The early years of the Historic European period (1540 CE to present), which began with the arrival of European explorers in Georgia, is told, in part, at several sites throughout the system, including Etowah Mounds, Fort King George in McIntosh County, and Hardman Farm. The establishment of the Georgia Colony in 1732 and arrival of English settlers in 1733 mark a transformation in Georgia history as it evolves from being "the Debatable Land" between the English colony of South Carolina and the Spanish colony of Florida into part of the British Empire in North America. The story of the precolonial and early colonial periods is interpreted at Fort King George and Wormsloe in Chatham County, while the Revolutionary War (1775–1783) and War of 1812 (1812–1815) stories are presented at Fort Morris in Liberty County.

The state historic site system is rich with nineteenth-century sites, including the Chief Vann House (Murray County), New Echota (Gordon County), and Dahlonega (Lumpkin County), all of which interpret Native American (Cherokee) history and the conflict that arose as white settlers pushed into Cherokee lands in the first half of the nineteenth century. Several plantation sites, Hofwyl-Broadfield in Glynn County, Traveler's Rest in Stephens County, and Jarrell in Jones County, relate stories about the development of farms and commercial enterprises in the first half of the nineteenth century. These sites have recently begun to include in their interpretation stories about the enslaved people who worked at these plantations.

The story of the great cataclysm of the Civil War is featured at A. H. Stephens's Liberty Hall in Taliaferro County, Pickett's Mill Battlefield in Paulding County, and Fort McAllister in Bryan County. Hardman Farm, which incorporates Native American history by virtue of its Mississippian period mound and a remnant of the Cherokee-era Unicoi Turnpike, focuses on agricultural developments in rural Georgia in the late nineteenth and early twentieth centuries. Roosevelt's Little White House in Meriwether County, among the most visited of the state sites, takes visitors from the Great Depression to the end of World War II through the lens of the nation's thirty-second president.

What the state has preserved and the stories told at those places reveal a great deal not only about what happened in the past but about the identity of Georgians and what we value in the present. The ways in which interpretation at these sites has evolved, or, in some cases, not evolved, is also illuminating. Few of the sites focus on women's stories, and none of the sites covered in this book prominently mention African American history. All the plantation sites now include some interpretation of slavery, and efforts have been made to give the names and, in some cases, the faces of the enslaved people who were instrumental in the success of these enterprises. However, there is no site devoted to the modern civil rights movement, a national story that had deep roots in Georgia. This seems to be a glaring omission but is not surprising given the time (1950s–1970s) during which most of the state system was developed. While it seems unlikely that the system will expand given the budget constraints under which it is currently operating, the addition of a site such as the Dorchester Academy in Liberty County, a school for African American students established in 1872 that later became a training center for civil rights leaders, would be a meaningful addition to the state's historic sites system.

Former Dorchester Academy dormitory.

How to Use This Book

This book is intended to serve as a guidebook to Georgia's state historic sites. In addition to a history of the events that happened at each site, the authors provide a brief history of how the site became part of the state system along with basic information about the site's interpretive experience, as well as a list of further reading for anyone interested in learning more about each site or its related topics.

Rather than a chronological or thematic organization, the sites are presented geographically in four sections representing the four regions into which the Department of Natural Resources divides the state—North Georgia Mountains, Piedmont, Coastal Plains, and the Coast. A map indicating the sites within each geographical region is presented along with a short summary of the site or sites in that region at the beginning of each section. The appendix provides a listing of the sites organized thematically according to categories created by GSPHSD.

The GSPHSD website (https://gastateparks.org/) provides current information about opening hours and special events at each of the sites. Readers are encouraged to visit the website for the most up-to-date information. The website provides very little information about the history that happened at each site and no information about how each site came to be part of the state system. The authors hope this book will help fill that gap.

Notes

1. "There's Lots to See in Georgia," *Atlanta Constitution*, August 22, 1949, 13.

2. Jann Haynes Gilmore, "Georgia's Historic Preservation Beginning: The Georgia Historical Commission 1951–1973)," *Georgia Historical Quarterly* 63, no. 1 (Spring 1979): 9.

3. Joseph B. Cumming, "Georgia Historical Commission," *New Georgia Encyclopedia*, last modified April 27, 2013, https://www.georgiaencyclopedia.org/articles/arts-culture/georgia-historical-commission/.

4. Joseph B. Cumming to Carl E. Sanders, December 9, 1963, Georgia Historical Commission—Director's Office—Administrative Records—1952–1964, RCB 9951, 061-01-001, Georgia Archives.

5. Gilmore, "Georgia's Historic Preservation Beginning," 15–20.

6. Elizabeth R. Lyon, "Georgia's Historic Preservation Office: A Brief History," *Georgia Historical Quarterly* 63, no. 1 (Spring 1979): 30.

7. Owen Smith, "2021 Marks 90th Anniversary of Georgia State Parks and Historic Sites," State Parks Blog, accessed January 20, 2023, https://gastateparks.org/state-parks-blog/2021-marks-90th-anniversary-georgia-state-parks-and-historic-sites.

8. Georgia Heritage Trust brochure, n/d, Box 1, Folder 10, G. A. Rogers Papers, "Georgia Heritage Trust Records," Zach S. Henderson Library Special Collections, Georgia Southern Henderson University, Statesboro, Ga.

9. Georgia Heritage Trust brochure.

10. Caleb Pirtle III, "The Sacred Trust of Georgia," *Southern Living*, December 1974, 81.

11. John Reetz, "Heritage Trust Has Rough Days as Funds Dry Up," *Atlanta Journal and Constitution*, November 4, 1979, 2B.

12. "Divisions," Georgia Department of Natural Resources website, accessed January 20, 2023, https://gadnr.org/divisions.

13. National Register of Historic Places, National Park Service website, accessed May 21, 2024, https://www.nps.gov/subjects/nationalregister/index.htm.

14. National Historic Landmarks, National Park Service website, accessed May 21, 2024, https://www.nps.gov/subjects/nationalhistoriclandmarks/index.htm.

15. David G. Anderson, "Paleoindian Period," *New Georgia Encyclopedia*, last modified June 8, 2017, https://www.georgiaencyclopedia.org/articles/history-archaeology/paleoindian-period-overview/.

16. Georgia Department of Transportation, "Cultural History of Georgia," accessed November 11, 2023, https://www.dot.ga.gov/InvestSmart/Environment/CulturalResources/Documents/History/CulturalHistoryOfGeorgia.pdf.

17. Georgia Department of Transportation, "Cultural History of Georgia," accessed November 11, 2023, https://www.dot.ga.gov/InvestSmart/Environment/CulturalResources/Documents/History/CulturalHistoryOfGeorgia.pdf.

REGION 1

The North Georgia Mountains

The North Georgia Mountains region includes the first historic sites acquired by the state in the 1950s, Etowah Indian Mounds and the Chief Vann House, and the most recent acquisition, Hardman Farm, as well as the Dahlonega Gold Museum. All of these sites have a Native American component in their interpretation, and at three of the sites—Etowah Indian Mounds, Chief Vann House, and New Echota—Native American history is the central focus. Etowah Mounds tells the story of the native inhabitants of the Mississippian period (900 to 1700 CE), while the Chief Vann House and New Echota focus on the history of the Cherokee Nation, which existed in northwest Georgia in the late eighteenth and early nineteenth centuries. The discovery of gold in 1828 in the heart of the Cherokee Nation led to the nation's first "notable" gold rush and, a decade later, contributed to Cherokee removal. The Dahlonega Gold Museum tells the story of the discovery of gold in North Georgia and its consequences. Hardman Farm was the summer retreat of Dr. Lamartine Hardman, Georgia's governor from 1927 to 1931. Located at the west end of the Nacoochee Valley, Hardman Farm features remnants of Native American history, including a Mississippian period mound and traces of the Unicoi Turnpike, a Cherokee-era roadway that linked South Carolina to Tennessee through North Georgia.

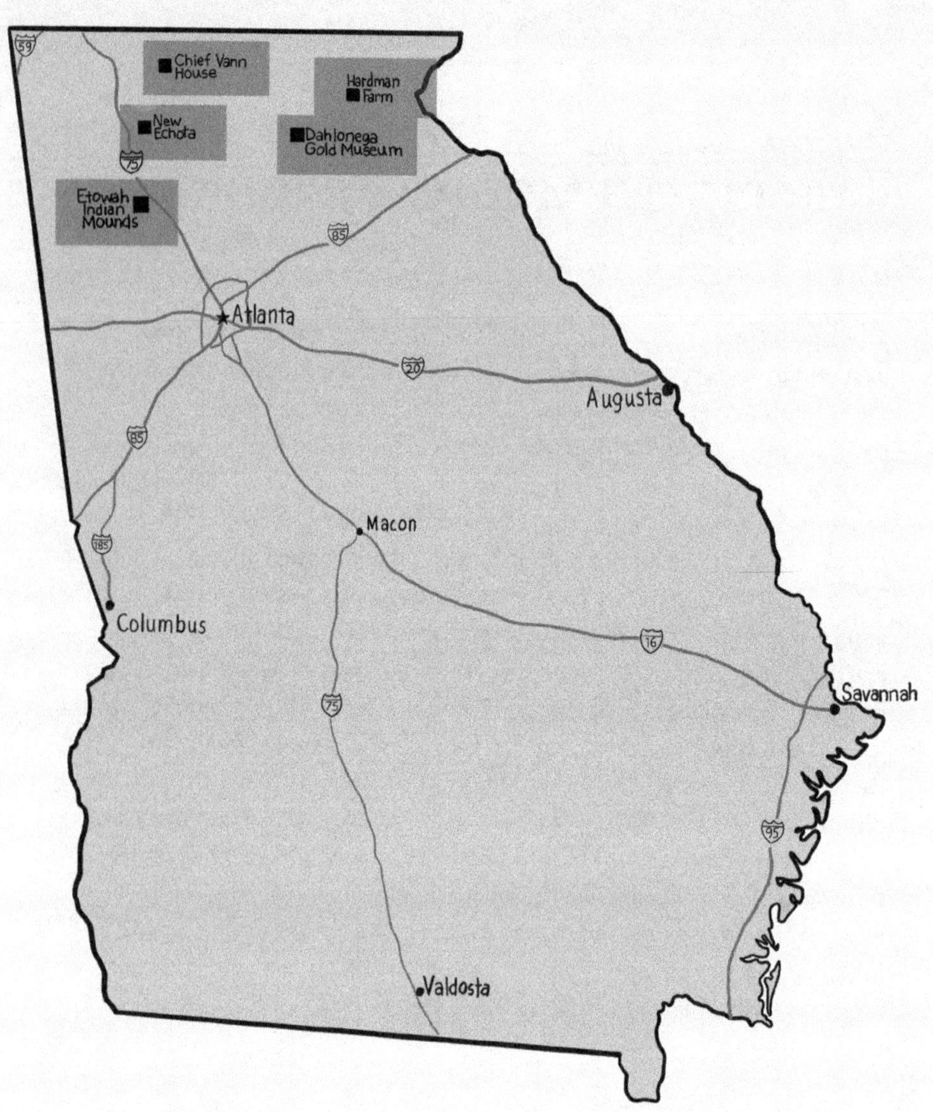

59
Chief Vann House
Hardman Farm
New Echota
Dahlonega Gold Museum
75
Etowah Indian Mounds
85
Atlanta
20
Augusta
85
Macon
185
Columbus
16
Savannah
75
95
Valdosta

CHAPTER 1

Chief Vann House

Donovan Schumpert and Jennifer W. Dickey

Basic Information

PERIOD OF SIGNIFICANCE: c. 1798–1834

DATE ESTABLISHED AS A HISTORIC SITE: 1952

ACREAGE: 137 acres

LOCATION: 82 Highway 225 N, Chatsworth, Ga. 30705, Murray County

Among the first sites acquired by the Georgia Historical Commission in 1952, the Chief Vann House remains a crown jewel of the state historic site system. When nominated for inclusion in the National Register of Historic Places in 1969, the house was described as "the showplace of the Cherokee Nation . . . significant as a mansion house of architectural and historical distinction deep in Indian country."[1] The Vann House plantation, also known as Diamond Hill, was the home of one of the wealthiest Cherokee families as well as more than one hundred enslaved Black people in the early nineteenth century. James Vann established the plantation in the late 1790s, and upon his death in 1809, his son Joseph inherited much of James's property. Diamond Hill served as headquarters for the far-flung business operations of both father and son for more than three decades. At a time when most Cherokee and white settlers in the region were living in log buildings, the Vann family resided in this two-story brick house that demonstrated their wealth and power.

The story of the Vann family in North Georgia came to an end in the 1830s when the Cherokees were forcibly removed to present-day Oklahoma.

Front entrance of the Chief Vann House.

However, the brick house survived into the twentieth century, when it became a focal point for local preservationists keen to see it restored to its former glory. That effort coincided with the state of Georgia's efforts to promote tourism through the acquisition, preservation, and interpretation of historic sites across the state. Acquired by the state in 1952 and opened to the public in 1958, the Chief Vann House, as it would come to be known, was the first historic site owned and operated by the Georgia Historical Commission.

History of the Chief Vann House

The son of Joseph Vann (a Scottish trader) and Wali Vann (the daughter of a white man and a Cherokee woman), James Vann was born around 1768. Joseph and Wali (also spelled Wah-li and Wai-Li) had migrated to Georgia from South Carolina in the early 1760s, settling first along the Savannah River before moving north into Cherokee territory. Moravian missionary accounts indicate that James Vann claimed to be born at a site located about twenty-five miles away from the place where he would later develop one of the largest plantations in the Cherokee Nation.[2] Intermarriage between white traders and Native women was not uncommon as European settlers moved into backcountry areas in the South Carolina and Georgia colonies. According to historian Theda Perdue, the mixed-race children of these unions almost always identified as Indian. Regardless of their appearance, they affiliated with the Native tribes from which their mothers descended and were claimed by their respective tribes as members. Such was the case with James Vann, who identified himself as Cherokee throughout his life and became an important political and business leader within Cherokee society.[3]

Although not much is known about James's childhood, historian Tiya Miles attributes James's mercurial personality and propensity to violence at least partially to the upheaval created by Revolutionary War battles between the Cherokees, who sided with the British, and the Americans. Miles notes that Vann "lived amid war or its aftermath for his entire life." He was "enterprising, clever, bold—but hostage to historical trauma and the personal flaws of arrogance and avarice."[4]

Joseph, Wali, and their three children—Jenny, Nancy, and James—likely settled in North Georgia in the latter years of the American Revolutionary War, and it was there that James would build his fortune. He directly inherited from his father several hundred acres of land and nearly seventy Black slaves, and he also claimed for himself the inheritance of his two sisters as well as his mother. Included in his mother's inheritance, according to Moravian missionary John Gambold, were "19 horses and 15 or 16 heads of cattle," which Vann sold. Each of his sisters inherited an enslaved woman, whom Vann claimed and kept for his own household.[5]

Like his father before him, James Vann established a trading post. To his mercantile operation he added a ferry service on the Conasauga River at a site that became known as Vannsville. Vann was recognized as "a leading character" who was "daily growing in consequence and importance in his nation," according to James Orr in 1798.[6] He acquired additional land and Black enslaved people to work the land on what became one of the largest plantations in the Cherokee territory. By 1800, the plantation, which Vann called Diamond Hill likely because of the large quantity of quartz rock in the soil, extended more than eight hundred acres. Vann invited a group of Moravian missionaries to settle on his land in 1800, not to bring Christianity to the Cherokees but to develop a school where Cherokee children could receive a formal education.[7]

Vann's wealth and power enabled him to persuade the Cherokee Council to allow the U.S. government to build a federal road through Cherokee territory and to negotiate with the U.S. government to route that road through his property. Vann then proceeded to expand his business holdings by developing other businesses, including another ferry and trading post and three taverns along the federal road.[8] He also convinced the U.S. government to allow him to handle U.S. mail distribution along the road. In 1806, Vann was elected to serve on the Cherokee Council, the governing body of the tribe, and by 1808, Vann was considered to be one of the most powerful men in the Cherokee Nation.[9] A sizeable portion of Vann's wealth was the population of enslaved people who lived and worked on his plantation. The enslavement of Black people by the Cherokees was, by the early 1800s, a common practice, especially among the wealthier members of Cherokee society. Miles notes that more than 580 Black people were enslaved within the Cherokee Nation in 1809, with the Vann family accounting for 115 of them. The enslaved population within the Cherokee Nation had almost tripled to 1,592 by 1835.[10]

Polygamy was common among the Cherokees, and although an exact count of James Vann's wives is not known, at least five have been identified, including three sisters, Elizabeth, Mary Polly, and Peggy Scott. The Scott sisters were the daughters of a Cherokee woman (Sarah Hicks) and an English trader (Walter Scott) who had served as assistant commissioner in the Cherokee Nation for the British before and during the Revolutionary War. The Cherokees were a matrilineal society in which men would usually join the family household of their wives; however, in the case of James Vann, the wives joined his household, although most of them did not stay for long. Vann was abusive to his wives, and most of them left of their own accord. By the time the Moravian missionaries arrived in 1801, Vann had two principal wives living in his household, Peggy and one of her older sisters. Peggy would be the only wife who remained with Vann until his death in 1809.[11]

Vann's abusive tendencies were not limited to women. He enslaved more than one hundred people who worked on his plantation, and his brutality toward these workers was well documented by the missionaries who lived nearby. In September 1805, the missionaries recorded that in the aftermath of a robbery of his household by four enslaved people, Vann took his revenge in an especially horrific way by burning to death one of the robbers, an enslaved man named Isaac. Vann killed Bob, another enslaved man who had participated in the robbery, and tortured two other enslaved people, Peter and April, and a white girl, Crawford, whom he suspected were coconspirators. While the manhunt for the robbers was underway, Vann vented his rage by repeatedly beating and torturing other enslaved people on his plantation.[12]

Much of what we know about Vann comes from the records of the Moravian missionaries whom Vann invited to settle on his property in an area known as Spring Place in 1800. The Moravian Church, headquartered in North Carolina, began petitioning the Cherokees for permission to establish a mission in Cherokee territory in the 1780s, but it was not until 1799, when James Vann attended a Cherokee Council meeting at which Moravian envoys pled their case, that the missionaries gained any traction. Although he was not the least bit interested in Christian conversion for himself or the Cherokee people, Vann was concerned about education. He met privately with the missionaries and offered to provide them with land for their mission if they would operate a school in addition to their church.

By 1801, the Moravians had settled on a forty-acre tract, which they called Springplace Mission, adjacent to Vann's Diamond Hill plantation. The Moravians met with disappointment in their efforts to Christianize the Cherokees, but their school became an important resource in the area. Many Cherokee children who would later become leaders of the Cherokee Nation attended the Springplace Mission School, including Elias Boudinot and John Ridge, both of whom signed the Treaty of New Echota, and Vann's favorite son, Joseph, who later inherited most of his father's estate and became an important political leader within the Cherokee Nation in his own right.[13]

Around 1804, Vann began construction of a two-story home atop a prominent hill on his plantation, and on March 24, 1805, the Moravians wrote in their diary that the Vann family moved into their new home.[14] Although the existing brick house has long been attributed to James Vann, Miles argues that the house constructed by Vann in 1804 was, in fact, a two-story log home. Miles bases her conclusion on documentary records related to an 1825 court case in which the builders of an "elaborate brick house" sued Joseph Vann for payment. Upon further review of the records in the Moravian Archives, Miles found no mention that the new house into which James Vann moved in March 1805 was made of brick, something she posits "would have been quite noteworthy at the time."[15] Nowhere, it seems, is James Vann's plantation home, which reflected his wealth and status within the Cherokee Nation, described as a brick structure. According to Miles, the two-and-a-half-story brick house that stands today was built by James's son Joseph around 1819, a position with which former interpretive ranger Julia Autry agrees.[16] The Georgia Department of Natural Resources, which owns and operates the Chief Vann House Historic Site, has continued to attribute construction of the brick house to James Vann with an acknowledgement that Joseph made improvements to the house around 1819.[17]

While the Springplace Missionary School served an important purpose in educating the Cherokee children in the area, the detailed records kept by the missionaries should be acknowledged as being equally if not more important. Anna Rosina Kliest Gambold kept the mission logs between 1805 and 1821, which chronicled daily life at both the mission and Vann's plantation. The records of Springplace Mission are today part of the Moravian Archives held in Winston-Salem, North Carolina. Based on translations of these logs done by Dr. Rowena McClinton, as well as correspondence and court records, Miles and her students at the University of Michigan were able to identify more than one hundred enslaved people by name and gain insight into what life was like for these people who constructed the buildings, tended the house, and worked the fields of Vann's plantation.[18] Autry used McClinton's and Miles's research to develop an exhibition on slavery at the Vann House, which opened in one of the log outbuildings in 2008 on the fiftieth anniversary of the opening of the house as a state historic site.[19]

Enslaved men, women, and children played a crucial role in making sure that the plantation functioned according to Vann's liking. The enslaved people worked in the fields and in the buildings on the plantation, including the main house. They constructed the buildings, the fences, and even a baking oven. They also built numerous barns and a new meeting house for the missionaries.[20] Enslaved men were responsible for "haul[ing] building materials and [raising] new structures." They also "cleared forested land, worked Vann's fields and orchards, and were periodically dispatched to his Chattahoochee River plantation to do the same." Enslaved women were responsible for the care of the Vann family "in times of sickness." Enslaved boys "search[ed] the woods for stray pigs or other items," and enslaved girls were sent to the Moravian mission to "assist with domestic work and childcare."[21] In addition to the demands of the physical labor, the enslaved people suffered mental anguish, as Vann sold them with complete disregard for familial ties. He frequently terrorized his labor force with beatings and other punishments.[22]

The Moravian logs and correspondence also provided documentation about other aspects of life at Diamond Hill. The Moravians were horrified by James Vann's "weakness for whiskey" as well as his "increasingly irrational and extremely violent behavior," which they chronicled during the final years of Vann's life. Although most historians have attributed Vann's erratic and violent behavior to his excessive drinking, more recent biographers have speculated that Vann suffered from mental illness, perhaps schizophrenia or brain damage as the result of possibly contracting syphilis. Whatever the cause, Vann has been described as "a thoroughly godless man" who was as "deadly as a water moccasin."[23]

James Vann was killed on February 19, 1809. During his stay at Buffington's Tavern in what is today Forsyth County near the Etowah River, an intoxicated Vann was shot by an unknown assailant. Vann's favorite son, eleven-year-old Joseph, who was traveling with his father, was asleep inside the tavern, along with one of Vann's enslaved men, who quickly transported young Joseph back to his father's home at Diamond Hill. John Norton, a Mohawk chief of Cherokee descent, later wrote, "It is said, that the deceased, altho' of considerable natural talents and capable of serving his country: on account of his violent disposition was not generally beloved: this perhaps may be the reason why no greater exertions have been made to bring the culprit to justice." Very little effort was made to identify Vann's killer, as numerous historians have reported, likely because Vann had made so many enemies and most people felt that his murder was a long overdue act of blood vengeance.[24] After Vann was murdered in 1809, Anna Gambold wrote, "Thus ended the life of one who was feared by many and loved by few."[25]

Even after his death, Vann continued to cause controversy among the Cherokees, which was still a matrilineal society in which mothers and sisters usually inherited property from sons and brothers. Vann left to his wife Peggy his household furniture and "all the rest & residue" of his property to Joseph, completely overlooking his mother, who was still alive, as well as his sisters and his other children. Vann's will was so out of step with what was the norm in the Cherokee Nation that the Cherokee Council modified the terms to distribute Vann's property among all eight of his children, although they did reserve the largest share for Joseph, and gave Peggy Vann, in addition to the furniture, the right to continue living in the main house.[26] Even with the council's reallotment Joseph's inheritance was substantial and included the land, hundreds of horses, an estimated thousand cattle, and 115 Black slaves.[27] Joseph, who was enrolled in school in South Carolina for several years, returned to Springplace to begin managing his inheritance in 1817 at age nineteen.

Joseph expanded and developed the Diamond Hill plantation, acquiring more land and enslaved workers, and he soon became known as "Rich Joe." He was, by all accounts, as ambitious and greedy as his father, although he was not predisposed to violence in the same way that James had been. Nevertheless, Joseph believed in corporal punishment for his enslaved workers, and he tightened control over the workers on his plantation by reducing their time off and increasing his surveillance of them. By the 1820s, Black slavery was so widespread among the Cherokees that the council imposed regulations on the practice, including authorizing "patrolling" companies to oversee slave activity, limiting the ability of slaves to trade or sell property, and outlawing marriage between Cherokees and "negro slaves." For the Black enslaved workers on Vann's plantation, life became more difficult, just as it did on plantations throughout much of the South in the first half of the nineteenth century.[28]

Like his father, Joseph Vann was a well-known figure within the Cherokee Nation and more broadly within the adjacent United States. President James Monroe was a guest at the Vann House in May 1819, an event that was remarked upon by Moravian missionary John Gambold in his correspondence. Two months after Monroe's visit, Gambold noted, "Our neighbor Joseph Vann is building a large brick house," which seems to support the assertions by Autry and Miles that the brick house that stands today was built by Joseph rather than by his father.[29]

The house, built atop a hill that overlooked the Federal Road, was designed in the Federal style with fanlight windows above the doorways. Each floor features two large rooms (twenty by thirty feet), one on each side of the central hallway. The attic is a finished space with two rooms of the same dimensions as the floors below and low, rounded ceilings. A notable feature is the cantilevered staircase with its hand-carved ornamentation. For nearly two hundred years the staircase, which rises from the first floor to the attic, had no visible external support. A steel rod connected to the ceiling and a wooden post between the floor and the outer corner of the staircase were installed when the house was restored to shore up what was, by that time, a sagging, cantilevered staircase. The interior of the house is decorated with "intricate carpentry" notable for its "expert joinery, fine carving and workmanship, good proportion, and striking color combinations."[30] In the late 1820s, Juliana Margaret Conner, a wealthy white woman who visited Vann's house, described it as a "fine large brick house—finished in a most extravagant style," although she found the interior, with its red, gold, blue, and green color scheme, to be "gaudily painted."[31]

Dining room of the Chief Vann House.

The exterior of the house had equally interesting details. Built of brick manufactured by enslaved workers on the plantation, the house featured two different bonding patterns. The south and east sides of the house, which faced the work yard and outbuildings, was constructed using a five-course, common bond pattern—a row or course of headers (the short end of the brick) followed by five rows of stretchers (the long end of the brick). The north side, which was the main entrance, and west side, which overlooked the Federal Road, were built with a more elaborate and decorative Flemish bond, which was created by alternating headers and stretchers in each course. Building a brick wall using Flemish bond would have been more expensive and difficult than the simpler common bond pattern—an indication that the masons who constructed the brick walls were highly skilled. The use of two different brick bonding patterns also reveals that while Vann understood the importance of presenting a beautiful and decorative appearance to the public, he also understood the value of economizing where he could on the non-public-facing sides of the house. Other notable features include the white pilasters and the two-story gabled porches on both the front and back of the house.[32]

Joseph's wealth and power helped him achieve political success within the Cherokee Nation. He was selected in 1827 to serve on the National Council, one of two legislative branches of the Cherokee Nation established in the Cherokee Constitution of 1827. However, neither the Constitution nor Joseph's position in Cherokee society could protect him from the forced removal of the Cherokee from Georgia in the 1830s. The Georgia General Assembly enacted legislation in December 1830 that claimed "all the Territory within the limits of Georgia, and now in the occupancy of the Cherokee tribe of Indians," and the following year the state legislature established Cherokee County, which encompassed the territory that had previously comprised the Cherokee Nation in Georgia.[33]

Vann's property was included in the 1832 Georgia land lottery that redistributed Cherokee lands to white settlers who qualified for a draw under rules set forth by the state legislature. By 1834 Joseph Vann and his two wives and eight children were forced to occupy a single room in the brick house, while Spencer Riley, who claimed to have drawn the lottery ticket that included Vann's house, and Colonel William Bishop, head of the Georgia Guard who claimed the site of the Moravian Mission at Springplace, fought over possession of Vann's home. Vann was accused of violating a Georgia law that prohibited Cherokees from hiring whites

Rear entrance of the Chief Vann House.

within the state's boundaries, the penalty for which was forfeiture of all property. Bishop, and his militia, seized Vann's house at gunpoint, forcing both Riley and the Vann family to flee.[34]

Joseph Vann and his family settled temporarily on a plantation that he owned in Hamilton County, Tennessee, before moving west to Webber Falls, Oklahoma, in 1836 following the ratification by the U.S. Congress of the Treaty of New Echota. He took with him to the Oklahoma Territory his family and at least forty-eight enslaved Black people. At Webber Falls, Vann built a brick house that was "a replica" of his brick house in Georgia.[35] Vann sued the federal government for the loss of his property in Georgia and was awarded a little over $19,000 (more than $600,000 in 2023) in compensation. The inventory of that property included "one fine brick house, 800 acres of cultivated land, 42 cabins, six barnes [*sic*], five smokehouse [*sic*], a grist mill, blacksmith shop, eight corn cribs, a shop and foundry, a trading post, a peach kiln, a still, 1,133 peach trees, 147 apple trees, etc."[36] As he had done in Georgia, Joseph Vann developed his landholdings and businesses in Oklahoma and remained one of the wealthiest members of the Cherokee tribe. In addition to his land-based businesses, Vann began operating a steamboat along the Arkansas and Mississippi Rivers. He was killed when his steamboat, *Lucy Walker*, exploded near New Albany, Indiana, on October 23, 1844.

Unlike his brick home in Oklahoma, which was destroyed during the Civil War, Vann's brick house in Georgia has survived for over two hundred years. Between the 1830s and 1952, the house was occupied by a series of owners and tenants. In 1920, a local physician, J. E. Bradford, acquired the house, although he did not live in it. Photographs taken by government employees of the Historic American Building Survey (HABS) in 1934 show a house that was described as in "poor condition."[37]

By 1950, the long-abandoned home was on the cusp of demolition by neglect, with no roof, partially collapsed floors, shattered windows, and cracks in the brick arches above the doors.[38] The next year, a group of individuals interested in restoring the Vann House convened at the Henry Grady Hotel in Atlanta to form the Joseph Vann Historical Association. Led by Gertrude Ruskin of Decatur and attended by prominent citizens from Atlanta, Dalton, Chatsworth, and Calhoun, the group hoped "to raise $5,000 to buy the home of Joseph Vann at Spring Place near Chatsworth and to preserve it as a museum-memorial of the Cherokee Indian." The Historical Association offered "a chance to give more than lip service to the campaign for the marking and maintenance of historic sites in order to preserve the Georgia heritage."[39]

The Historical Association rode the wave of interest in preserving the state's history that culminated in 1951 with the state legislature creating the Georgia Historical Commission (GHC), a state agency charged with "promoting understanding of the history of the state from prehistory to the present, permanently preserving and marking historic sites, publicizing Georgia's history, and advising local entities on historical matters."[40] Among the attendees at the Joseph Vann Historical Association meeting was Ivan Allen Sr., a leading businessman in Atlanta who had grown up near Springplace and who contributed the first $500 to the preservation cause. By July 1952, the organization had acquired the property and donated it to the GHC.[41]

The condition of the house, according to architect Francis Smith, who was hired by the GHC to perform an inspection, was "deplorable," although Smith reasoned that the house could be restored at a cost of $15,000.[42]

Smith's estimate proved dramatically low. GHC secretary C. E. Gregory reported that "the State gave us $40,000 for the Vann House restoration, which was not enough," noting that Governor Marvin Griffin had given the GHC an additional $30,000 to finish the restoration of the house and grounds and to furnish the house. Two months before the planned grand opening of the GHC's first historic site, Gregory noted that he had about $7,000 left in his budget, which he planned to spend on furnishings.[43]

The restoration of the Vann House, led by Maryland architect Henry Chandlee Forman, took over five years and included, in addition to returning the house to its former glory, an archaeological survey of the grounds conducted by Dr. Clemens de Baillou. Local community members also became involved in the restoration process, none more so than Dicksie Bradley Bandy, president of the Whitfield-Murray Historical Society, who became an important liaison between the state and the Cherokee Nation in Oklahoma, which named Bandy as "an official ambassador for the Cherokee Nation because of her interest and work on restoration of the Chief Vann House."[44] Bandy was instrumental in getting donations of furnishings for the house as well as serving as a leading promoter of the Chief Vann House as a historic site.

The grand opening of the Chief Vann House, the GHC's first historic site, was held on July 27, 1958, at 2:00 p.m. before "a sweltering, sun-baked crowd of several thousand persons, including state dignitaries and representatives of the Cherokee Nation." GHC chairman Joseph B. Cumming presided over the ceremonies, while Rev. J. Raymond Vann of New York City, a direct descendant of James Vann, offered an invocation. The keynote speaker was Governor Marvin Griffin, who proclaimed that "the $70,000 spent for its restoration 'is a wise investment, not only for the cash returns the people of this area will receive in tourist trade but is equally as important for restoring and preserving a priceless treasure of our glorious history.'" Griffin added that two additional Native American sites, Etowah Mounds and New Echota, which were under development by the GHC, were generating international interest.[45] Five days after the opening, Ivan Allen wrote to GHC secretary C. E. Gregory that the "Georgia Historical Commission is an answer to my dreams and prayers." Recalling that as a child he had dreamed of buying the Vann House to mark where his grandmother had "lived among the Cherokees at Spring Place," Allen could now say that his "dream became reality when nearly five thousand people in the beaming hot sun attended the opening."[46]

The GHC billed the Chief Vann House as the "Showplace of the Cherokee Nation" when it opened in 1958, a description that was also used a decade later when the site was added to the National Register of Historic Places. The site resurrected an interest in Cherokee history in Georgia as well as an interest in atoning for Cherokee removal. Three months after the opening, Joseph Cumming wrote to Earl Boyd Pierce, chief attorney for the Cherokee Nation, that he hoped to approach the governor about "effecting a repeal of the restrictive and punitive legislation that was enacted during the mid-1830's, depriving the Cherokees of their civil rights, almost their human rights."[47] Pierce, who had attended the Chief Vann House opening in July, expressed his enthusiasm for such a repeal, hoping that it could happen before the dedication of New Echota, the former Cherokee capital, located seventeen miles south of the Vann House, which the GHC had acquired in 1956 and was planning to develop as a historic site.[48]

Completion of the restoration and opening of the Vann House did not mean that the site was out of danger. A decade after the grand opening, Mary Gregory Jewett, who had succeeded her father as secretary of the GHC, wrote to William Murtaugh, Keeper of the National Register, that the Army Corps of Engineers were seeking approval to build a dam in the area that would create a lake within three hundred feet of the Vann House. Noting that the Vann House was "one of the most important structures in the State of Georgia," Jewett appealed to Murtaugh for the Vann House to be "on the first consensus list for the National Register inclusion for the State of Georgia."[49] The National Register of Historic Places had been created by the National Historic Preservation Act two years earlier, and listing on the National Register provided historic sites with some degree of protection from damage caused by federal undertakings, such as the construction of a dam or roadway. Jewett was eager to get the Vann House listed, and her efforts bore fruit when the Vann House was inscribed in the National Register of Historic Places on October 28, 1969.

Additional structures were added to the site over time. A log building was constructed on the site in an area near where the kitchen was once located to serve as the caretaker's house. That building was later converted into an office and, in 2002, exhibit space. Several other log buildings that date to the Cherokee period, including two cabins and a corn crib, were also moved to the site. In 2002, a visitor center that features an exhibition about the Cherokees and the Vann family, as well as a theater, gift shop, and public restrooms, was added. That same year, the Springplace Moravian Mission

Site of the Springplace Moravian Mission.

Cemetery was donated to the state and became part of the Chief Vann House historic site. In 2005, the State Department of Transportation, the Trust for Public Land, and the Friends of the Vann House raised $1.5 million to buy an additional 85 acres that had once been part of Vann's plantation. The land, which was slated for development as a trailer park and strip mall, is located within two hundred feet of the brick house and is preserved as green space to protect the viewshed from the house.[50]

Touring the Site

Visitors who are traveling to the historic home of the once prominent Vann family enter the site from the "Trail of Tears Highway" through a gate that is to the north of Georgia Highway 52 and Highway 225. A driveway, lined with wooden fences, leads to the visitor center, which houses exhibits, a classroom/theater, offices, and restrooms. A fifteen-minute introductory film entitled *Walking in Two Worlds: The Vann Family and the Cherokee Nation*, also available online at https://gastateparks.org/ChiefVannHouse, introduces visitors to the story of the Vann family. The exhibition provides additional information about the history of the

Outbuildings at the Chief Vann House, including the reconstructed kitchen (left) and Cherokee homestead (right).

Cherokees in the area as well as information about the Vann family, their plantation, and their fate following Cherokee removal.

Although tours of the museum and outbuildings are self-guided, tours of the main house are guided by staff or volunteers, so visitors should check with staff to confirm the schedule of the guided tours. The house tour offers visitors a glimpse into the lifestyle of James Vann and his son, including an uncensored look at the vices, drinking and gambling, that contributed to James's demise. Visitors are guided through the two main floors of the house as well as the attic and basement.

Among the self-guided buildings are the cluster of Cherokee-era buildings near the visitor center—two cabins and a corn crib—that were relocated from another site. These buildings provide insight into how most of the Cherokees in this area lived during the early nineteenth century.

Nature trail from the visitor center to the Moravian Mission site.

The two-story log building located in the area where the kitchen stood during the Vann period is a twentieth-century reconstruction that once served as the residence of the site's caretaker and later as an office for staff. Converted to exhibit space following the opening of the visitor center in 2002, the building, which has recently undergone significant repairs, now houses an exhibit on the enslaved people who lived and worked on the Vann plantation. Nearby is a reconstructed blacksmith forge.

Visitors can follow the half-mile nature trail, which originates in the field across the parking lot from the visitor center and winds past the ruins of a stone spring house through the woods to the Moravian Mission cemetery. The trail is well marked and is rated as medium difficulty because of the uneven terrain.

Notes

1. William R. Mitchell Jr., "Chief Vann House," National Register of Historic Places Nomination Form (Washington, D.C.: U.S. Department of the Interior, National Park Service, 1969), section 8.

2. Tiya Miles, *The House on Diamond Hill: A Cherokee Plantation Story* (Chapel Hill: University of North Carolina Press, 2010), 40–41.

3. Theda Perdue, *"Mixed-Blood" Indians: Racial Construction in the Early South* (Athens: University of Georgia Press, 2003), 23.

4. Miles, *House on Diamond Hill*, 48.

5. Miles, 48.

6. *Walking in Two Worlds: The Vann Family and the Cherokee Nation*, produced by Jim Couch and Becky Marshall (Georgia Department of Natural Resources, 2002), 0:37, YouTube, https://www.youtube.com/watch?v=BH7q_ETh-_o.

7. Rowena McClinton, ed., *The Moravian Springplace Mission to the Cherokees* (Lincoln: University of Nebraska Press, 2010), 26.

8. Miles, *House on Diamond Hill*, 4–5.

9. Miles, 63.

10. Miles, 88.

11. Miles, 53–54.

12. Miles, 118–120.

13. McClinton, *Moravian Springplace Mission*, 26–27.

14. Mitchell, "Chief Vann House."

15. Miles, *House on Diamond Hill*, 206–207.

16. Julia Autry, telephone interview by Jennifer Dickey, July 21, 2023.

17. "Chief Vann House," History of Georgia State Parks & Historic Sites, accessed June 12, 2023, https://gastateparks.org/ChiefVannHouse; Department of Natural Resources, *Chief Vann House* (Atlanta: Department of Natural Resources, 2023).

18. Tiya Miles, telephone interview by Jennifer Dickey, July 20, 2023.

19. Autry, telephone interview.

20. Jennifer Jones, Jessica Jones, Tiffany Teasley, Neika White, and Cachavious English, "African American Life, Culture, and Community," in *African American History at the Chief Vann House*, ed. Tiya Miles, Alexandria Cadotte, and Merwin Moss (Ann Arbor: University of Michigan, 2006), 8.

21. Miles, *House on Diamond Hill*, 77.

22. Brittany Marino, Erica Coleman, Alisha Humphrey, Ollie Ganz, Kelly Shalifoe, Rachael Howery, Alexandria Cadotte, and Ashley Payne, "The Vann Family as Slaveholders," in Miles, Cadotte, and Moss, *African American History*, 6.

23. *Walking in Two Worlds*, 0:37.

24. Miles, *House on Diamond Hill*, 30.

25. Miles, 133.

26. Miles, 143–144.

27. N. Michelle Williamson, "Chief Vann House," *New Georgia Encyclopedia*, last modified August 31, 2013, https://www.georgiaencyclopedia.org/articles/history-archaeology/chief-vann-house/; Miles, *House on Diamond Hill*, 164.

28. Miles, *House on Diamond Hill*, 165.

29. Miles, 166.

30. Mitchell, "Chief Vann House."

31. Miles, *House on Diamond Hill*, 167–168.

32. Mitchell, "Chief Vann House."

33. Mary Johnson, "Cherokee County," *New Georgia Encyclopedia*, last modified June 17, 2022, https://www.georgiaencyclopedia.org/articles/counties-cities-neighborhoods/cherokee-county/.

34. Miles, *House on Diamond Hill*, 175–176; N. Michelle Williamson, "Joseph Vann," *New Georgia Encyclopedia*, last modified Jul 20, 2021, https://www.georgiaencyclopedia.org/articles/history-archaeology/joseph-vann-1798-1844/; Murray County Museum, "Murray County Characters: Joseph 'Rich Joe' Vann," accessed June 12, 2023, https://www.murraycountymuseum.com/mcc_12.html.

35. "Webbers Falls—Old Settlers, New Homeland," National Park Service, accessed June 12, 2023, https://www.nps.gov/articles/000/webbers_falls_old_settlers.htm.

36. Mitchell, "Chief Vann House."

37. Historic American Buildings Survey, "Chief James Clement Vann House, U.S. Route 76 & State Route 255, Spring Place, Murray County, Ga.," documentation compiled after 1933, https://www.loc.gov/item/ga0291/.

38. Tiya Miles, "'Showplace of the Cherokee Nation': Race and the Making of a Southern House Museum," *Public Historian* 33, no. 4 (November 2011): 15.

39. "The Vann House Is Worth Saving," *Atlanta Constitution*, October 8, 1951, 4.

40. Jann Haynes Gilmore, "Georgia's Historic Preservation Beginning: The Georgia Historical Commission (1951–1973)," *Georgia Historical Quarterly* 63, no. 1 (Spring 1979): 9.

41. Miles, "Showplace of the Cherokee Nation," 18–20.

42. Miles, 20.

43. C. E. Gregory to Joseph B. Cumming, May 15, 1958, GHC Director's Office, Historic Sites Operations Correspondence—1954–1967, RCB 23851, 061-01-002, Georgia Archives (hereafter, GHC Director's Office).

44. "Mrs. Bandy Honored by Cherokee Nation," *Chattanooga Daily Times*, August 27, 1958, 18.

45. Warren Bosworth, "Restored Vann House Dedicated," *Atlanta Constitution*, July 28, 1958, 1.

46. Ivan Allen to C. E. Gregory, August 1, 1958, GHC Director's Office.

47. Joseph B. Cumming to Earl Boyd Pierce, October 25, 1958, GHC Director's Office.

48. Earl Boyd Pierce to Joseph B. Cumming, October 30, 1958, GHC Director's Office.

49. Mary Gregory Jewett to William J. Murtaugh, GHC Director's Office.

50. "Grant Provided for Vann House Project," *Atlanta Constitution*, April 26, 2004, E2.

Further Reading

Boulware, Tyler. "Cherokee Indians." *New Georgia Encyclopedia*, last modified August 24, 2020. https://www.georgiaencyclopedia.org/articles/history-archaeology/cherokee-indians/.

Garrison, Tim Alan. "Cherokee Removal." *New Georgia Encyclopedia*, last modified July 23, 2018. https://www.georgiaencyclopedia.org/articles/history-archaeology/cherokee-removal/.

Duncan, Barbara R., and Brett R. Riggs. *Cherokee Heritage Trails Guidebook*. Chapel Hill: University of North Carolina Press, 2003.

McClinton, Rowena. *The Moravian Springplace Mission to the Cherokees*. Vols. 1–2. Lincoln: University of Nebraska Press, 2007.

Miles, Tiya, ed. *African American History at the Chief Vann House*. Ann Arbor: University of Michigan, 2006.

Miles, Tiya. *The House on Diamond Hill: A Cherokee Plantation Story*. Chapel Hill: University of North Carolina Press, 2012.

Perdue, Theda. *"Mixed-Blood" Indians: Racial Construction in the Early South*. Athens: University of Georgia Press, 2005.

Perdue, Theda. *Slavery and the Evolution of Cherokee Society, 1540–1866*. Knoxville: University of Tennessee Press, 1979.

Williamson, N. Michelle. "Chief Vann House." *New Georgia Encyclopedia*, last modified August 31, 2013. https://www.georgiaencyclopedia.org/articles/history-archaeology/chief-vann-house/.

Williamson, N. Michelle. "Joseph Vann, 1798–1844." *New Georgia Encyclopedia*, last modified July 20, 2021. https://www.georgiaencyclopedia.org/articles/history-archaeology/joseph-vann-1798-1844/.

CHAPTER 2

New Echota

Izzabella Barrett and Jennifer W. Dickey

Basic Information

PERIOD OF SIGNIFICANCE: 1825–1838

DATE ESTABLISHED AS A HISTORIC SITE: 1962

ACREAGE: 200 acres

LOCATION: 1211 Chatsworth Highway NE, Calhoun, Ga. 30701, Gordon County

Perhaps the most haunting of the state's historic sites, New Echota symbolizes the Cherokee people's attempt to preserve their culture in the changing world of the early nineteenth century. The site was declared a National Historic Landmark in 1973 for its significance as "a high point in the cultural transition of the Cherokee Nation" and for being the "first truly 'national' capital of the Cherokees."[1]

With European settlement encroaching on their lands, the Cherokees had lost much of their territory by the 1820s. In an effort to preserve what was left of their lands in the east, the Cherokees adopted a republican form of government in 1820, and on November 12, 1825, they established the town of New Echota as the capital of the Cherokee Nation. New Echota would serve that function for less than five years. During that time, government buildings were erected, including a Council House, a Supreme Courthouse, and a print shop in which the *Cherokee Phoenix* newspaper was printed. The capital was abandoned after the Treaty of New Echota, signed by a group of Cherokee leaders in 1835, which ceded Cherokee lands in the southeast to the United States government in exchange for money and land in what is today Oklahoma.[2]

The reconstructed Supreme Courthouse at New Echota.

Restoration of the former Cherokee capital of New Echota began in the early 1950s when a group of Gordon County residents spearheaded the acquisition and excavation of the site and donated the land to the State Historical Commission. The site opened to the public in 1962 with two restored buildings and two reconstructed buildings. As of 2022, there were thirteen buildings at the site, including a museum/visitor center, which opened in 1969. The site serves as a celebration of and memorial to the Cherokee people who occupied the area for centuries and gives visitors a brief but well-rounded interpretation of Cherokee life and culture.

History of New Echota

The Cherokees inhabited the southern Appalachian Mountains, including the northern third of what would become Georgia, hundreds of years prior to European contact. By the early 1800s, however, white settlers had encroached into the area that the Cherokees had occupied for centuries. The Cherokees were not a united people; they shared kinship networks that identified them, but most activity centered around individual towns.[3]

At a meeting in 1820, Cherokee legislators approved a resolution to create a new town to serve as the capital. The town was planned and was to have "one hundred town lots, of one acre square." Streets throughout the town were to be fifty feet wide, and the main street was to be sixty feet wide. A public square of two acres would house the Council House and the Supreme Court buildings. Lots were to be sold to the highest bidder, and the proceeds from the sales were to be used for construction of the public buildings.[4] At the time New Echota was founded by the Cherokees on November 12, 1825, to serve as the new capital of the Cherokee Nation, almost 90 percent of their land had been taken from them.

The capital was named New Echota after the town Echota (sometimes Chota), the former capital of the Overhill Cherokees located in Tennessee. Echota had been largely destroyed during the Revolutionary War and never recovered.[5] The new capital was an attempt to preserve the Cherokee Nation by giving up the localized government systems and creating a government modeled on the three branches of the U. S. government: legislative, executive, and judicial. The Cherokee Nation was divided into eight districts with four delegates elected from each district; these delegates made up the National Council. The National Council, in turn, elected twelve members to the National Committee. The National

Committee then chose the top officials in the government, the principal chief, assistant principal chief, and treasurer. New Echota would become the meeting place of the legislative branch.[6]

New Echota was a small town with about six buildings clustered together in the center and others "scattered nearby." Although the town's permanent population was only about eighty people, when the National Council was in session, the population exceeded three hundred.[7] A visitor from Connecticut, Benjamin Gold, described New Echota as "an interesting and pleasant place. The ground is level and smooth as a floor; the center of the Nation, a new place, laid out in city form; a hundred lots of an acre each . . . six new framed houses in sight, besides a Council House, Court House, printing office and four stores."[8]

Most Cherokees did not live in towns such as New Echota. Instead, they lived in villages scattered throughout their lands.[9] The centerpiece of New Echota was the Council House where the legislature met. The town was surrounded by Cherokee-owned plantations that were maintained by enslaved workers.[10]

A unifying force within the Cherokee Nation was the development of a writing system for the Cherokee language. In 1821, a "mixed-blood" Cherokee named Sequoyah, or George Guess, created symbols for each syllable of the Cherokee language.[11] The Cherokee syllabary enabled written communication across the Cherokee Nation in the Native language. In 1826, the Cherokee Council authorized the construction of a printing office for publishing a national newspaper. This log building, described as a hewn-log structure that measured thirty feet long by twenty feet wide, would serve as the headquarters for the *Cherokee Phoenix*, a bilingual (in Cherokee and English) newspaper that was published from 1828 until 1834.[12]

The *Cherokee Phoenix* covered various topics, but "most significant of all the contents of the *Phoenix*, however, were its political editorials. They inveighed against the abuses" of the state of Georgia and the white settlers who encroached on Cherokee land.[13] The paper's first editor, Elias Boudinot, was also involved in printing religious texts such as portions of the Bible and a new edition of an Indian hymn book. Boudinot had a string of health issues, so the *Phoenix* was not printed regularly. Boudinot also published pro-removal editorials, a stance that likely led to his resignation at the behest of Chief John Ross, who opposed Cherokee removal.[14] Elijah Hicks became editor of the *Phoenix* in August 1832, and the paper's

Interior of the reconstructed print shop at New Echota.

tone became increasingly favorable for Cherokee independence and education.[15] The paper raged against the U.S. government, the Georgia state government, and Cherokee removal. Georgia state leaders began to see the *Phoenix* as a threatening voice, so state authorities confiscated the press and type in October 1834.[16]

Efforts by the state of Georgia to expand westward and force the Cherokee and Muscogee (Creek) Indians out of the state had been underway since the eighteenth century. In the Compact of 1802, the state agreed to cede its western lands to the federal government in exchange for $1.25 million and a pledge by the federal government to remove the Indians from within the state's borders "as early as the same can be peaceably obtained, on reasonable terms."[17] The federal government failed to take quick action on Indian removal, however, and the Cherokee Nation stood fast in northwest Georgia, even as white settlers began to trickle into the area. The 1828 election of President Andrew Jackson, who was strongly in favor of Indian removal, changed the tenor of U.S.-Cherokee relations. The discovery of gold in North Georgia in 1828 led to a rush of white settlers into Cherokee territory in 1829 and further increased the pressure for removal of the Cherokee people to Indian Territory in the west. The U.S. Congress passed the Indian Removal Act in 1830, which empowered President Jackson to negotiate removal treaties with Indian tribes.[18]

Meanwhile, the state of Georgia had passed a series of anti-Indian laws that "outlawed the Cherokee national government and began distributing Cherokee lands to Georgia citizens by lottery."[19] The Cherokees responded through multiple channels, seeking allies in Congress and filing appeals through the court system in an effort to combat the state's actions. The U.S. Supreme Court claimed it had no jurisdiction in *Cherokee Nation v. Georgia* (1831), in which the Cherokees sought an injunction against Georgia's anti-Indian laws. However, in 1832, another case came before the court. Samuel Worcester, a white missionary who had moved to New Echota in 1827 and was involved in the Cherokee resistance, had been arrested by Georgia authorities for violating a state law that prohibited "white persons" from living within the Cherokee Nation. Worcester was tried and convicted and sentenced to four years in prison in the state penitentiary. Upon his appeal to the U.S. Supreme Court, the court ruled "that the Cherokee Indians constituted a nation holding distinct sovereign powers" in *Worcester v. Georgia* (1832), and that the Cherokees retained "a legitimate title to its national territory."[20]

The *Worcester* decision notwithstanding, Georgia continued distributing Cherokee lands to white settlers through land lotteries and increased the pressure for removal of the Cherokees from within the borders claimed by the state. A faction of Cherokees led by Elias Boudinot, John Ridge, and his father, Major Ridge, determined that the best alternative for the survival of the Cherokee Nation was to accept removal and to negotiate a deal with the U.S. government for lands in the west. This minority faction, known as the Treaty party, began talks with the U.S. government and in October 1835 presented a proposal to the Cherokee Council, which was unanimously rejected. In spite of this rebuff, the Treaty party continued their negotiations with the U.S. government and in late 1835 agreed to a deal that ceded Cherokee lands in the east in exchange for territory in the west in what is today Oklahoma. The U.S. government would also pay the Cherokees $5 million plus the costs of removal and subsistence for the Cherokees for one year.[21]

The Treaty of New Echota was signed by Major Ridge, John Ridge, and Elias Boudinot at New Echota on December 21, 1835, in spite of overwhelming opposition by tribal members and without the approval of Principal Chief John Ross. President Andrew Jackson sent the treaty directly to the Senate, which passed it in a close vote in 1836. President Jackson then signed the treaty on May 23, 1836.[22] The treaty was the final action that sealed the deal on Cherokee removal, an event now known as the Trail of Tears.

According to Article 18 of the treaty, the Cherokees had two years to move westward, and the U.S. federal government would cover all moving costs.[23] However, because most Cherokees ignored the treaty, much as they did with any legislation passed by Georgia or the federal government about Cherokee affairs, only about two thousand, or 10 percent, of the Cherokees moved westward over the next two years.[24] In May 1838, federal troops arrived in the Cherokee Nation to enforce the treaty. They forced Cherokee citizens from their homes into forts and military camps. Military leaders reported that they had completed the roundup of Cherokees in Georgia within three weeks.[25] The march westward began shortly thereafter and continued into 1839. Over the course of the next year, almost twenty thousand Cherokees were forced to move west; an estimated four thousand Cherokees died along the way.[26]

As payback for their role in signing the Treaty of New Echota, John Ridge, Major Ridge, and Elias Boudinot were murdered by unknown assailants after they arrived in what is today Oklahoma. According to Cherokee law, as of October 26, 1829, it was illegal for a person or persons to sign a treaty that went against the will of the National Council under penalty of death. Most Cherokees felt the death of the Treaty party leaders was justified because of "the ancient law of blood, which demanded vengeance for the deaths on the Trail of Tears."[27] After the forcible removal of the Cherokees, most of the buildings in New Echota were burned or torn down, and the site became cotton farmland.[28]

By the 1950s, the site of the former Cherokee capital, which had been farmed for over a century, was slated for redevelopment. However, local business leaders in Calhoun raised money to purchase the site and petitioned the Georgia government to make it a state historic site. The county hired historian Henry Malone to conduct a survey of the property in an effort to identify the exact location of the Cherokee town.[29] The site was excavated in 1954 by a group of archaeologists from the Georgia Historical Commission led by Lewis Larson, who worked alongside the National Park Service archaeologist Joe Caldwell.[30]

Unable to afford the cost of reconstruction and eager to have the site developed as the former Cherokee capital, the community donated the land to the state in 1956 following the excavation.[31] The community wanted to get the site excavation done before it was officially a state historic site to avoid needing to obtain state approval for the excavation. There have been no excavations since the 1950s after the state acquired the land and no plans for further excavations at the site, but interpretive ranger Kevin Mardell admits it would be interesting to see what might be revealed by nondestructive methods such as Light Detection and Ranging (LIDAR), a remote sensing method that uses laser-light pulses to generate three-dimensional information about the characteristics of the earth.[32]

Historian Andrew Denson notes the irony of Georgia's white leaders supporting the creation of a state historic site commemorating the Cherokee Indians at the same time they were fighting furiously to keep in place a system of race-based segregation in Georgia. Denson speculates, "For most Georgians, Native American history might have been distant enough to be unthreatening. . . . Georgia's Indian history, as far as many whites were concerned, had ended in the Age of Jackson. While the Civil Rights Movement ensured that modern southerners would struggle over the legacies of slavery, the history of Indian dispossession must have seemed rather safe."[33] Reconstructing the former Cherokee capital served as a way for the state to commemorate the previously excluded "non-white racial groups and oppressed peoples," explains Denson.[34]

However narrow the commemorative focus may seem in retrospect, in the 1950s the true driving force was tourism rather than a perceived need to make amends for past transgressions by white leaders. Inspired by the success of the reservation of the Eastern Band of the Cherokees in North Carolina as a tourist site, local leaders thought New Echota could become equally popular. The success of Colonial Williamsburg, the reconstructed colonial capital in Virginia, as a living history site also informed the plans for New Echota. Local and state advocates for the reconstruction of New Echota envisioned the site as an "Indian Williamsburg" that would include costumed interpreters and other living history programs.[35]

The original plan for the site was for most of the town to be reconstructed, but due to a combination of factors, including disagreement among experts about the location and configuration of some of the buildings and a shortage of funds, only nine buildings were built.[36] The Georgia Historical Commission settled on a modest reconstruction of the town that "was planned and placed so that visitors might see at a glance what New Echota was like at its finest hour."[37] Reconstruction efforts began in 1956 and continued, in fits and starts, until the 1990s.

Not everyone wanted the site to be reconstructed. The site's excavations were inconclusive about the size, shape, and location of some buildings, including the Council House. In a letter from architectural historian Harold N. Cooledge Jr. to the Georgia Historical Commission on January 11, 1971, regarding the reconstruction of the Council House, Cooledge wrote, "Insufficient evidence, either physical or literary, has been presented to allow any sound reconstruction of the history of the Council (and/or Town) House at New Echota."[38] A Council House Committee was created, which in 1971 recommended that reconstruction of the Council House should not happen without further evidence and that reconstruction should move forward only for the buildings with enough evidence.[39] Commission director Joseph B. Cumming encouraged staff "to go on with the reconstruction based on the best evidence possible."[40]

Two years later, debate about how to proceed with reconstruction continued, and Benjamin Levy, author of the New Echota National Historic Landmark nomination, argued that "the reconstructed buildings were not essential to the value of the site."[41] Most of the staff at the Georgia State Historical Commission wanted the site to be reconstructed but wanted it to be done with careful research to ensure the reconstructions were done correctly. The research was carefully done, and since the town was planned, there were records of the town map and the buildings. Ranger Kevin Mardell explained that "some records show us how many nails were used in the floorboards."[42] This allowed the buildings to be reconstructed in their original position, give or take five feet in any direction.[43]

At the time of the opening in 1962, only the print shop and the Supreme Courthouse were reconstructed. The Worcester Mission, the only building that was original to the site from the Cherokee period, was restored to its 1820s appearance. Vann's Tavern, originally built and operated by James Vann, a Cherokee citizen, was moved to New Echota from its original location at the Chattahoochee River crossing near Oscarville, Georgia. A visitor center/museum was added in 1969.[44] In spite of the slow pace and incomplete nature of the town's reconstruction, the site was added to the

The restored Worcester House at New Echota.

National Register of Historic Places in 1970 and designated as a National Historic Landmark in 1973, when it was recognized by the Department of the Interior as “a high point in the cultural transition of the Cherokee Nation.”[45]

According to Andrew Denson, when the site first opened in 1962, “the interpretive effort focused on the story of Cherokee Removal, and the moral message was atonement.” Rebuilding the town, preserving the land, and telling the story of the Cherokee removal was a way for Georgia to apologize for the removal and an acceptance of historical guilt.[46] Three decades later, a sense of tragedy pervades the site, both for the historical events that happened here in the nineteenth century and for the incomplete reconstruction effort in the twentieth century.

Interpretive ranger Kevin Mardell, who disagrees with Denson’s perspective about atonement and historical guilt, argues, “While it is very important to recognize the fallibility of humans and their errors through

The relocated Vann's Tavern at New Echota.

history, including the events of the Cherokee removal, interpretation at its core is to inform, not necessarily persuade."[47] According to Mardell, "We have what we need to say, and what we are trying to say is very much set in stone."[48] That message provides a glimpse into the lives and culture of the Cherokee people in Georgia and the tragedy of Cherokee removal. The museum exhibition was last updated in 2001, and in 2021, many of the interpretive panels across the site were revised by the Cultural and Interpretive Resource Unit of Georgia State Parks and Historic Sites to bring out-of-date language "up to modern sensitivity standards."[49]

In August 1990, the Gordon County Historical Society began a fund-raising campaign to continue rebuilding the Cherokee capital, including reconstruction of the Council House, which was considered to be the most important building in the town. Members of the Cherokee Nation of Oklahoma and the Eastern Band of Cherokees from North Carolina met with an "advisory committee of historians specializing in Cherokee

The reconstructed Council House at New Echota.

history" in an effort "to ensure the restoration [was] done in a historically correct manner." The president of the Gordon County Historical Society stated: "New Echota needs to be fully restored not only to educate the public on the Cherokee Indians of the early 1800s, but also as a lasting legacy to Cherokee accomplishments and as a tribute to the thousands of Cherokees who died on the Trail of Tears. We as a Nation owe the Cherokees such a memorial."[50] Reconstruction of the Council House was completed in 1994.

New Echota is a site that remembers Cherokee culture and history from initial Cherokee occupation of the land to the forcible removal of the Cherokees in the late 1830s. Significant developments in Cherokee history, such as the invention of a written version of the Cherokee language, the creation of the *Cherokee Phoenix* that was first printed in New Echota, and the centralization of the Cherokee government, are memorialized here. This is also the site of the signing of the Treaty of New Echota, which led to Cherokee removal. History happened here, and the landscape and reconstructed buildings help visitors understand this period of history.

Despite its historical significance and its location near a major north-south interstate, New Echota ranks in the bottom half of the state's historic sites in terms of visitation. The dreams of creating an "Indian Williamsburg" that would be an economic engine for Gordon County never came to fruition. Although the site remains a popular destination for school groups, it only attracts around ten thousand visitors a year. The site excels at showing the events that happened at New Echota to the public in a meaningful and respectful way, and the workers at the site are determined to maintain the site's integrity and tell a truthful account of the historical events. The site is a peaceful and quiet memorial to the Cherokee people and what they built in the early nineteenth century.

Touring the Site

New Echota is located less than a mile off I-75 in Calhoun, Georgia, and fewer than twenty miles south of the Chief Vann House, another of Georgia's state historic sites, on Highway 225. Visitors enter the site through a gate into a parking lot. There is no fence surrounding the site, so the grassy landscape and the buildings scattered across it are visible from the parking lot.

The visitor center includes a single, self-guided exhibition, a theater, and a small gift shop as well as restrooms. Visitors can watch the seventeen-minute film *The Cherokee Nation: The Story of New Echota* on-site or through the New Echota website (https://gastateparks.org/NewEchota).

As of 2023, there were twelve restored, relocated, or reconstructed buildings on the site. Visitors exit the museum onto the historic landscape, where they encounter the first outdoor panel with a map of the site and the trail to follow to see all the buildings. The recommended course to go through the site is the Middle-Class Cherokee Farmstead, Council House, Supreme Courthouse, common Cherokee cabin and outbuildings, Worcester House, Vann Tavern, print shop, and the Boudinot House Site before returning to the museum. The trail follows the historic paths of New Town Road and Town Street.

The Middle-Class Cherokee Farmstead includes a house, a smokehouse, a barn, and a corn crib. The buildings were not originally in New Echota

The relocated Middle-Class Cherokee Farmstead at New Echota.

but were disassembled at their original locations and put back together at New Echota. The house was originally in Calhoun, while the barn and smokehouse were from Tennessee. The fully furnished house is usually closed, although visitors can arrange to go inside on a guided tour.

The reconstructed Council House and Supreme Courthouse are both open to the public. Behind the courthouse are a cluster of relocated buildings that represent a Common Cherokee Farmstead from the New Echota period. The small house and its outbuildings once belonged to the family of John Roger.

Farther along the trail is the former home of Reverend Samuel A. Worcester, the only building from the Cherokee period that is original to the site. Constructed in 1828 by Worcester to serve as a residence and mission, the house was significantly modified over the years. It was restored in 1958–1959 to its historic appearance from the Cherokee period. The house is furnished as it would have been when the Worcester family lived there.

The oldest building on the site is the tavern, which was relocated from its original site on the Chattahoochee River in 1954. Built in 1805 by James Vann, the tavern served as an inn, general store, and ferry house.[51] The Vann family did have a house on the lot where the store now sits. Vann was the dominant chief of the Cherokees by 1800. James Vann's son, Joseph, continued his father's trading business and was elected to the National Council.[52] Inside, the store looks much like it would have looked in the early 1800s.

The print shop, reconstructed in the mid- to late 1950s, houses a fully working printing press. On a guided tour, the guide will put ink on the press and then print a page of the newspaper. There are also cabinets full of printing keys or letters that would have been used in the press.

The last stop on the tour is not a structure but four stones marking the location of the Boudinot house. Elias Boudinot was the original editor of the *Cherokee Phoenix* who fell out of favor because of his support of relocation for the Cherokee people. Boudinot's home was burned down in what is believed to be arson because of his involvement in the signing of the Treaty of New Echota. A well at the house site that served as a dumping ground for Cherokee possessions left behind following removal was excavated in the 1950s and proved to be a repository of many artifacts.

The site hosts multiple events throughout the year. Your State Parks Day includes free admission and parking at any Georgia State Park and Historic Site, usually at the end of September. On Native American Heritage Day, held in November, the site features living history and craftspeople who help bring alive the history of the Cherokee Nation.[53]

Notes

1. Benjamin Levy, "New Echota," National Register of Historic Places Nomination Form (Washington, D.C.: U.S. Department of the Interior, National Park Service, 1973), section 8.

2. Tyler Boulware, "Cherokee Indians," *New Georgia Encyclopedia*, last modified August 24, 2020, https://www.georgiaencyclopedia.org/articles/history-archaeology/cherokee-indians/.

3. Boulware.

4. Henry T. Malone, "New Echota—Capital of the Cherokee Nation, 1825–1830," *Early Georgia* 1, no. 4 (Spring 1055): 6–7.

5. Levy, "New Echota."

6. Kimberly Macenczak, "Educators to the Cherokees at New Echota, Georgia: A Study in Assimilation" (PhD diss., Georgia State University, 1991), 13.

7. Malone, "New Echota," 9; *The Cherokee Nation: The Story of New Echota*, produced by Jim Couch and Becky Marshall (Georgia Department of Natural Resources, 1990), https://www.youtube.com/watch?v=YmoAr9LQwEc&t=1014s.

8. Malone, "New Echota," 9.

9. Kevin Mardell, interview by Izzabella Barrett, October 8, 2022, digital recording in possession of the author.

10. "Sequoyah," Georgia Historical Society, accessed December 2, 2022, https://www.georgiahistory.com/resource/sequoyah-innovative-creator-of-the-cherokee-syllabary/.

11. Devon Ellen Pawloski, "Stolen Lands, Stolen Stories: Colonizing and Decolonizing Cherokee Historic Sites in Georgia" (MHP thesis, University of Georgia, 2021), 40.

12. Malone, "New Echota," 6; Ovid Andrew McMillion, "Cherokee Indian Removal," 27; *The Cherokee Nation: The Story of New Echota.*

13. Hugh R. Autry, "New Echota: Birthplace of the American Indian Press," National Park Service Popular Studies Series, History no. 6 ([Washington, D.C.:] United States Department of the Interior, 1941), 9, Secretary of State—Front Office—Secretary of State Subject Files, 1972–1973, RCB-27620, Georgia Archives.

14. Macenczak, "Educators to the Cherokees," 85.

15. Autry, "New Echota," 18.

16. Macenczak, "Educators to the Cherokees," 43.

17. "Articles of Agreement and Cession Regarding Georgia's Western Lands, 1802," Governor's Subject Files, Executive Dept., Governor, RG 1-1-5, Georgia Archives, accessed October 3, 2023, https://vault.georgiaarchives.org/digital/collection/adhoc/id/416.

18. Boulware, "Cherokee Indians."

19. Andrew Denson, *Monuments to Absence: Cherokee Removal and the Contest over Southern Memory* (Chapel Hill: University of North Carolina Press, 2017), 26–28.

20. Tim Garrison, "*Worcester v. Georgia*," *New Georgia Encyclopedia*, last modified February 20, 2018, https://www.georgiaencyclopedia.org/articles/government-politics/worcester-v-georgia-1832/.

21. Denson, *Monuments to Absence*, 28–29.

22. Denson, 30.

23. John B. Wilson, *Indian Treaties and Cessions of Land in Georgia. 1705-1837*, 484, transcript by W.P.A., project no. 7158, Georgia Department of Archives and History, Atlanta, Georgia.

24. Macenczak, "Educators to the Cherokees," 82.

25. Denson, *Monuments to Absence*, 35.

26. *The Cherokee Nation: The Story of New Echota.*

27. Macenczak, "Educators to the Cherokees," 88.

28. "Restoration of New Echota Set to Continue," *Pickens Country Progress*, August 16, 1990.

29. Andrew Denson, "Remembering Cherokee Removal in Civil Rights–Era Georgia," *Southern Cultures* 14, no. 4 (Winter 2008): 86–90.

30. Mardell, interview.

31. Edward Woodward, "Capital City of New Echota Shows Progressiveness of Cherokee Nation," *Atlanta Constitution*, August 22, 1992.

32. Mardell interview.

33. Denson, "Remembering Cherokee Removal," 95.

34. Denson, 88.

35. Denson, 93.

36. "Restoration of New Echota Set to Continue," *Pickens County Progress* (Jasper, Ga.).

37. New Echota Restoration, Georgia Historical Commission—Director's Office—Administrative Records, RCB-13557, Georgia Archives (hereafter, GHC Director's Office).

38. Harold N. Cooledge Jr. to Georgia Historical Commission, January 11, 1971, GHC Director's Office.

39. Billy Townsend, Report on Recommendations of Council House Committee, March 5, 1971, GHC Director's Office.

40. Joseph B. Cumming to Members of Georgia Historical Commission, April 19, 1971, GHC Director's Office.

41. Levy, "New Echota," 2.

42. Kevin Mardell tour of New Echota, October 8, 2022.

43. Kevin Mardell tour of New Echota.

44. Georgia State Parks & Historic Sites Division, "New Echota Historic Site," *History of the Georgia State Parks and Historic Sites Division*, accessed on February 3, 2023, https://gastateparks.org/sites/default/files/parks/pdf/HistoryOfGSPHSD.pdf.

45. U.S. Department of the Interior, "National Survey of Historic Sites and Buildings: New Echota, Gordon County, Georgia" September 8, 1973, accessed January 3, 2023, https://npgallery.nps.gov/GetAsset/15090938-2870-4737-9b12-7ebcc1f24508.

46. Denson, "Remembering Cherokee Removal ," 87–89.

47. Kevin Mardell, email to Izzabella Barrett, October 20, 2022.

48. Mardell interview.

49. Mardell interview.

50. "Restoration of New Echota Set to Continue."

51. *New Echota Cherokee Capital State Historic Site* (pamphlet), Georgia Department of Natural Resources, n.d.

52. N. Williamson, "Joseph Vann," *New Georgia Encyclopedia*, last modified July 20, 2021, https://www.georgiaencyclopedia.org/articles/history-archaeology/joseph-vann-1798-1844/.

53. Mardell interview.

Further Reading

Boulware, Tyler. "Cherokee Indians." *New Georgia Encyclopedia*, last modified August 24, 2020. https://www.georgiaencyclopedia.org/articles/history-archaeology/cherokee-indians/.

Denson, Andrew. *Monuments to Absence: Cherokee Removal and the Contest over Southern Memory*. Chapel Hill: University of North Carolina Press, 2017.

Duncan, Barbara R., and Brett H. Riggs. *Cherokee Heritage Trails Guidebook*. Chapel Hill: University of North Carolina Press, 2003.

Garrison, Tim Alan. "Cherokee Removal." *New Georgia Encyclopedia*, last modified July 23, 2018. https://www.georgiaencyclopedia.org/articles/history-archaeology/cherokee-removal/.

Inskeep, Steve. *Jacksonland: President Andrew Jackson, Cherokee Chief John Ross, and a Great American Land Grab*. New York: Penguin Books, 2016.

Macenczak, Kimberly Portwood. "Educators to the Cherokees at New Echota, Georgia: A Study in Assimilation." PhD dissertation, Georgia State University, 1991.

McMillion, Ovid Andrew. "Cherokee Indian Removal: The Treaty of New Echota and General Winfield Scott." MA thesis, East Tennessee State University, 2003.

National Park Service. "Discover the Trail of Tears: A Lightning Lesson from Teaching with Historic Places." Accessed August 2, 2023. https://www.nps.gov/subjects/teachingwithhistoricplaces/lightning-lesson-006_trail-of-tears-major-ridge.htm.

Williamson, N. "Joseph Vann." *New Georgia Encyclopedia*, last modified July 20, 2021. https://www.georgiaencyclopedia.org/articles/history-archaeology/joseph-vann-1798-1844/.

CHAPTER 3

Etowah Indian Mounds

Kathryn Graham and Jennifer W. Dickey

Basic Information

PERIOD OF SIGNIFICANCE: ca. 1000–1600 CE

DATE ESTABLISHED AS A HISTORIC SITE: 1953

ACREAGE: 54 acres

LOCATION: 813 Indian Mounds Road SE, Cartersville, Ga. 30120, Bartow County

Listed in 1933 as one of Georgia's "seven natural wonders" during the state's bicentennial celebration, Etowah Indian Mounds is one of the most well-preserved Mississippian period mound sites in the Southeast.[1] The home of at least three chiefdoms over almost a six-hundred-year period, Etowah has offered insight into the Mississippian cultures that occupied the Mississippi River valley and much of the Southeast from around 900 to 1700 CE. The Etowah site is renowned for its three large mounds and the rich array of artifacts that have been recovered by archaeologists at the site. The site was designated as a National Historic Landmark in 1964 and was among the first sites added to the National Register of Historic Places upon its creation in 1966. The site is considered "important as an expression of the eastern expansion of Mississippian culture and of cultural traditions" and for the "vast quantity of unusual and elaborate ceremonial material which the site has yielded."[2]

Approach to Mound A (right) and Mound B (left) at the Etowah Indian Mounds.

History of the Etowah Indian Mounds

The Mississippian period covers almost eight hundred years during which complex societies developed and evolved in the midwestern and southeastern United States. The prevalence of mound-culture sites along the Mississippi River valley led archaeologists to apply the name of the river to the period of history during which these sites developed. Archaeologists further divide the Mississippian period into three phases—Early (900–1200 CE), Middle (1200–1500 CE), and Late (1500–1700 CE).[3]

Characteristic of the Mississippian period was the organization of Native peoples in the Midwest and Southeast into chiefdoms—a political organization with two ranks, ruling elites and commoners.[4] Chiefdoms were societies in which power was transferred hereditarily among the elites who ruled over the commoners. The Cahokia site, located near present-day East St. Louis, was the largest and most densely populated

Mississippian site, reaching a population within the city of perhaps 16,000, with another 35,000 residents living in the surrounding areas between 1050 and 1150 CE.[5]

At its peak between 1325 and 1375 CE, Etowah was likely home to as many as three thousand people. Over the span of six centuries, Etowah was occupied three times for periods ranging from 125 to almost 200 years with gaps in occupancy ranging from around 50 to 100 years. A much-diminished Etowah was part of the larger Coosa chiefdom when Hernando de Soto and his men marched through the Southeast in 1540. The Spanish explorers spent several days at Etowah in August of that year.[6]

By 1600, Etowah was once again abandoned, likely a consequence of diseases brought by the Spanish in combination with environmental factors. Etowah, like much of the Southeast over which Spanish explorers trod in the sixteenth century, was part of what historians have called a "shatter zone" in which Native societies were transformed during the late sixteenth through early eighteenth centuries. The collapse of the Mississippian societies happened through the "combined conditions of the structural instability of the Mississippian world and the inability of Native polities to withstand the full force of colonialism." The collapse unfolded over the course of two centuries, and although the Native societies changed dramatically, the Native peoples survived, "regrouped and reformed new kinds of polities."[7]

By the time the English arrived in the area that is today Georgia, the descendants of the people of the Etowah chiefdom had coalesced into a group of allied peoples that were referred to by the English as "Creeks." The Creek Indians occupied western and southern Georgia as well as much of Alabama into the early nineteenth century, when they were forcibly removed by the U.S. and state governments to the Oklahoma Territory.[8]

The world into which Hernando de Soto and other Spanish explorers ventured in the 1500s was characterized by hereditary chiefdoms in which the commoners were farmers and the ruling elite organized the labor to build mounds and fortified towns and managed the agricultural surpluses produced by the farmers. Critical to the success of the Mississippian peoples was the rise of corn agriculture in the tenth century. While corn agriculture had existed in the American Southeast since around 200 CE, the development of a variety of corn that thrived in the southeastern climate seems to have occurred around 900. Anthropologist Eric Bowne explains that "with the adoption of corn as the major crop, southerners went from being gardeners to being farmers," and "nascent chiefs used the ability to store corn for long periods to their political advantage."[9]

The earliest archaeological features discovered at Etowah indicate that the site was first settled between 1000 and 1100. This first chiefdom on the site was likely the period when construction began on what is today known as Mound A, which is among the largest mounds remaining in the Southeast. Mound A served as the platform upon which the chief would build his house and ceremonial structures. Construction of Mound B, thought to have been used for ceremonial purposes, may have begun during this period as well. This first village at Etowah, which existed for a little over a century, was unusual because it had no palisade, or protective walls. This could indicate that the chiefs of Etowah developed conciliatory relations with groups in the surrounding area. Several other chiefdoms developed during this period in the Etowah Valley, although none of them rivaled the Etowah site in terms of mound building. Perhaps the most formidable chiefdom in the region was Ocmulgee in the area of present-day Macon. The Etowah Valley chiefdoms were abandoned around 1200 and would remain so for about fifty years.[10]

Around 1250, the Etowah site was reoccupied, and over the next 125 years, the chiefdom reached its peak of power and population. Artifacts found on the site from this period indicate that the new chiefs brought "foreign artifacts" that helped establish their leadership claims. Archaeologists have speculated that some of these artifacts may have come from Cahokia. Four other mound centers, which were subsidiary to Etowah, developed during this time in the Etowah Valley. The Etowah chiefdom was engaged in long-distance trade that extended into the Midwest and as far south as northern Florida. Mound A was expanded; Mound C, which was the site of a temple and served as a burial mound, was constructed; and a public plaza was developed between the mounds.

Mound A, at more than 60 feet tall, is approximately the height of a six-story building, and its flat top is a half acre. The base of the mound, which is second in size in the United States only to Monks Mound at Cahokia, measures about 330 feet by 380 feet.[11] Ground-penetrating radar surveys conducted in 2005 indicated that a complex of buildings existed on the top of Mound A, likely the home and ceremonial buildings of the chief.[12] Across the 54-acre town site, archaeologists using ground-penetrating radar have identified the location of more than 140 buildings ranging from houses clustered around small plazas to one structure that is almost 100 feet long, giving them a sense of how the town appeared during its period of peak occupancy.[13] A 3-foot-high raised plaza estimated to be 300 square feet was built out of clay next to Mound A during the middle period. Archaeologists believe that Mound B, which was begun during the first phase of occupancy and expanded during the middle phase, was built in what was once a residential area. Mound C, which was constructed and used only during the middle period of occupancy, was a burial mound for the town's elite. It is the only one of the three large mounds to have been completely excavated, and it is from Mound C that most of the artifacts as well as human remains—more than 350 burials—were recovered.[14] At its peak, the site featured eight mounds and a moat and wall surrounding the town. Unfortunately, the moat and wall proved insufficient when the town was attacked around 1375, and the chiefdom collapsed. The site was abandoned and would not be reoccupied for about a century.[15]

The final phase of occupancy began around 1475, but this time Etowah was a subsidiary chiefdom of the larger Coosa chiefdom. Three small mounds were constructed during this period—Mounds D, E, and F—but the existing mounds were not expanded. Mound C, which had been used as a burial mound during the Middle Mississippian period, was not used during this Late Mississippian period. The arrival of de Soto's Spanish expedition in August 1541 contributed to the decline of the larger Coosa chiefdom as well as to Etowah, which was abandoned by 1600.[16]

A Cherokee guide led the Reverend Elias Cornelius to the Etowah site in 1818, and miscommunication between the guide and Cornelius likely led to the spread of the "Moundbuilder theory," which held that the mounds had been built by a "superior" race of people who had since been slaughtered by Indians in the area. In 1832, the Etowah Mounds were part of the lands distributed to white settlers following the forced removal of the Indians. Lewis Tumlin drew the lot that contained the mounds, and his family would own the property for more than one hundred years. The Tumlins allowed the Smithsonian Institution to conduct investigations into Mound C in the 1880s. The findings by John Rogan, including intricately embossed copper plates found among the burials on the summit of Mound C, helped discredit the Moundbuilder theory.[17]

The Tumlin family guarded the site and largely kept looters at bay well into the twentieth century. They allowed further archaeological investigations in the 1920s by Warren Moorehead, who spent three seasons excavating Mound C and began investigations of Mound B and the village area. Like Rogan before him, Moorehead uncovered burial artifacts from Mound C, including copper plates as well as shell sculptures, effigies in clay, and stone sarcophagi. By the 1930s, Moorehead had concluded that the Etowah Mounds "were built by members of the great Muskhogean family, composed of the Creek, Chickasaw, Choctaw, Natchez, and Seminole tribes."[18]

The Tumlin family retained ownership of the mound site until 1953, when they sold it to the Georgia Historical Commission for $20,000. Dr. A. R. Kelly, state archaeologist of the University of Georgia, declared that the price paid was "more than a bargain," and that "no price could be placed on the historical information concerned."[19] Lewis Henry Tumlin Jr., the great-grandson of Lewis Tumlin, was asked to serve as the "resident custodian" after the state's acquisition of the site, and he was often on-site during the archaeological excavations carried out by archaeologists William Sears and Lewis Larson, which took place between 1952 and 1958. In 1954, Larson's team uncovered what is considered to be among the finest Mississippian artifacts—a pair of marble effigies, one male and one female—in a log-lined tomb (Burial 15) at the base of Mound C. The position of the twenty-four-inch-tall marble effigies, along with the haphazard placement of the other contents of Burial 15, including the disarticulated remains of four individuals, supported Larson's theory that Etowah had come under attack and was destroyed by fire around 1375.[20]

As the archaeological investigations were underway, Governor Marvin Griffin earmarked $50,000 for the construction of a museum in which to display the artifacts recovered from the site. On Sunday, October 19, 1958, Governor Griffin, Secretary of State Ben Fortson, and Historical Commission chairman Joseph Cumming attended the opening ceremonies for the state's newest historical site. A crowd of four thousand people attended the ceremony at which Griffin declared, "With the development of these historical sites we are going to make progress and ol' Georgia is going to move forward," referencing the commission's other sites in nearby Murray (the Chief Vann House) and Gordon (New Echota) Counties. The mounds as well as the other new state historic sites were expected to draw tourists to the area, something that was considered vital to the state's economy.[21] Among the objects on display at the museum were pearls, copper axes, flint swords, shell gorgets, embossed copper shields and ornaments, the two marble effigies, and human remains that were displayed in the ground and covered by glass.[22]

Much to the dismay of the Muscogee (Creek) descendants of the Etowah people, those skeletons remained on display until 1987. Following the passage of the Native American Graves Protection and Repatriation Act (NAGPRA) in 1990, the state was required to conduct an inventory of all the objects and human remains that had been removed from the site—at least 404 individuals and more than 187,000 funerary objects.[23] The inventory was completed in 1996, but not until 2021 did the Muscogee (Creek) Nation file a repatriation claim for the items under the control of the Department of Natural Resources (DNR). The repatriation process began in January 2023.[24] The removal of the objects from display has led to a "reimagining" of the exhibit space, according to interpretive ranger Keith Bailey, who explains that going forward the museum will "focus on the people and the culture of Etowah, not the artifacts." According to tribal representative Raelynn Butler, the Etowah site is still a "sacred and religious place" to the Muscogee people, and the objects associated with the site are a "physical representation of Muskogean culture and lifeways."[25]

Despite the removal of the objects from display, the site remains well worth a visit with the most spectacular of the artifacts, the mounds themselves and the fish weir in the Etowah River, as the principal sights for visitors.

Touring the Site

Visitors enter the Etowah Mounds through a gate off a backroad near Highway 41 in Cartersville, Georgia.[26] A cluster of picnic tables are located adjacent to the parking lot.

The visitor center includes a museum, a gift shop, a theater, and restroom facilities. The small gift shop is located behind the counter where visitors pay admission. A diorama located in the hallway shows how the chiefdom would have appeared at the height of its power. The museum is located across the hall from the diorama, and the theater, where a film, *The Southeastern Indians*, is shown, is located at the back of the exhibit space. The film is also available on the website at https://gastateparks.org/EtowahIndianMounds.

The museum once featured a variety of artifacts that were recovered from the site by archaeologists, including the two marble effigy sculptures as well as numerous ceremonial objects made of copper. Most of the artifacts were found in Mound C. These objects were repatriated to the

Diorama of the Etowah Indian Mounds showing the settlement at its peak.

Muscogee (Creek) tribe in early 2024 following the NAGPRA guidelines. The museum now features interpretive panels that explain the history of the site and its people.

Large windows across the corner of the visitor center allow a view of the mounds as well as of a reconstructed wattle-and-daub building and adjacent seating for outdoor educational programs. Staff use this space for annual demonstrations of the basic skills used by the Mississippian period people, such as flintknapping (creating tools out of flint), fire building, weaving, and food preparation, and for programs with school groups. Consult the website for details of scheduled events.

The borrow pit from which earth was dug for construction of the mounds still surrounds much of the site. A mown path across the grass-covered plaza leads to the cluster of the three largest mounds—Mounds A, B, and C. The sixty-three-foot-high Mound A, once the site of the chief's residence and ceremonial temple, towers over the site. Mound B, located south of Mound A, served as the temple platform for a lesser chief. Mound C, which was built in numerous stages, once featured temple structures and served as a funerary mound. It is the only mound in the complex that

Education area and wattle-and-daub house at the Etowah Indian Mounds.

has been completely excavated. Visitors can access the top of each of these mounds via wooden steps. The view from atop Mound A is especially worth the climb.

Interpretive panels across the site offer information on the archaeological surveys that have been conducted at the site, including the most recent ground-penetrating radar survey, as well as explanations of the various spaces—from the borrow pit to the plaza and the mounds themselves.

Visitors should be sure to walk the trail along the Etowah River at the back side of the site. Still visible is the stone fish weir constructed during the prehistoric period of Etowah's occupation.

The trail loops along the eastern edge of the site, from which visitors can get a good view of the complex, including three smaller mounds located in the field east of the plaza in front of Mound A. The height of these mounds has been reduced by erosion and farming practices over the centuries, but they mark the sites of residences of revered village leaders.

Borrow pit at the Etowah Indian Mounds.

View of Mound C from atop Mound A at the Etowah Indian Mounds.

Fish weir in the Etowah River at the Etowah Indian Mounds.

Notes

1. "State's Seven Natural Wonders Are Selected for Bicentennial," *Atlanta Constitution*, January 30, 1933, 9.

2. Francine Weiss, "Etowah Indian Mounds," National Register of Historic Places Nomination Form (Washington, D.C.: U.S. Department of the Interior, National Park Service, 1983), section 8.

3. Adam King, "Mississippian Period," *New Georgia Encyclopedia*, last modified Jan 6, 2021, https://www.georgiaencyclopedia.org/articles/history-archaeology/mississippian-period-overview/.

4. Robbie Ethridge, introduction to *Mapping the Mississippian Shatter Zone: The Colonial Indian Slave Trade and Regional Instability in the American South*, ed. Robbie Ethridge and Sheri M. Shuck-Hall (Lincoln: University of Nebraska Press, 2009), 5.

5. Eric Bowne, *Mound Sites of the Ancient South* (Athens: University of Georgia Press, 2013), 79.

6. Adam King, *Etowah: The Political History of a Chiefdom Capital* (Tuscaloosa: University of Alabama Press, 2003), 82.

7. Ethridge, introduction to *Mapping the Mississippian Shatter Zone*, 2.

8. Claudio Saunt, "Creek Indians," *New Georgia Encyclopedia*, last modified August 25, 2020, https://www.georgiaencyclopedia.org/articles/history-archaeology/creek-indians/.

9. Bowne, *Mound Sites*, 3–4.

10. Bowne, 155.

11. Weiss, "Etowah Indian Mounds."

12. Greg Bluestein, "Excavators Utilizing Eco-Friendly Techniques to Probe Sacred Ground," *Macon Telegraph*, July 6, 2006, 14.

13. Mike Toner, "City beneath the Mounds," *Archaeology Magazine* 61, no. 6 (November/December 2008).

14. Bowne, *Mound Sites*, 150–151.

15. Bowne, 156.

16. Bowne, 157.

17. Bowne, 153.

18. Ben Cooper, "Dr. Moorehead Writes of Findings in Excavating Etowah Mounds," *Atlanta Constitution*, May 8, 1932, 27.

19. Ken Hogg, "Cartersville Mounds Purchased by State," *Atlanta Constitution*, March 12, 1953.

20. King, *Etowah*, 78–80; George E. Stuart, "The Education of an Archaeologist: The 1954 Season at Etowah, Georgia," *Southeastern Archaeology* 23, no. 2 (Winter 2004): 146–149.

21. George Evans, "Griffin Dedicates Mounds," *Atlanta Constitution*, October 20, 1958, 18.

22. "Etowah Mounds Museum to Open Sunday," *Columbus Enquirer*, October 17, 1958, 12.

23. Diane Wagner, "Control of Items Excavated from Prehistoric Burial Mounds in Cartersville Is Passing to Descendants in Oklahoma, Alabama," *Rome News Tribune*, September 13, 2009.

24. "Georgia Begins Repatriation of Native American Artifacts from Etowah Indian Mounds," Georgia Department of Natural Resources State Parks & Historic Sites, last updated December 20, 2022, https://gastateparks.org/press-release-parks/georgia-begins-repatriation-native-american-artifacts-etowah-indian-mounds.

25. Keith Bailey and Raelynn Butler, Evening Lecture—Repatriation at Etowah, Bartow History Museum, May 25, 2023.

26. Keith Bailey interview by Kathryn Graham, October 2022.

Further Reading

Bowne, Eric, E. *Mound Sites of the Ancient South: A Guide to the Mississippian Chiefdoms.* Athens: University of Georgia Press, 2013.

Ethridge, Robbie, and Sheri M. Shuck-Hall, eds. *Mapping the Mississippian Shatter Zone: The Colonial Indian Slave Trade and Regional Instability in the American South.* Lincoln: University of Nebraska Press, 2009.

Hudson, Joyce Rockwood. *Looking for DeSoto: A Search Through the South for the Spaniard's Trail.* Athens: University of Georgia Press, 1993.

King, Adam. *Etowah: The Political History of a Chiefdom Capital.* Tuscaloosa: University of Alabama Press, 2003.

King, Adam. "Mississippian Period." *New Georgia Encyclopedia*, last modified January 6, 2021. https://www.georgiaencyclopedia.org/articles/history-archaeology/mississippian-period-overview/.

Larson, Lewis. "Etowah Mounds." *New Georgia Encyclopedia*, last modified October 13, 2021. https://www.georgiaencyclopedia.org/articles/history-archaeology/etowah-mounds/.

Pauketat, Timothy R. *Ancient Cahokia and the Mississippians.* New York: Cambridge University Press, 2004.

CHAPTER 4

Dahlonega Gold Museum

Jennifer W. Dickey

Basic Information

PERIOD OF SIGNIFICANCE: 1836 to 1965

DATE ESTABLISHED AS A HISTORIC SITE: 1966

ACREAGE: 1 acre

LOCATION: 1 Public Square N, Dahlonega, Ga. 30533, Lumpkin County

The city of Dahlonega owes its existence to the North Georgia gold rush that began in 1828–1829—what is often described as the "first major gold rush" in the history of the United States. The gold rush in North Georgia followed earlier discoveries in North Carolina from 1799 and the early 1800s along a vein that ran all the way to Georgia. The land upon which gold was discovered in the 1820s in what is now Georgia, however, belonged neither to the state nor the United States at the time. It belonged to the Cherokees, a sovereign nation of Native peoples who had their own government and who had been negotiating for several decades to preserve the sovereignty and boundaries of their homeland. The North Georgia gold rush led to an invasion by prospectors and the eventual seizure and redistribution of Cherokee land by the state and the removal of the Cherokee people by the federal government to Indian Territory in what is now Oklahoma. Among the new counties carved out of the former Cherokee Nation was Lumpkin, named after Governor Wilson Lumpkin, whose county seat of Dahlonega was established in 1833. By 1836, the boom town of Dahlonega boasted a brick courthouse in the town square. That courthouse, which is today home to the Dahlonega Gold Museum,

Main entrance to the Dahlonega Gold Museum.

was listed on the National Register of Historic Places in 1971 for its significance in "the story of the nation's first notable gold rush" and as "the oldest public building in North Georgia," which is "itself part of the gold story having witnessed most events associated with gold fever in that part of Georgia."[1]

History of the Dahlonega Gold Museum

Although historians disagree about who first discovered gold in the area that is today Lumpkin County, they largely agree that the events that occurred in the late 1820s constitute the first major gold rush in what is today the United States. To describe what happened in this area in the 1820s as the "first discovery" of gold, however, is indisputably false. In 1935 historian Fletcher M. Green noted that "there is indubitable proof that the

Indians of Georgia had knowledge of the gold buried in the region," and that they "vaguely report[ed] this to the Spanish" and "had crude jewelry made of gold." The Cherokees, who lived in this area at the time of the settlement of the Georgia colony, were aware of the gold deposits but wisely kept this knowledge to themselves. Green offered examples of what are "some of the dozens of 'first discoveries'" in the nineteenth century but noted that none of them can definitively be deemed "the first." He recounted that by 1828–1829, a gold vein that was being mined in North Carolina was "traced southward into Georgia; and several discoveries were made about the same time in various places in the state."[2]

In 1828 gold was found in a creek in White County by an enslaved man who was returning from working in the mines in North Carolina, and another discovery was made by a Black man in Bear Creek near the site that would become Dahlonega. Additional gold finds occurred that same year in Ward's Creek in what would become Lumpkin County and in Duke's Creek in Habersham County. A discovery by Benjamin Parks in 1828 is often cited as the event that precipitated the Georgia gold rush, but as Green noted, "the early discoveries came so thick and fast that it is practically impossible to definitively establish priority of discovery."[3]

Benjamin Parks frequently recounted his story about kicking an unusual stone while deer hunting and noticing a gold-colored vein. More than six decades later, Parks stated, "Within a few days it would seem as if the world must have heard of it, for men came from every state. They came afoot, on horseback, and in wagons, acting more like crazy men than anything else. All the way from where Dahlonega now stands to Nuckollsville there were men panning out of the branches and making holes in the ground."[4] However the word spread about the presence of gold in North Georgia, according to historian David Williams, the first "documentary evidence" appeared in the *Georgia Journal*, a Milledgeville newspaper, on August 1, 1829, which ran a notice announcing, "Two gold mines have just been discovered in this [Habersham] county, and preparations are making to bring these hidden treasures of the earth to use."[5] By the fall of 1829, thousands of prospectors had arrived in North Georgia, an area that belonged to the Cherokee Nation. The Cherokees referred to the event as the "Great Intrusion." From its base in New Echota, the *Cherokee Phoenix* reported, "Our neighbors who regard no law and pay no respects to the laws of humanity are now reaping a plentiful harvest. . . . We are an abused people."[6]

The influx into Cherokee territory by the miners set in motion a series of events that would lead to the dispossession of the land from the Cherokee people and their removal to the west as well as the creation of Cherokee County in 1831. The Cherokees, who themselves had periodically mined gold in the area, appealed to the U.S. government in early 1830 for protection against the invaders, and following a warning from the U.S. agent to the miners that they should leave the area, many miners agreed to do so. However, the "intruders," as they were called in the *Cherokee Phoenix*, soon returned when they realized that the agent had no intention of procuring warrants against them.[7] In an effort to keep the peace, U.S. troops were sent to Georgia to help quell the unrest and remove the miners who were illegally panning and digging for gold on Cherokee land.

Georgia governor George Gilmer had issued proclamations in July 1830 declaring the extension of state laws to the territory and ordering all mining to cease.[8] Gilmer appealed to President Andrew Jackson to remove the troops, noting that the General Assembly had passed an act stating that "all the Cherokee territory, and the persons occupying it, were subjected to the ordinary jurisdiction of the state," and that the federal troops were no longer necessary in Georgia.[9] Jackson complied and removed federal troops from Georgia, although federal troops returned at the reluctant request of Gilmer two months later in an effort to keep the peace in what was becoming an increasingly lawless area.[10]

Reflecting on the early years of the gold rush some fifty years later, Judge Junius Hillyer recalled: "Within the short space of a year after the first precious metal was found from 5,000 to 10,000 people congregated in the Indian territory west of Hall and Habersham counties searching for gold. These intruders were lawless and turbulent men. By their numbers, with the ferocity of their Anglo-Saxon blood, they successfully resisted the civil powers and also a portion of the army which the United States government sent to drive them out and protect the rights of the Indians." Hillyer added that "the soldiers succumbed to gold fever themselves and were induced to join slyly in the digging. Besides this, the section was overrun by thieves, gamblers and murderers—quarrelsome, drunken and malicious—forming altogether a lawless, ungovernable community."[11]

The Cherokee Nation filed suit against the state for its extension of state laws into Cherokee territory. Gilmer sent into the area members of the Georgia militia, who arrested several missionaries, including Reverend S. A. Worcester, who lived in New Echota and who filed suit against the state for his imprisonment. Both suits made their way to the U.S. Supreme Court. In 1831 in *Cherokee Nation v. the State of Georgia*, the court declined to rule on the merits of the case in which the Cherokees argued that they were a sovereign nation and not subject to the laws of Georgia, but a year later the court ruled in *Worcester v. Georgia* that the Cherokee Nation was a sovereign territory "in which the laws of Georgia can have no force."[12] President Jackson, empowered by the Indian Removal Act of 1830, which allowed him to negotiate treaties directly with the Indian nations, refused to enforce the Supreme Court decision, and the depredations of the Cherokees continued.[13]

The state sent surveyors into the newly designated Cherokee County in 1831 to partition the area into 160-acre agricultural land lots and 40-acre gold lots, all of which would be redistributed to white Georgia residents through a series of land lotteries in 1832 and 1833. As the lottery winners arrived to claim their land, the Cherokees were dispossessed. While Principal Chief John Ross continued to fight to maintain the Cherokee Nation, another faction within the tribe negotiated the Treaty of New Echota with the U.S. government, which ceded their ancestral lands to the United States in return for land in what was then the Arkansas Territory (present-day Oklahoma) and $5 million.[14] Beginning in 1838, U.S. troops rounded up the remaining Cherokee people in Georgia and escorted them, either overland or via waterways, to the designated Indian Territory west of the Mississippi River. This event, during which thousands of Cherokees died, has become known as the Trail of Tears.

In December 1832, the Georgia General Assembly divided Cherokee County into ten smaller counties, including the county of Lumpkin. The first town settled in this new county was called Nuckollsville, after Nathaniel Nuckolls, who established a tavern and an inn to house the miners who were pouring into the area. Among the new landowners in the area was the former vice president and current South Carolina senator John C. Calhoun, who sent his son-in-law, Thomas Clemson, along with twenty enslaved men to work his mine.[15] Calhoun allegedly suggested that the name of the town be changed. Local resident John Powell suggested "Auraria," derived from the Latin word for "gold," which won the approval of the town's residents and was adopted in November 1832.[16]

Auraria grew quickly, and by 1833 the town had "one hundred dwelling houses, twenty stores, fifteen law offices, five taverns, and two newspapers" to support the population of about one thousand residents and a "floating population of ten thousand." Surprisingly, when the county seat was selected by the inferior court in December 1833, a mining camp known alternately as Licklog or New Mexico was chosen. Green argues that although Auraria, with its many buildings and growing population, seemed like the logical choice to serve as the county seat, controversy surrounding a "fraudulently drawn" land lot in which Auraria was located led the court to choose the smaller settlement located six miles northeast of Auraria.[17] In October 1833, the court "unanimously agreed upon the name of Talonega for the village," the Cherokee word for "gold." According to the *Georgia Journal and Messenger*, "the village was improving with unprecedented rapidity."[18] By 1834, the spelling had been changed to "Dahlonega."

A log building was constructed to serve as the county courthouse, but by most accounts, Dahlonega, as well as much of Lumpkin County, was a lawless land. In the town, "gambling houses, dancing houses, drinking saloons, houses of ill fame, billiard saloons, and tenpin alleys were open day and night," according to a Dahlonega resident, who noted that the women of the town, who were almost equal in number to the men, were "equally as vile and wicked." Dahlonega was described as an "unmoral community" where "drunkenness, fighting, lewdness, and every other vice" existed "to an awful extent."[19]

Among the throngs of miners who flocked to the area were several Black men, both enslaved and free. The enslaved miners were sent there by their enslavers to work after the fall harvest or sent there by planters who had given up growing cotton to try their hand at mining. In some cases, notes David Williams, enslaved workers were acquired specifically to work in the gold mines. Newspapers from the period abounded with advertisements offering "liberal prices" for Black men who could be put to work in the mines as well as notices for runaways who had escaped enslavement while working in the mines.[20]

Although they were excluded from owning land or enjoying any of the entertainment venues of Dahlonega, several free Blacks also came to the area in search of gold. Some worked as sharecroppers and panned for gold in their spare time, while at least one, James Boisclair, managed to accumulate significant wealth. Boisclair, known locally as "Free Jim," was emancipated in Augusta, Georgia, in 1826 and arrived in Dahlonega in 1833, where he set up a "cake and fruit shop." Boisclair also began searching for gold, and he discovered a vein on a lot east of Dahlonega that looked promising. By law, free Blacks were not allowed to own property in Georgia, so Boisclair arranged for the superintendent of the Dahlonega Mint, Joseph Singleton, to buy the lot, while Boisclair operated the mine. Boisclair worked his mine, known as the "Free Jim mine," for over a decade, and it proved productive. He was able to expand his business operations to include "the largest dry-goods and general merchandise store in Dahlonega" as well as an ice house and a saloon. Like many residents of Dahlonega, Boisclair left Georgia for California following the discovery of gold on the West Coast. According to David Williams, Boisclair was killed in a fight over a claim in California.[21]

The construction in the mid-1830s of two major brick buildings—a courthouse and a U.S. Mint—changed the appearance of the gold rush town that up until that time had been dominated by wood frame and log buildings. The U.S. Mint, which opened in 1838, operated until 1861. Here, miners could have their gold assayed (tested for quality) and made into gold coins. During its twenty-three years of operation, the mint produced about 1.5 million gold coins valued at over $6 million, but it never provided the boost to the nation's coin shortage that its advocates had predicted.[22] By the late 1840s, news of gold discoveries in California signaled the beginning of the end of Georgia's gold rush, as prospectors headed west.

The mint operated for several months following Georgia's secession from the United States in 1861, although there was confusion about to whom it belonged—the U.S. government, the state of Georgia, or the Confederate States of America. The latter would have the final say in the fate of the mint when the Confederate Congress voted to close the mints in Dahlonega and New Orleans on June 1, 1861.[23]

During the Reconstruction Period, the mint facility served as a base for federal troops from 1867 to 1869. After a failed attempt to sell the building in 1870, the Treasury Department gave it to the new North Georgia Agricultural College in 1871. The building, which had throughout its existence suffered from a leaky roof and structural problems, burned in December 1878. All that remained was the stone foundation upon which the college built a new building that still stands today. Coins from the Dahlonega Mint bearing the mint mark "D" became increasingly valuable as collector's items in the twentieth century.[24]

The courthouse, located in the public square in the center of the town, was built by Ephraim Clayton, a native of North Carolina who "gained widespread fame as a builder" during the nineteenth century.[25] Clayton received the commission after another contractor, John Humphries, who was paid $2,000 to build the courthouse in February 1834, "absconded from the county of Lumpkin" without ever beginning the project.[26] Described as a "country version of Classic Revival" with "a Jeffersonian flavor" and "partly Greek, partly Roman and partly Federal," the two-story brick courthouse dominated the town's central square. Its exterior brick walls were 22.5 inches thick, and its interior brick walls were 12 inches thick. The brick for the courthouse was made from clay quarries from nearby Cane Creek and is flecked with tiny traces of gold. The second floor was reached by a set of external stairs located beneath a Tuscan-columned portico on the southeastern side of the building. Upon its opening in 1836, the first floor of the courthouse served as a marketplace, and the second floor housed the county offices and courtroom.[27]

It was on the steps of the courthouse that the assayer of the Dahlonega Mint, Matthew Stephenson, pleaded with an assembly of some two hundred miners in 1849 that they should not go to California in search of gold. Pointing to nearby Findley Ridge, Stephenson declared: "In that ridge lies more gold than man ever dreamt of. There's millions in it." Stephenson's words allegedly inspired the phrase "There's gold in them thar hills" spoken by the character Mulberry Sellers in Mark Twain's 1892 book, *The American Claimant*. Stephenson's pleas aside, most of the twenty-niners who had flocked to Georgia in 1829 in search of gold became forty-niners as they headed to California to participate in that gold rush.

Although the California gold rush of 1849 led to an exodus of miners, many of them would return to the area in the 1850s and bring with them new mining techniques, such as hydraulic mining, that were much more aggressive and ravaged the landscape across the North Georgia gold veins. Gold fever ebbed and flowed over the next century in Georgia. The last of the large-scale attempts to mine gold in North Georgia occurred in the late nineteenth and early twentieth centuries, when several companies set up large operations in the area. In 1899, the Dahlonega Consolidated Gold Mining Company constructed the largest gold-processing plant east of the Mississippi River on Yahoola Creek. Chartered at a half-million dollars, the Dahlonega Consolidated Gold Mining Company failed to turn a profit and closed in 1903. The other mining companies soon followed suit. Another wave of mining ensued in the 1930s, but that too proved to be short-lived.[28]

The legacy of the Dahlonega Consolidated Gold Mining Company lives on today in the form of a tourist attraction, Consolidated Gold Mining

External staircase on the south side of the Dahlonega Gold Museum.

Company, a private company that offers tours of the underground mines last worked in the early twentieth century. However, the most comprehensive history of the gold rush, as well as the story of Cherokee removal, is found in the 1836 courthouse, the state historic site that houses the Gold Museum. The 1836 courthouse served the county for 129 years before it was sold to the Georgia Historical Commission in 1966 following the opening of a new courthouse about a mile south of the public square in 1965.

In March 1966 Governor Carl Sanders announced that he was making available $100,000 for the acquisition of the courthouse and conversion of the building into a gold museum. Upon accepting the deed to the courthouse from Lumpkin commissioner Clyde Fortner, Sanders declared, "There is a great deal of history in Dahlonega," adding, "The courthouse will serve generations to come as a reminder of what it was in the past and what we're trying to make it today." Secretary of State Ben Fortson, who was jubilant about the acquisition of the courthouse by the state, stated that the courthouse was "a great historic site that should be preserved for all Georgians" and predicted that people would come from all over the United States to visit the site.[29]

The courthouse, restored to its 1830s appearance, reopened on July 1, 1967, as the Dahlonega Gold Museum. The building was described by reporter Andrew Sparks as "the biggest surviving souvenir of America's first gold rush," adding, "No matter what is displayed inside the gold museum, the building itself—like Frank Lloyd Wright's Guggenheim Museum in New York—will always be one of the chief exhibits."[30] William Mitchell, historian for the Historical Commission, noted that the building's original moldings, crafted by Ephraim Clayton, were identical to those in the 1835 "Carpenter's Handbook" published by New England architect Asher Benjamin. Benjamin was a prolific architect who worked in New England from the 1790s until his death in the 1840s, and his influence on American architecture in the first half of the nineteenth century was substantial because of his seven handbooks of architecture, published between 1797 and 1856.[31] A carpenter by trade, Ephriam Clayton likely brought with him to Dahlonega a copy of Benjamin's book, published under the title *The Practical House Carpenter*, tying the county courthouse in Dahlonega to the latest fashion in architectural style in the United States.

Restoration architect Garland Reynolds described the character of the building as "pioneer Georgian," explaining: "People came here to the mountains and tried to copy things being done on the east coast, and they did it with heart pine and native clay, using handmade tools. The builder probably arrived in a wagon with that carpenter's handbook." The north side of the building was the "best elevation," according to Reynolds, who described it as "something you'd expect to see in Philadelphia."[32] He described the exterior stairs under the columned porch as "a bastard thing, added to make the plan work." Clayton was "thoroughly versed" in the Georgian style, according to Reynolds, "but out of his element in Greek Revival," which was a new style in the United States in the 1830s.[33]

Prior to the restoration of the courthouse, the city of Dahlonega had long celebrated its link to the gold rush with an annual festival known as Gold Rush Days held in late October.[34] The Dahlonega Chamber of Commerce also ran a small gold museum in a barn located about half a mile from the courthouse square.[35] But the opening of the Historical Commission's Gold Museum in September 1970 in the restored courthouse created a focal point for the gold rush history that was comprehensive and professionally curated. The museum included artifacts from the early days of the gold rush as well as objects related to the courthouse function of the building. The judge's chambers and jury room, for example, remained furnished as they had been historically, while the courtroom served as a theater for a slide show about the gold rush. Most of the gold rush–related artifacts were displayed on the first floor.

In 2018, the state undertook a $550,000 renovation of the exhibitions following a three-year planning and design process.[36] Reopening in June 2018, the museum included an expanded space for the Cherokee Trail of Tears story and displays focused on the three themes of the gold rush of 1829, the Dahlonega Mint, and the courthouse itself.[37] With more than twenty thousand visitors a year, the site is among the most visited of Georgia's state historic sites. The once-lawless frontier town of Dahlonega has evolved into a tourist destination anchored by the museum and the surrounding shops and restaurants. The former North Georgia Agricultural College, chartered in 1871 and opened in 1873, is now the University of North Georgia, a public senior military college. Price Memorial Hall, a two-story brick building constructed on the foundation of the U.S. Mint and the oldest building on the university's Dahlonega campus, serves as the university's main administrative office building. In celebration of the school's centennial in 1973, the steeple atop Price Memorial Hall was clad in gold leaf mined in the Dahlonega area—a reminder, along with the Dahlonega Gold Museum, of the city's history as the site of the nation's first major gold rush.

Touring the Site

The Dahlonega Gold Museum State Historic Site is located in the center of Dahlonega on the public square. Outdoor interpretive markers provide a brief history of the Georgia gold rush and the courthouse. Visitors enter the building through the east side, where they encounter an information desk and gift shop as well exhibits about Benjamin Parks, the geology of gold, and America's first major gold rush. Additional exhibits about the Cherokee Nation, the Great Intrusion triggered by the gold rush, and the ensuing forced removal remembered as the Trail of Tears are located in the southwest corner of the first floor, along with a display about the "wild frontier" of North Georgia during the early gold rush days. An exhibit about the U.S. Mint is located across the hall. Included in the mint display is a rare complete set of Dahlonega Gold Coins from 1838 to 1861.

Exhibit explaining “The Great Intrusion” into Cherokee lands as the result of the gold rush in the Dahlonega Gold Museum.

Exhibit about the U.S. Mint in the Dahlonega Gold Museum.

Gold rush exhibit on the second floor of the Dahlonega Gold Museum.

The second floor of the building contains a theater in what was the old courtroom, where visitors can view an eighteen-minute video titled *America's First Gold Rush.*[38] The theater is ringed with discovery drawers that visitors can open to view a variety of minerals and gold-related artifacts. Adjacent to the theater space are displays about the process of gold mining and the lives of the miners. On display are tools of the trade ranging from pans to equipment used in hydraulic mining.

On the east side of the second floor, the former judge's chamber and the jury room are presented as they were in 1942 when *Life* magazine featured a story about the Superior Court of the Northeastern Judicial Circuit of Georgia. The second-floor exhibits and film are not wheelchair accessible.

The shops and restaurants that surround the square and the Gold Museum draw tourists year-round, especially in the fall. Dahlonega has

Former judge's chambers at the Dahlonega Gold Museum.

embraced its identity as the site of the nation's first major gold rush and continues to host a Gold Rush Days Festival in October each year. While the arts and crafts vendors and strolling tourists lend an air of excitement to the town, the festival crowds make access to parking downtown and the museum difficult during Gold Rush Days.

Notes

1. William R. Mitchell Jr., "Dahlonega Courthouse Gold Museum," National Register of Historic Places Nomination Form (Washington, D.C.: U.S. Department of the Interior, National Park Service, 1971), section 8.

2. Fletcher M. Green, "Georgia's Forgotten Industry: Gold Mining, Part I," *Georgia Historical Quarterly* 19, no. 2 (June 1935): 98–100.

3. Green, "Georgia's Forgotten Industry," 99.

4. Green, "Georgia's Forgotten Industry," 100.

5. David Williams, "'Such Excitement You Never Saw': Gold Mining in Nineteenth-Century Georgia," *Georgia Historical Quarterly* 76, no. 3 (Fall 1992): 696.

6. David Williams, "Georgia's Forgotten Miners: African Americans and the Georgia Gold Rush," *Georgia Historical Quarterly* 75, no. 1 (Spring 1991): 77–78.

7. "Intruders," *Cherokee Phoenix*, April 7, 1830, 2.

8. Green, "Georgia's Forgotten Industry," 104.

9. George R. Gilmer, "Communication &c. between the Governor and the War Department, Executive Department," *Georgia Journal and Messenger*, November 20, 1830, 2.

10. David Williams, *The Georgia Gold Rush: Twenty-Niners, Cherokees, and Gold Fever* (Columbia: University of South Carolina, 1995), 32.

11. "Georgia's Indian Troubles," *Atlanta Journal*, October 28, 1928, 98.

12. *Cherokee Nation v. Georgia*, 30 U.S. 1 (1831), accessed July 24, 2023, https://supreme.justia.com/cases/federal/us/30/1/; *Worcester v. Georgia*, accessed July 24, 2023, https://www.oyez.org/cases/1789-1850/31us515.

13. "Chief John Ross Protests the Treaty of New Echota," National Park Service, accessed July 31, 2023, https://www.nps.gov/articles/000/protest-treaty-of-new-echota.htm.

14. Tim Alan Garrison, "Cherokee Removal," *New Georgia Encyclopedia*, last updated July 23, 2018, https://www.georgiaencyclopedia.org/articles/history-archaeology/cherokee-removal/.

15. Williams, "Georgia's Forgotten Miners," 80.

16. Green, "Georgia's Forgotten Industry," 109; Department of Natural Resources, Parks & Historic Sites Division, *Dahlonega Gold Museum State Historic Site* (Atlanta: Department of Natural Resources), 1995; Williams, *Georgia Gold Rush*, 59.

17. Green, "Georgia's Forgotten Industry," 109.

18. "The Western Herald," *Georgia Journal and Messenger*, October 17, 1834, 3.

19. Williams, "Georgia's Forgotten Miners: African Americans and the Georgia Gold Rush," 79.

20. Williams, 82–83.

21. Williams, 86.

22. Sylvia Head and Elizabeth W. Etheridge, *The Neighborhood Mint* (Macon, Ga.: Mercer University Press, 1986), ix.

23. Head and Etheridge, 186.

24. Head and Etheridge, 189.

25. "Clayton, Ephriam (1904–1892)," North Carolina Architects & Buildings: A Biographical Dictionary, accessed July 31, 2023, https://ncarchitects.lib.ncsu.edu/people/P000070.

26. Head and Etheridge, *Neighborhood Mint*, 1986, 5.

27. Mitchell, "Dahlonega Courthouse Gold Museum."

28. Williams, *Georgia Gold Rush*, 122.

29. William O. Smith, "State Finances Gold Museum," *Atlanta Journal*, March 8, 1966, 2.

30. Andrew Sparks, "Home for Memories of the Gold Rush," *Atlanta Journal*, June 4, 1967, 16.

31. Jack Quinan, "Asher Benjamin and American Architecture," *Journal of the Society of Architectural Historians* 38, no. 3 (October 1979): 244.

32. Sparks, "Home for Memories of the Gold Rush," 14.

33. Sparks, 16.

34. "Gold Tarnishing on Gold Rush Day," *Atlanta Journal*, September 4, 1963, 2.

35. Jack Spalding, "Dahlonega's History 'Gilt Edged,'" *Atlanta Journal*, July 16, 1962, 22.

36. "Still Pure Gold: Renovated Dahlonega Gold Museum State Historic Site Reopens June 18," Explore Georgia, accessed August 1, 2023, https://www.exploregeorgia.org/still-pure-gold-renovated-dahlonega-gold-museum-state-historic-site-reopens-june-18.

37. Layne Saliba, "The Dahlonega Gold Museum Is Open Again," *Atlanta Journal-Constitution*, June 26, 2018, accessed August 1, 2023, https://www.ajc.com/travel/the-dahlonega-gold-museum-open-again-here-why-you-should-visit/ZVddZnaWGiFwjhIzOM37HO/.

38. *America's First Gold Rush*, produced by Becky Marshall (Georgia Department of Natural Resources, 2008), https://www.youtube.com/watch?v=eDfUC1bdqvw&t=1073s.

Further Reading

Coulter, E. Merton. 1956. *Auraria: The Story of a Georgia Gold-Mining Town*. 1956; rpt., Athens: University of Georgia Press, 2009.

Etheridge, Elizabeth W. "Branch Mint at Dahlonega." *New Georgia Encyclopedia*, last modified October 11, 2016. https://www.georgiaencyclopedia.org/articles/history-archaeology/branch-mint-at-dahlonega/.

Harshaw, Lou. *The Gold of Dahlonega: The First Major Gold Rush in North America*. Asheville, N.C.: Hexagon, 1979.

Head, Sylvia, and Elizabeth W. Etheridge. *The Neighborhood Mint: Dahlonega in the Age of Jackson*. Macon, Ga.: Mercer University Press, 1986.

Johnson, Edward A. "Dahlonega." *New Georgia Encyclopedia*, last modified September 9, 2014. https://www.georgiaencyclopedia.org/articles/counties-cities-neighborhoods/dahlonega/.

U.S. Department of the Interior. 1895. *The Gold Fields of the Southern Appalachians*. Scotts Valley, Calif.: CreateSpace Independent Publishing Platform, 2014.

Williams, David. *The Georgia Gold Rush: Twenty-Niners, Cherokees, and Gold Fever*. Columbia: University of South Carolina Press, 1995.

Williams, David. "Gold Rush." *New Georgia Encyclopedia*, last modified September 12, 2018. https://www.georgiaencyclopedia.org/articles/history-archaeology/gold-rush/.

CHAPTER 5

Hardman Farm

Deiah Brue and Jennifer W. Dickey

Basic Information

PERIOD OF SIGNIFICANCE: 1869–1937

DATE ESTABLISHED AS A HISTORIC SITE: 2014

ACREAGE: 173 acres

LOCATION: 143 Ga.-17, Sautee Nacoochee, Ga. 30571, White County

The newest addition to Georgia's state historic site system is Hardman Farm. Acquired by the state in 1999 and opened to the public in 2014, Hardman Farm provides a glimpse into the life of a series of well-to-do families who used this site as a getaway destination. The centerpiece of the 173-acre site is the Italianate-style home built in 1869 by James Hall Nichols, but the namesake of the site was its third owner, Dr. Lamartine Griffin Hardman. Hardman, who served two terms as governor of Georgia from 1927 to 1931, acquired the house in 1903 from Calvin W. Hunnicutt.[1]

Whereas Nichols had used this magnificent home in the west end of the Nacoochee Valley as a primary residence and refuge because of his and his wife's health issues, Hunnicutt and Hardman used the home as a summer residence to escape the hubbub of Atlanta. For Nichols, the property was a working farm, and most of the outbuildings at the site date to the time of his residence. Although Hunnicutt did not engage in farming, his successor, Lamartine Hardman, did and applied the latest scientific techniques to the endeavor. The property remained in the Hardman family for almost one hundred years, and the main house and outbuildings have been preserved much as they were during the heyday of Lamartine Hardman's

The main house at Hardman Farm.

residence. Two important cultural resources at the site that predate the Nichols residency are a Mississippian period mound and a section of the Unicoi Turnpike, a Cherokee-era roadway.

History of Hardman Farm

The Nacoochee Valley, located in northeast Georgia in an area known as the Appalachian Highland region, was designated as a 2,500-acre National Register Historic District in 1980 by the National Park Service for its "nineteenth and early-twentieth-century architecture" as well as "its prehistoric and historic archaeology." This rich array of natural and cultural resources includes an Indian mound, several structures that date to the early period of white settlement (1830s), and Hardman Farm. Described in the National Register nomination as "the most elaborate structure in the district," the main house at Hardman Farm, built in 1869 by James Nichols, is located in the west end of the valley and was known historically as "West End."[2] The property includes the prehistoric Indian burial mound with its picturesque gazebo. Although the mound is one of the most photographed sites in Georgia, the Department of Natural Resources no longer uses images of the mound to promote its historic sites out of respect for the interests of the Muscogee (Creek) people who are descendants of the Native Americans buried there.

Long before James Nichols arrived in the Nacoochee Valley in 1869, the site was occupied by Native people of the Woodland era as far back as 100–500 CE. However, the principal period of occupation during which the mound was built was during the Middle Lamar Period (1350–1600 CE) of the Mississippian period. During the Nichols period of ownership (1869–1893), several stone box graves were uncovered when fields west of the mound were plowed. Nichols himself removed an estimated two feet of earth from the top of the mound and built a wooden gazebo that remains atop the mound today.

The only formal excavation of the site, however, was conducted in 1915 under sponsorship of the Heye Foundation at the invitation of Lamartine Hardman. Archaeologists excavated an estimated 20–30 percent of the mound and uncovered seventy-five burials as well as several fire pits, pottery, copper objects, and a variety of pipes. They concluded, erroneously, that the mound had been built by Cherokees and was inhabited by them from prehistoric times until 1819.[3] Additional artifacts were collected from the fields surrounding the mound by University of Georgia archaeologist Robert Wauchope in 1939, which suggested that there was a village settlement in the area. No additional archaeological research was conducted until 2004 when Mark Williams of the University of Georgia conducted a summer field school at the site. Williams and his team focused on the village site surrounding the oval mound and concluded that the village was likely three to four hectares in size. The 2004 excavations confirmed the early-to-middle Woodland occupation as well as a long occupation during the Lamar period of the Mississippian period. In contrast to Heye's conclusions from 1918, Williams concluded that Cherokee occupation of the site was minimal.[4] However, there is historical evidence of two Cherokee villages in the Nacoochee Valley—Nacoochee and Chota—documented by Colonel George Chicken in 1715. The Cherokee villages appeared on maps until the mid-eighteenth century, although their precise location is not known.[5]

Traces of Native American occupation—the Unicoi Turnpike and the Indian mound—at Hardman Farm.

The opening of the Unicoi Turnpike in the 1810s brought travelers through the area that was still part of the Cherokee lands. The Treaty of 1819, which ceded Cherokee lands in the Sautee and Nacoochee Valleys to Georgia, was followed by a land lottery in 1820, which distributed land to white settlers.[6] White settlement in the mountainous region was sparse, as the area was not suited to large-scale agriculture.[7] In March 1822, sixty-two families arrived in the valley and began developing industries such as gristmills, a blacksmith shop, and a foundry.[8] The discovery of gold in North Georgia in 1828 led to the gold rush in the region. The gold vein that ran through nearby Lumpkin County, where Dahlonega was established as the county seat in 1833, also ran through what would eventually become known as White County, and the flow of white settlers increased. White County (created from Habersham County in 1857) would prove to be second only to Lumpkin County in Georgia in terms of the richness of the gold vein. Matthew Stephenson, who would later become the assayer at the Dahlonega Mint and beseech local miners to stay in Georgia rather than go to California, got his start in the Nacoochee Valley, where he owned interests in several gold mines in the 1830s.[9] As gold mining waned in the mid-1800s, dairy farming was introduced in the valley.

By the Reconstruction era, White County had a population of 4,609, and the county seat of Cleveland, established in 1857, had a population of 145.[10] The area was still rural and relatively remote. It also became a refuge for James Hall Nichols, a Confederate veteran from Milledgeville who had contracted malaria during the war. Upon his return to Milledgeville at the end of the war, James discovered that his wife, the former Kate Latimer, whom he had left behind with his daughter, Anna Ruby, had been assaulted by U.S. soldiers while he was away. According to the diary of Anna Maria Green, a neighbor of the Hall family, Kate, who was already in fragile health following a miscarriage, had a mental breakdown from which she would never recover.[11] As James struggled to regain his health following repeated bouts of malaria, he discovered the Nacoochee Valley area during a stay at the White Sulphur Springs resort near Gainesville. Believing that the North Georgia climate would benefit him, and that the relative seclusion of the area would benefit Kate, James acquired the property known at the time as the Brown Homestead for $5,994 in February 1869.[12]

James removed the Brown house and began construction of an Italianate mansion that was patterned after his sister's home, Rose Hill, near Milledgeville. Described as a "weatherboarded Italianate Villa–style house" in the 1980 National Register nomination, the Nichols home, West End, was the most ornate and elaborate residence in the valley. James's landholdings included the pasture in which the Indian mound was located. He leveled the top of the mound, removing two feet of earth, and built a gazebo that mimicked the architectural style of the main house. He built an array of outbuildings to support his farm, including a kitchen, which was connected to the main house by a breezeway, a smokehouse, a gashouse, a spring house, a greenhouse, and a game room. To the east of his home, he built a small wooden church in the Gothic Revival style. Completed in 1872, the church was first known as the Nacoochee Presbyterian Church and held services until the early 1900s, after which the church was unused until 1921, when Lamartine Hardman allowed a

Baptist congregation to use the facility. The church is still in use and is now known as the Crescent Hill Baptist Church.[13]

James thrived in his new environment where he farmed and explored the beauty of the surrounding mountains and valleys. He experimented with rice cultivation, which was highly unusual for the area. In addition to his farming activities, James and his daughter, Anna Ruby, often went horseback riding in the mountains surrounding West End, and among their favorite spots was a double waterfall on Smith Creek located eight miles north of West End. James named the waterfall Anna Ruby Falls, the name by which the falls are still known today. Anna Ruby married George Payne, a pharmacist, in 1885, and the couple relocated to Atlanta.

While James flourished and became a prominent resident of the Nacoochee Valley, Kate struggled with mental illness. She was secluded at West End under the care of her mother, Augusta Latimer, for several years. In the 1880s, as Kate's mental health declined further, James hired a nurse to assist with her care. By 1892, he felt that Kate's illness had progressed to the point where he and the nurse could no longer care for her at home, and he had her committed to Central State Hospital in Milledgeville as a "certified lunatic." Kate remained institutionalized there until her death in 1909. Evidence of her treatment while a resident of West End remains in an upstairs bedroom where large hooks that were used to hold a hammock-like device are still visible.[14]

Not wishing to live alone in the Nacoochee Valley mansion, James Nichols sold the property to Calvin W. Hunnicutt, an Atlanta businessman, in 1893 and moved to Atlanta himself. Although his Atlanta residence allowed him to be closer to his daughter, he struggled with myriad health issues. After he suffered another malaria relapse in 1897, he once again retreated to the Nacoochee Valley. While staying in the area, Nichols suffered a fatal heart attack.[15]

While James Nichols had been a full-time resident at West End, C. W. Hunnicutt used the home as a summer residence where he could escape the heat and bustle of Atlanta. Hunnicutt had arrived in Atlanta in 1847 when the town was still known as Marthasville, and he had been a leader in the development of the city. Described as "Atlanta's oldest pioneer and one whose efforts in business and public life have aided strongly in the upbuilding of the city," Hunnicutt had served for a year on the city council and fourteen years on the Fulton County Commission, which he chaired for eight years. Prior to the Civil War, Hunnicutt made a fortune running a dry goods store and a pharmacy. Finding himself "penniless" after the war, he started a plumbing business that became one of the "best known concerns in the city."[16]

Hunnicutt's tenure at West End, while restful for him and his family, proved uneventful for the property itself. Hunnicutt made few changes to the house and grounds during the decade in which he owned West End. In 1903, he began divesting himself of some of his real estate holdings, including land in Atlanta, which would become the site of the city's expanded waterworks system at Hemphill station, and his summer retreat in the Nacoochee Valley. Dr. Lamartine Hardman, a well-known medical doctor, farmer, and state representative from Commerce, Georgia, purchased West End from Hunnicutt for $15,500.[17]

When he acquired West End, Hardman was one of the wealthiest men in the state of Georgia. Historian Pamela Hackbart-Dean described Hardman as a "Renaissance man," whose career was "one of the most versatile of his generation."[18] Born in the town of Harmony Grove (now Commerce), in Jackson County, Georgia, in 1856, Lamartine Hardman attended Georgia Medical College, from which he graduated in 1877, as well as the University of Pennsylvania, where he pursued postdoctoral studies. He received a second degree in 1890 from Guy Hospital in London. After nearly fifteen years away from his home state, Hardman returned to his hometown and, along with his brother, William, established a hospital in Commerce, the Hardman Sanatorium. The brothers "introduced into the hospital advanced apparatus" and became well known throughout the state. Hardman also began buying real estate in Jackson County, and in 1892, he acquired the Harmony Grove Cotton Mills.

By the turn of the century, Hardman owned land in seven counties and was one of the most successful farmers in the state. He applied scientific farming techniques and was committed to agricultural innovation. In 1901, the forty-five-year-old Hardman was introduced to twenty-year-old Emma Wiley Griffin, from Valdosta. After a six-year courtship, the couple married in 1907 and eventually had four children—Lamartine Jr., Josephine, Sue, and Emma. Hardman launched his political career in 1902 when he successfully ran for office as the representative from Jackson County. He served in the state house for five years, and in 1907, he was elected to the state senate, where he served until 1910. Hardman reached the peak of his political powers when he was elected governor of Georgia in 1926. Pledging to "give the state a businesslike administration, eliminating waste and extravagance," he served two terms from 1927 to 1931.[19] During Hardman's tenure as governor, he oversaw the donation of Rhodes Hall to serve as a depository for state records. The Georgia General Assembly had created the Georgia Department of Archives and History in 1918, and the move to Rhodes Hall was a vast improvement over the previous state archives space in a room on the third floor of the state capitol.[20]

Throughout his political career, Hardman maintained a residence in his hometown of Commerce and his farm in the Nacoochee Valley, which he renamed Elizabeth on the Chattahoochee in memory of his mother.[21] In contrast to the Hunnicutt era, the Hardman era at what was formerly known as West End would be a period of major change. Hardman introduced his scientific farming techniques to the area, including the tile drainage technique, which improved water flow in poorly drained areas and dramatically increased field productivity. While campaigning for governor in 1926, Hardman spoke about how his introduction of tile drainage in Georgia had made "thousands of acres of swamp lands that were too wet to be cultivated" into some of "the most fertile land in Georgia."[22] Other innovations introduced on the farm by Hardman were soil testing and crop rotation. He established a dairy on the property in 1907. Although Hardman and his family only stayed at the farm during the summer months, farming and dairy operations continued year-round.[23] It was also during Hardman's ownership that archaeologists carried out the excavation of the Indian mound in 1915.

Lamartine Hardman died in 1937, but his family retained ownership of the farm until the 1990s. Throughout the twentieth century, Hardman's children and grandchildren continued to use the property as a retreat. Hardman's descendants, led by the youngest of his children, Emma Hardman Thompson, began negotiations in 1993 with the Trust for Public Land for a donation of the 173-acre farm to the Trust with the contingency that the Trust would raise $3 million to restore the property and then transfer ownership to the state. At the time of the transfer in March 1998, Governor Zell Miller stated that Hardman Farm was "the most significant unprotected historic site in the state of Georgia." Miller pledged over half a million dollars toward the project, and the state and federal departments of transportation pledged an equal amount to erect signage, construct a parking lot, and improve access.[24]

The state acquired the property from the Trust in 2002 for $570,000. Included in the purchase were the Nacoochee mound, the main house,

Outbuildings behind the main house, including the corn crib (left), carriage house (center), and dairy barn (right).

and twenty-one period farm buildings. Department of Natural Resources (DNR) commissioner Lonice Barrett declared the property a "key acquisition." Russ Marane, Georgia director for the Trust for Public Land, called Hardman Farm "a stunning project" that would "be one of the most significant projects on the Chattahoochee River and maybe one of the most historic projects in the state."[25]

While the Trust had begun stabilization efforts, the main house and many of the outbuildings were in poor condition when the state acquired the property in 2002. Over the next twelve years, the DNR began restoring the many buildings on the site using a methodical and conservative approach. The $2 million first phase involved the restoration of the seven-thousand-square-foot dairy barn and the gazebo atop the mound. Both projects won awards for excellence in preservation from the Georgia Trust for Historic Preservation in 2006.[26] Restoration of the main house, another $2 million project, was completed in 2011 and included a "building performance analysis" conducted by preservation architects from Lord,

Aeck and Sargent to determine the optimum way to introduce a centralized climate-control system that had minimal impact on the building's historic fabric.[27] A mix of state and federal funds were used for the projects with money from the State Stewardship Fund and the Tennessee Valley Authority.[28]

While the site was under restoration it was occasionally open to visitors. The DNR plans to have the site fully open to the public by 2009 were derailed by the discovery of asbestos in the house, which caused delays in the restoration process while remediation took place.[29] The 2008 financial crisis further delayed work as the state reduced funding to its historic sites. Hardman Farm finally opened to the public in 2014.

Touring the Site

Located on the corner of Georgia Highways 17 and 75, Hardman Farm is at the gateway to what is one of Georgia's most visited tourist sites, the city of Helen. A one-mile hiking trail that begins at the Hardman Farm visitor center provides a beautiful walk along the Chattahoochee River into downtown Helen. The parking lot for the Hardman Farm site is

Hardman Farm visitor center.

off Highway 17 at the end of a circuitous road to the top of the hill overlooking the visitor center, which is in a red brick building constructed by Hardman to serve as a store and post office. Here visitors can pay admission, explore the gift shop, and view several outdoor exhibit panels that provide background on the development of the property and the families who lived here.

An extant stretch of the Unicoi Turnpike crosses the property, and visitors walk along this route to access the main house, which can only be toured with a guide. The house has been preserved much as it was during the Hardman family's residency in the early twentieth century. Markings that recorded the heights of the Hunnicutt children and grandchildren have been preserved on the window trim in one of the upstairs bedrooms. Tours of the outbuildings are self-guided. Visitors can go inside many of the buildings, including the dairy and horse barns, corn crib, cistern, and bull pen. The site has fifteen outbuildings that are open to the public in addition to the main house and the red brick store/visitor center.

The prehistoric mound is protected by the federal government, and visitors are not allowed access. Interpretation of the Native American occupancy in Sautee Nacoochee is available at the Sautee Nacoochee

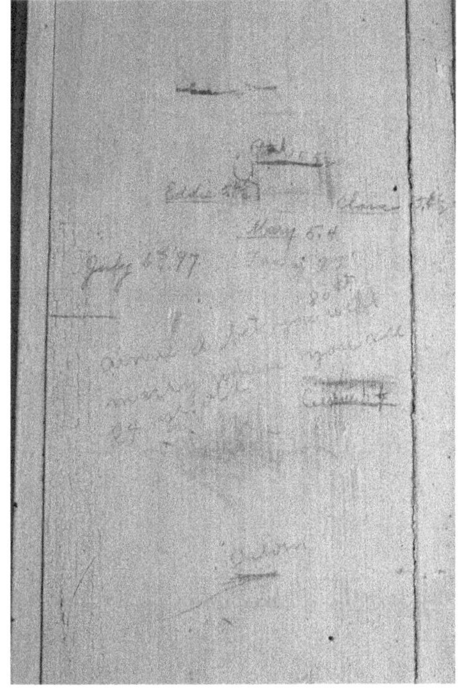

Notes on the window frame from the Hunnicutt family at Hardman Farm.

Kitchen at Hardman Farm.

Cultural Center, a separate entity located about two miles down the road from Hardman Farm. The main mission of the cultural center is to preserve and protect the culture of the Natives who once lived in the Sautee Nacoochee Valley.[30] The center fills in the gaps of the Native history that is not told at Hardman Farm.

Hardman Farm is supported by the Friends of Georgia State Parks chapter dedicated to Hardman Farm. Through this union, Hardman Farm is given aid that focuses on preserving the site and providing volunteers to help manage the site.[31] The volunteers help with events and the upkeep of the grounds. Among the most anticipated events is the annual Victorian Christmas held on Fridays and Saturdays throughout December. The Mountain Farm Celebration, held in mid-October, features arts and crafts as well as "hands-on pioneer skills exhibits." The site hosts more than thirty events a year, including living history programs, theater productions, and outdoor dances.[32]

Although not part of the site, the Crescent Hill Baptist Church is located one-tenth of a mile from the main house on Highway 17. The church, which was built by James Nichols in 1872, has been well preserved and is often open to the public. It is well worth a visit.

Notes

1. David Chapman, "Lamartine Hardman," *New Georgia Encyclopedia*, last modified March 11, 2020, https://www.georgiaencyclopedia.org/articles/arts-culture/lamartine-hardman-1856-1937/.

2. Dale Jaeger, Richard Cloues, and John R. Morgan, "Nacoochee Valley Historic District," National Register of Historic Places Nomination Form (Washington, D.C.: U.S. Department of the Interior, National Park Service, 1980), section 8.

3. George G. Heye, "The Nacoochee Mound in Georgia" (1918; rpt., Charleston: LeGare Street Press, 2022), 39, 99–100; Mark Williams, *Nacoochee Revisited: The 2004 Project* (Box Springs, Ga.: LAMAR Institute, 2004), 5.

4. Williams, *Nacoochee Revisited*, 28–29.

5. James Langford, "Nacoochee Mound," *New Georgia Encyclopedia*, last modified February 13, 2013, https://www.georgiaencyclopedia.org/articles/history-archaeology/nacoochee-mound/.

6. "Treaty with the Cherokee, 1819," Tribal Treaties Database, Oklahoma State University Libraries, accessed September 4, 2023, https://treaties.okstate.edu/treaties/treaty-with-the-cherokee-1819-0177#:~:text=The%20United%20States%20agree%20to,six%20hundred%20and%20forty%20acres.

7. Thomas Lumsden, "White County," *New Georgia Encyclopedia*, last modified June 27, 2022, https://www.georgiaencyclopedia.org/articles/counties-cities-neighborhoods/white-county/.

8. Carrie Anne Adams, *A Concise History of the Nichols-Hunnicutt-Hardman Property at Nacoochee Georgia* (Atlanta: Georgia Department of Natural Resources, 2005), 3.

9. Matt Gedney, *Living on the Unicoi Road: Helen's Pioneer Century and Tales from the Georgia Gold Rush* (Marietta, Ga.: Little Star Press, 1996), 14.

10. "White County, Georgia Genealogy," 1870 Census, accessed September 4, 2023, https://www.familysearch.org/en/wiki/White_County,_Georgia_Genealogy#cite_note-6.

11. Adams, *Concise History of the Nichols-Hunnicutt-Hardman Property*, 16.

12. Adams, 10.

13. "Crescent Hill Baptist," Historic Rural Churches, accessed September 4, 2023, https://www.hrcga.org/church/crescent-hill-baptist/.

14. Adams, *Concise History of the Nichols-Hunnicutt-Hardman Property*, 17–18.

15. Olin Jackson, *A North Georgia Journal of History*, vol. 2 (Alpharetta, Ga.: Legacy Communications, 1991), 360.

16. "Calvin Hunnicutt, Pioneer, Is Dead," *Atlanta Constitution*, January 21, 1915, 6.

17. White County History Book Committee, *A History of White County Georgia, 1857–1980* (Cleveland, Ga.: White County, 1981), 100.

18. Pamela Hackbart-Dean, "Georgia's Renaissance Governor: Lamartine Hardman—Physician, Millowner, Agriculturalist," *Georgia Historical Quarterly* 79, no. 2 (Summer 1995): 442.

19. Hackbart-Dean, 444–446.

20. Lydia Knight, "Georgia Archives," *New Georgia Encyclopedia*, last modified November 3, 2015, https://www.georgiaencyclopedia.org/articles/education/georgia-archives/.

21. White County History Book Committee, *History of White County Georgia*, 100.

22. "Dr. Hardman's Speaking Engagements Announced," *Macon Telegraph*, August 15, 1926, 5.

23. White County History Book Committee, *History of White County Georgia*, 101.

24. Charles Seabrook, "State Will Be Granted Historic Site near Helen," *Atlanta Journal*, March 17, 1998, 122.

25. Stacy Shelton, "Green Space to Expand by Five Tracts," *Atlanta Constitution*, September 24, 2002, B1.

26. Jerry Grillo, "Restoring a Sense of Community," *Georgia Trend*, September 1, 2010, accessed September 4, 2023, https://www.georgiatrend.com/2010/09/01/restoring-a-sense-of-community/; "Trust Presents Preservation Awards," *Atlanta Constitution*, April 23, 2006, D13.

27. Julia Arnold, Raman Koti, Susan Turner, and Sandeep Ahuja, "Applications and Validation of Building Performance Analysis for a Georgia Farmhouse," *APT Bulletin: The Journal of Preservation Technology* 50, no. 1 (2019): 16.

28. White County, HP-070406–045 Rehabilitate Horse Barn, Hardman Farm 030–04–020; C 657920; RCB 69852, Georgia Archives.

29. White County, HP-070406–045 Rehabilitate Horse Barn, Hardman Farm.

30. "Our Story," Sautee Nacoochee Cultural Center, accessed October 21, 2022, https://www.snca.org/snc/contact/ourStory/page.php

31. Tom Johnson, telephone interview by Deiah Brue, September 28, 2022.

32. Hardman Farm State Historic Site, accessed September 4, 2023, https://gastateparks.org/HardmanFarm; Scarlet Fuller and William Wagner, Zoom interview by Deiah Brue, October 31, 2022.

Further Reading

Chapman, David A. "Lamartine Hardman." *New Georgia Encyclopedia*, last modified March 11, 2020. https://www.georgiaencyclopedia.org/articles/arts-culture/lamartine-hardman-1856-1937/.

Gedney, Matt. *Living on the Unicoi Road*. Marietta, Ga.: Little Star Press, 1996.

Heye, George R. *The Nacoochee Mound in Georgia*. New York: Museum of the American Indian, Heye Foundation, 1918; rpt., Charleston, S.C.: Legare Street Press, 2022.

Inscoe, John C. "Helen." *New Georgia Encyclopedia*, last modified May 6, 2017. https://www.georgiaencyclopedia.org/articles/counties-cities-neighborhoods/helen/.

Jackson, Olin. *A North Georgia Journal of History*, vol. 2. Alpharetta, Ga.: Legacy Communications, 1991.

Langford, James B. "Nacoochee Mound." *New Georgia Encyclopedia*, last modified February 13, 2013. https://www.georgiaencyclopedia.org/articles/history-archaeology/nacoochee-mound/.

REGION 2

Piedmont

Stretching in a northeast to southwest direction from South Carolina to the Alabama border, the Georgia Piedmont lies between the North Georgia Mountains and the Coastal Plains. The northwest boundary is the Blue Ridge Mountains, while the southwest boundary is the fall line, which runs from Augusta through Macon to Columbus. Within this region are five state historic sites that tell pieces of Georgia's history from the early nineteenth century through World War II.

The remarkably well-preserved Traveler's Rest, a former stagecoach inn located on the Unicoi Turnpike in Stephens County, offers a glimpse into life on the Georgia frontier in the early 1800s. The former home of Alexander Stephens, Liberty Hall, located in Taliaferro County, is the centerpiece of a state park established in 1933 as a memorial to the vice president of the Confederate States. Pickett's Mill in Paulding County is one of the most well-preserved Civil War battlefields in the South. Jarrell Plantation in Jones County is a remarkably intact family farm on which generations of the Jarrell family carved out a living for nearly 130 years. The Little White House, the former retreat of U.S. president Franklin Delano Roosevelt, captures the story of the nation's thirty-second president, who came to Georgia seeking relief from the effects of polio in the 1920s. Roosevelt's former residence and the nearby historic pools complex offer insight into myriad aspects of the nation's history, including the Great Depression and World War II.

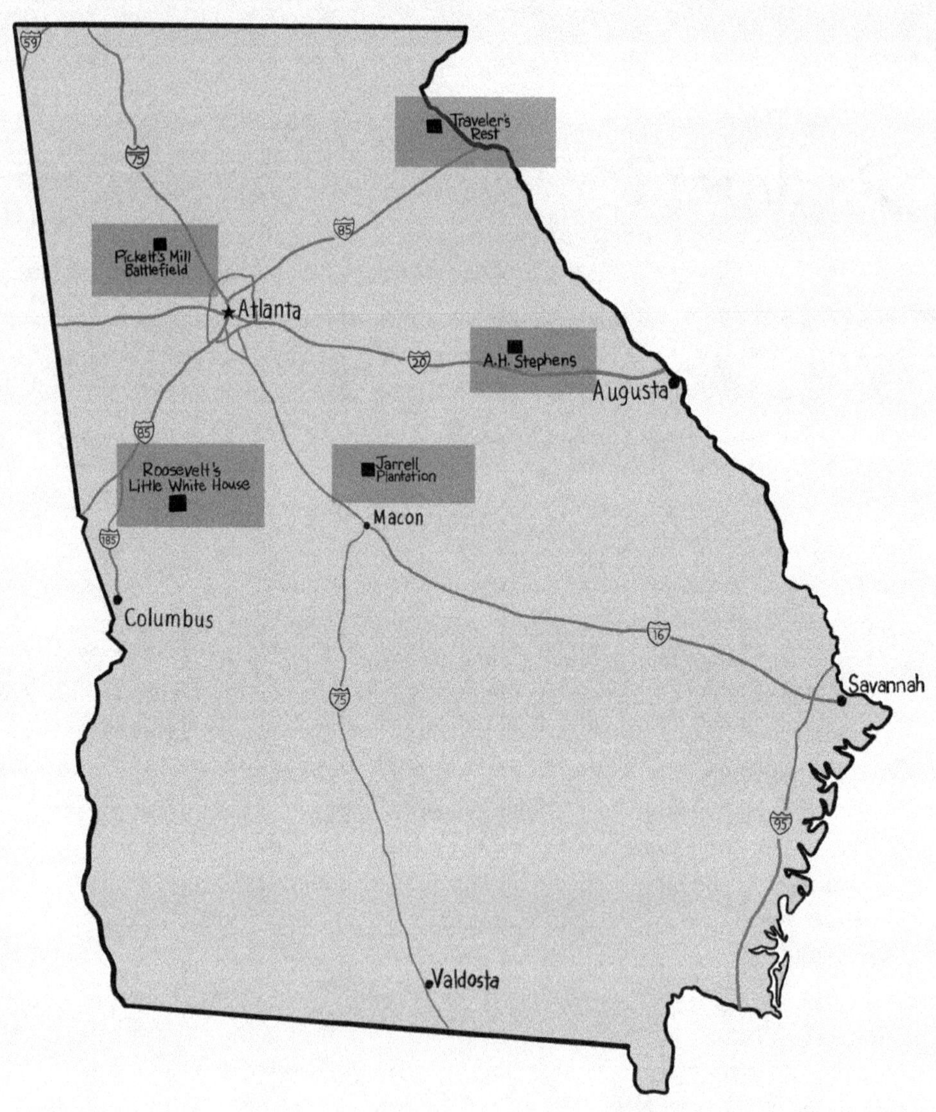
59
75
Traveler's Rest
85
Pickett's Mill Battlefield
Atlanta
20
A.H. Stephens
Augusta
85
Roosevelt's Little White House
Jarrell Plantation
Macon
185
Columbus
16
Savannah
75
95
Valdosta

CHAPTER 6

Traveler's Rest

Hannah Eslinger and Jennifer W. Dickey

Basic Information

PERIOD OF SIGNIFICANCE: 1815–1870
DATE ESTABLISHED AS A HISTORIC SITE: 1955
ACREAGE: 6 acres
LOCATION: 4339 Riverdale Road, Toccoa, Ga. 30577, Stephens County

Among the remnants of early white settlement in northeastern Georgia is Traveler's Rest, a former stagecoach inn located near the Tugaloo River (now Lake Hartwell) on the route of the Unicoi Turnpike. This rustic building, whose origins were for many years shrouded in mystery and tall tales of an Indian attack, has stood for almost two centuries in its current configuration. The building is over ninety feet long and features a shed porch that runs the full length of the front of the building. Originally the site of a prehistoric settlement, the land was later occupied by the Cherokees. Following the American Revolution, pioneer settler and Revolutionary War veteran Jesse Walton acquired the site in a land grant in 1785. Walton's death at the hands of Creek Indians in 1789 became the foundation for much of the mythology of the site that persisted well into the twentieth century.

Walton's descendants sold the property to James R. Wyly around 1815, and Wyly began building what would later become the premier inn along the turnpike. Traveler's Rest reached its peak in size and prosperity under the ownership of Devereaux Jarrett, who doubled the size of the main building in the 1830s. From the 1840s until the 1850s, Traveler's Rest

Main house at Traveler's Rest.

served as a plantation home, stagecoach inn, trading post, and post office and was the centerpiece of Jarrett's northeast Georgia empire, which included more than fourteen thousand acres.

The Jarrett family owned the property for more than a century before selling it to the state, which has preserved it as a historic site. Traveler's Rest was recognized by the National Park Service as a National Historic Landmark in 1964 and added to the National Register of Historic Places in 1978. The site is significant as "one of the oldest houses in northeast Georgia" and as a "well-preserved example of an early tavern in a rural frontier setting." The building is also significant for its "length of service as a stagecoach inn, until late in the nineteenth century."[1]

History of Traveler's Rest

The land along the Tugaloo River Valley adjacent to South Carolina was inhabited by Cherokee Indians during the eighteenth century—a period marked by occasional incursions by white settlers and the major armed conflicts of the Seven Years War and the American Revolution. The Treaty of Augusta in 1773 ceded to Georgia the land along the Tugaloo River, and land in this area was allocated to Revolutionary War veterans in the 1780s. Among those who made such a claim was Major Jesse Walton. A member of the North Carolina militia during the war and cofounder of the town of Jonesborough in Washington County (formerly in North Carolina, part of Tennessee as of 1790), Walton sold his considerable landholdings west of the Blue Ridge Mountains in 1784 and migrated with his family to Franklin County, Georgia, where the state was offering bounty grants to veterans.[2]

If life on the frontier in North Carolina had seemed insecure, settlement in the Tugaloo Valley quickly proved equally as perilous as Creek Indians, unhappy that they were being displaced in the Old Southwest (the southwestern frontier territories), began conducting raids into American settlements in northeast Georgia along the Tugaloo River. A raiding party stole horses from Walton in 1786, and one of his sons was wounded in another raid two years later. The "sporadic violence" of the Georgia frontier prompted Walton to move his family across the river to South Carolina, but he continued to work his plantation on the Georgia side of the river. He also was active in Georgia politics, serving as part of Georgia's Executive Council in 1786 and 1787 and in the General Assembly in 1789. In June 1789, Walton was tending his crops at his plantation when he was attacked by Creek Indians and severely wounded. Walton died three weeks later from his injuries but not before dictating a will in which he left his property, including his land and twenty-two enslaved people, to his wife, the former Mary Walker, and his surviving children—Achilles, Walker, George, and Mary Carter.[3]

Walton's death at the hands of the Indians would later be embellished, likely by the last private owner of Traveler's Rest, Mary Jarrett White, and escalated into pure mythology. According to the legend told by White and reprinted in countless newspaper articles, Walton and his family were massacred following a four-day battle in which the Walton family fought tirelessly for their lives and their home. As reported in 1930 by well-known Atlanta historian Franklin Garret in the *Atlanta Journal*, the Walton family were seated by the fire when "a horde of Cherokee Indians on the warpath" laid siege to the house. Walton hid his wife and children in a secret compartment on the staircase and ran to the attic, where he took aim at the attackers through the "loopholes cut for that purpose."[4] As late as 1965, the story was reprinted with additional embellishments that included how "first the Indians fell on the children at the top of the stairs and hacked off their scalps," and adding that "the blood stains with a footprint discernible are still there at the top of the stairs."[5]

Mary Gregory Jewett, executive director of the Georgia Historical Commission, attempted to set the record straight as the commission undertook an in-depth, architectural inspection in 1966. "For a long time stories persisted that Walton and his wife and all the children except one were massacred in the house, but it isn't true," said Jewett, adding that documentary evidence of Walton's ambush by Creek Indians and records of his surviving family members belied the legend.[6] The architectural inspection, carried out by Georgia Tech graduates Richard Hall and Larry Farrow, established that the "loopholes" in the attic gable ends through which Walton allegedly shot at the Indians were, in fact, for ventilation. Architect Larry Farrow noted, "If you try to sight through one of them, you find it's impossible." The "bloody footprint" at the top of the stairs, Farrow added, appeared to be from "the bottom of a red paint can."[7] Tests conducted in a laboratory at Georgia Tech revealed that the red stain was a type of paint thinner.[8]

A further architectural analysis conducted in 1977 by restoration architect Paul Buchanan revealed that the existing building was constructed in two phases, with the first phase beginning around 1815 and the second between 1835 and 1840, conclusively proving that the building that stands today did not exist during the time of Jesse Walton's ownership of the property.[9] The legend of the massacre of the Walton family in their home by "marauding Indians" died hard, however. The brochure published by the Historical Commission in the late 1960s included the story, noting it is one of the possible accounts of Jesse Walton's demise.[10] By the early 1970s, Jewett had asked the caretaker at Traveler's Rest to stop sharing the legend of the massacre with visitors, and future brochures no longer included the story.[11]

Following Walton's death, the security situation in the Tugaloo Valley improved. By the 1790s, Walton's wife and children prospered on "middle-sized farms" in the area. His daughter married Joseph Martin in 1803, and the couple settled on her father's former property. By 1813, all of Jesse Walton's sons had relinquished their shares of the Walton property to Mary Carter's husband, Joseph Martin, who sold a little over thirteen hundred acres at Walton's Ford to James R. Wyly for $2,000 around 1815. Wyly had been hired by the Unicoi Company to supervise the construction of the Unicoi Turnpike, a toll road across northeastern Georgia that linked South Carolina to Tennessee.[12] It was Wyly who would build the south section of the building that came to be known as Traveler's Rest.

The Unicoi Turnpike was the result of a treaty between a group of white men who established the Unicoi Turnpike Company and the Cherokee Indians, who occupied much of the land the road would traverse. The road, which opened in 1818, followed a Cherokee trading path between the Tugaloo River and the Tennessee River. The Unicoi Turnpike Company was granted a twenty-year charter during which time the company could construct and operate the toll road. The company had the right to collect tolls and open "stores, taverns, and inns" along the turnpike and were to pay the Cherokees $160 a year. At the end of the twenty years, the road would revert to the Cherokees.[13] Recognizing that the road, which took more than three years to build, would be a boon to businesses along its route, Wyly acquired the former Walton property from Martin as well as property along the route in the Nacoochee Valley and at Hiawassee and proceeded to build taverns at each location.[14]

According to archaeologists and architectural historians, Wyly's tavern on the Tugaloo was built between 1815 and 1820 on the site of a previous structure as evidenced by the discovery of a root cellar uncovered in archaeological excavations in 1968. Wyly backfilled the cellar when he began construction of his tavern around 1815.[15] The two-story frame building was approximately fifty feet long and about eighteen feet deep. The building featured a parlor and hall along with two rear bed chambers on the first floor and three rooms on the second floor as well as a shed-roof porch that ran the full length of the front (west) side.[16] A leading citizen in the area, Wyly operated his tavern and a ferry, farmed the land surrounding his tavern, and served as the river commissioner, militia officer, sheriff, and postmaster at Walton's Ford, as the area was known.

Among Wyly's acquaintances was Devereaux Jarrett, a local landowner who ran a nearby store and with whom Wyly had served on the Franklin County Grand Jury. Jarrett, born in 1785 in South Carolina, operated a store on the South Carolina side of the Tugaloo River in the early 1800s. In 1807 Jarrett married Sarah Patton, a native of North Carolina. By 1809 Jarrett had expanded his business operations across the river into Georgia, where he operated an additional store. By 1814, he began acquiring land in Georgia, and by 1820, Jarrett had moved his family, which had grown to include three children, to a two-thousand-acre farm along Toccoa Creek near James Wyly's residence and tavern on the Unicoi Turnpike. In 1833 Wyly agreed to sell his tavern to Jarrett, who was described as the "richest man in the Tugaloo Valley," for $6,000. By the time the deed transfer was recorded in 1838, Jarrett had moved his family along with as many as forty-five enslaved people to the site that he began to call Traveler's Rest.[17]

Following his acquisition of Wyly's inn, Jarrett doubled its size. By 1840, the building had been expanded to its current dimensions. According to restoration architect Paul Buchanan, the addition on the north end "was primarily a family residence attached to a tavern, allowing the original building to be devoted to tavern use only."[18] Among the important additions on the north end was a cellar kitchen, which replaced an outside kitchen. A dining room and drawing room were also added on the north end, as well as two new bed chambers on the second floor. On the south end of the building, a stairway that opened directly onto the front porch was added to provide direct access for travelers to the shared upstairs bed chambers. In 1844, Jarrett was named postmaster of Walton's Ford, and in addition to its functions as a family residence and stagecoach inn, Traveler's Rest served as the post office.[19]

Notable signatures in the Traveler's Rest guest book are those of English geologist and geographer George W. Featherstonhaugh, who chronicled his travels through the American South in his 1847 publication, *A Canoe Voyage up the Minnay-Sotor*; South Carolina senator John C. Calhoun, who often stayed at Traveler's Rest while en route to his gold mine in Auraria; and state representative and later vice president of the Confederate States Alexander H. Stephens. In July 1847, future Georgia governor Joseph E. Brown and his new bride, Elizabeth Grisham, spent their wedding night at Traveler's Rest on their way from West Union, South Carolina, to Tallulah Falls.[20]

At a time when travel through the relatively undeveloped area of northeast Georgia often meant rough roads, bad food, and poor accommodations, Jarrett's inn at Traveler's Rest stood out for its cleanliness, good food, and reasonable rates.[21] Featherstonhaugh wrote in almost glowing

Basement kitchen at Traveler's Rest.

terms about his stay at Traveler's Rest in the late 1830s, noting that he had been served "an excellent breakfast of coffee, ham, chicken, good bread, butter, honey, and plenty of good new milk for a quarter of a dollar." Jarrett was "a quiet, intelligent, well-behaved man . . . and seemed anxious to do what was obliging and proper," Featherstonhaugh noted, adding, "What a charming country this would be to travel in, if one was sure of meeting with such nice clean quarters once a day!" So impressed was Featherstonhaugh that he became a repeat customer of Traveler's Rest.[22]

Another Englishman who reflected on his stay at Traveler's Rest was James Silk Buckingham, who traveled across the South with his family in 1839. In his 1842 publication, *The Slave States of America*, Buckingham reported that he and his family "were put into a large room with four beds" and were fortunate that they "had no companions to share the room." The beds, he explained, "were of three kinds; one of the softest down, another of cotton, and another of straw; the former being usually preferred by the people of this country, but the latter by strangers." In addition to the variety of beds available, Buckingham noted that Traveler's Rest, which he described as “a large farm-house and inn united” was unique in the area because it was “the only house with glass windows in it on the road.”[23]

Between his acquisition of Traveler’s Rest in 1833 and his death in 1852, Devereaux Jarrett’s empire expanded dramatically. In addition to his plantation, which was tended by enslaved workers, Jarrett operated a toll bridge, a store, a cash-lending business, a cotton gin, a tanyard, a blacksmithy, a gristmill, and a sawmill. In the late 1840s, he operated a gold mine. In all these business endeavors, Jarrett relied heavily on enslaved people to do the work. They tended the crops and worked as blacksmiths, tanners, millers, and gold miners. Enslaved people constructed the buildings on Jarrett’s farm as well as the toll bridge from which he derived income.[24]

The success of Traveler’s Rest as both a business and as the center of Jarrett’s farm operations would have been impossible without the labor of enslaved people. Unfortunately, few details about the enslaved people who lived and worked on the Jarrett farm were recorded. It is known that they were offered distractions in the forms of festivities and were allowed to attend religious services. In addition to the work that they did for Jarrett, they tended their own gardens and “were allowed to own small personal items, many of which they purchased at the Jarrett store.”[25]

In 1850, Jarrett’s property holdings included over fourteen thousand acres and sixty-eight enslaved people. That same year, Jarrett began giving away land and enslaved people to his four children, all of whom established plantations along the Tugaloo River. Sarah Jarrett, who had given birth to four children between 1812 and 1831, died in 1842, and three years later, Jarrett married Sarah’s sister, Elizabeth. Both Devereaux and Elizabeth Jarrett died in 1852, he in February and she in October, leaving Devereaux’s and Sarah’s four children—Thomas Patton, Robert, Charles Kennedy, and Sarah Anne—to inherit their father’s sizable estate.[26]

Devereaux Jarrett deeded Traveler’s Rest to his and Sarah’s third son, Charles Kennedy, who continued to operate many of the family businesses, including the toll bridge, the blacksmithy, the store, and the inn. Kennedy, as he was known, expanded the store operations, which in the 1850s offered a wide range of products from medicines to food and clothing. Although traffic along the Unicoi Turnpike had dwindled by the 1850s, Traveler’s Rest continued to be a preferred “stopping-place” for much of the decade and into the Civil War period. During the war, soldiers were frequent guests at the inn. Kennedy also held an ongoing interest in a gold

Slave cabin at Traveler's Rest.

mine, but as with other mine investors during this period, Jarrett's mine was not especially lucrative.[27]

Kennedy married Elizabeth Lucas of Athens in 1855, and the couple had six children over the next nineteen years. During that time, the remote corner of Georgia where Traveler's Rest had long been an important stopping place became more well connected with the arrival in 1873 of the railroad and the establishment of the nearby town of Toccoa. By the turn of the twentieth century, Traveler's Rest still served as a family home, but it no longer welcomed travelers as it had done in its heyday in the first half of the nineteenth century. Kennedy, who died in 1877, left Elizabeth with a sizable estate that included the farm at Traveler's Rest and several thousand acres of land as well as interests in two gold mines. Elizabeth liquidated the mining interests and much of the landholdings, and by the 1890s, the farm consisted of 450 acres.[28] Upon Elizabeth's death in 1904, Traveler's Rest passed to the two surviving Jarrett children, Sally Grace and Mary Elizabeth.

Around 1915, Mary Elizabeth, recognizing that the name Traveler's Rest was no longer appropriate for what was by this time simply a family residence, changed the name to Jarrett Manor. Following Sally Grace's death in 1927, Mary Elizabeth, whose husband, Virgil A. White, had died in 1911, became the sole owner of Jarrett Manor. Mary Elizabeth White became a well-known figure throughout Georgia when she became the first woman in the state to vote in the election of 1920. Although the Nineteenth Amendment to the U.S. Constitution went into effect in August 1920, that date was too late for women to register to vote in the 1920 election. White, however, had anticipated the ratification of the amendment and "paid her poll tax and registered six months previous to the election," becoming the first woman to vote in the state's history.[29] White was politically active and served as a Democratic presidential elector in 1932. She hosted a party at Jarrett Manor in November 1932 celebrating Franklin D. Roosevelt's victory, an event that was reported in the *Atlanta Journal*.[30]

By the mid-1950s, White, who was approaching ninety years of age, decided that she could no longer live in the home where she had spent most of her life, and she began to make plans to move to Macon to live near her son, Edward. White had long advocated for the ongoing preservation of her historic home, and in 1954 she offered to sell the property to the Toccoa Chamber of Commerce. It created the Jarrett Manor Foundation, which partnered with the Georgia Historical Commission to acquire the house and three acres of land for $8,000. The acquisition was finalized in the summer of 1955. Aided and abetted by White's decades of mythmaking, the *Atlanta Journal* dated the tavern to the Revolutionary War period and reported the now-debunked tale of the Indian slaughter of the Walton family, a perspective that the Historical Commission seemed to endorse.[31]

The Historical Commission opened the site to the public almost immediately after acquiring it from Mary Jarrett White, even while they assessed the main building's condition and inventoried its contents. The commission hired Mabel Ramsey, a Jarrett descendant, to serve as the on-site caretaker and hostess at the site, a job that Ramsey carried out with great enthusiasm.[32] Among the changes that the state attempted was rebranding the site as Traveler's Rest, the historic name under which Devereaux Jarrett had operated the site as a stagecoach inn. Ramsey, however, insisted on calling the place Jarrett Manor. In a letter to commission historian William Mitchell on January 28, 1966, Ramsey wrote: "If you don't stop trying to change the name of Jarrett Manor to Travelers [*sic*] Rest you are going to bring down a Civil War on your head. The more than two hundred 'Jarretts' up this way are furious about it and it will be as strong as Sherman's Army once they get started. . . . I think it has been Jarrett Manor too long for you to change it now."[33] Mitchell's reply was swift and unequivocal. The name Traveler's Rest was the "older and more historic name," with Jarrett Manor being a relatively recent moniker for the historic building. "Evidently the family had forgotten the name's significance to those in the past who used it and praised your great-grandfather's hospitality under its sign," argued Mitchell. Citing renowned architectural consultant Harold Cooledge as well as the U.S. government, which had listed the site as a National Historic Landmark under the name Traveler's Rest in 1964, Mitchell was emphatic that the site should be called Traveler's Rest.[34] Ramsey, who continued to refer to the site as Jarrett Manor, retired in 1968.[35]

Only after the architectural inspection of the mid-1960s did the commission begin to understand that the building dated from the nineteenth, not the eighteenth, century. Cooledge reported to the commission in July 1968 that the study carried out by Larry Farrow and Richard Hall two years earlier, combined with the archaeological excavations underway in 1968 by William Kelso, made it "unlikely" that "any part of Walton's construction is now standing." Cooledge further concluded that "none of the existing structure pre-dates 1816–1819."[36]

Kelso's report, published in February 1969, concluded that the site had been "briefly occupied by Early Mississippian Period [American] Indians," that a former root cellar located under the south end of the main house was backfilled after 1815, and that the south half of the main house was the oldest structure on the property.[37] The investigations done by Kelso and the two architects, which were endorsed by Cooledge, enabled the Historical Commission to move forward with the reconstruction of the smokehouse and well house and restoration of the main house to reflect its appearance during the period when it was a stagecoach inn. Interventions included necessary repairs to replace rotten wood, mostly in areas most exposed to the weather.[38] By 1971, most of the restoration work at the site was complete with the exception of repairs to the porch.[39]

In addition to the in-depth architectural investigation conducted in 1966 and the archaeological survey done in 1968, the state engaged Paul E. Buchanan, director of architectural research for Colonial Williamsburg, to conduct an analysis of the house in 1977. Buchanan confirmed the historical evolution of the main house during two main periods, 1815 and 1835–1840. Buchanan's report was included as an appendix in historian Robert Bouwman's 1980 book, *Traveler's Rest and the Tugaloo Crossroads*, which was commissioned by the Historic Preservation Section of the Department of Natural Resources.

Bouwman's book offers the most detailed and comprehensive history of Traveler's Rest and the people associated therewith. Reprinted by the University of North Georgia Press in 2015, the book also includes archaeologist William Kelso's report on his excavations. The preface to the new edition chronicles the site's evolution from a well-staffed operation that was open six days a week in the 1970s to a site that as of 2012 was open three Saturdays a month and had been selected as a "place in peril" by the Georgia Trust for Historic Preservation. Bouwman bemoaned that "Traveler's Rest is neglected by the State of Georgia and most of the state's citizens." The site "is a treasure that is still appreciated by visitors and those who love it," he added.[40] Despite its limited hours, Traveler's Rest continues to wow those visitors who come to the site. As the last remaining stagecoach inn along what was once the Unicoi Turnpike, the site provides a unique glimpse into Georgia's past.

Touring the Site

Traveler's Rest is interpreted as a mid-nineteenth-century stagecoach inn and residence. The main house has been restored to its historic appearance, and several outbuildings have been reconstructed to reflect how the site appeared during its heyday. The wooden building stretches ninety feet across and is two stories tall. The shed porch spans the entire front of the building. Three brick chimneys, one on each end and one in the middle that demarcates the original north end of the building, are visible from the front of the house. Two additional chimneys that vent the fireplaces in the back rooms are visible from the back of the house.

A set of stone steps, which were once used to facilitate stagecoach boarding, are located in front of the house. Scattered around the grounds are smaller outbuildings, including a reconstructed smokehouse; a reconstructed well house; an early twentieth-century son-in-law cabin, constructed by Sally Grace's husband, Sam; and a small cabin to the rear of the main house that dates to the 1850s and was the home of the family's enslaved nanny. Near the cabin is a large boulder with Indian petroglyphs,

Front porch of Traveler's Rest.

reportedly brought to the site by Devereaux Jarrett after it was discovered along the Tugaloo River by several of his enslaved workers.

Visitors are free to walk around the property and through all the rooms in the main house, which is furnished with many items that belonged to the Jarrett family. Several of the pieces were made by Caleb Shaw, a cabinet maker who migrated to the Tugaloo Valley from Massachusetts. One of the back rooms in the south section of the house is used as the viewing room for a ten-minute film about the site, which is also accessible on the Traveler's Rest website (https://gastateparks.org/TravelersRest). An appendage on the north end of the house, known as the loom room, is connected by a wooden walkway. Used in later years as a weaving room, the wood-framed loom room sits atop a brick structure that was originally a dairy and later served as a cocoonery for raising silkworms during the late 1830s. James Buckingham reported on a silk-producing operation at Traveler's Rest during his visit in 1839.

Interpretive markers located near the parking lot and behind the house provide information about the development of the site by Wyly and Jarrett as well as information about the "Indian Rock" and enslaved workers at Traveler's Rest. Tours are self-guided, although a ranger is on site during

Wash pot and reconstructed well house at Traveler's Rest.

Common room on second floor at Traveler's Rest.

opening hours (Saturday and Sunday, 9:00 a.m.–5:00 p.m.) to answer questions. Parking for disabled visitors is located immediately behind the main house on the south end, and a ramp provides access into the slave cabin and the main house.

Special events at the site include Pioneer Day in October, when volunteers demonstrate "the skills and daily life of early settlers," and Christmas at the Inn in December, when the house is decorated for Christmas as it would have been during the 1800s.

Notes

1. Blanche Higgins Schroer, "Traveler's Rest," National Register of Historic Places Nomination Form (Washington, D.C.: U.S. Department of the Interior, National Park Service, 1978), section 8.

2. Robert Bouwman, *Traveler's Rest and the Tugaloo Crossroads* (Dahlonega, Ga.: University of North Georgia University Press, 2015), 35–36.

3. Bouwman, 40–42.

4. Franklin Garrett, "Georgia Manor Built in 1775," *Atlanta Journal*, September 14, 1930, 74.

5. Tom Ramsay, "Manor Has Bloody Past," *Tiger Clemson*, January 8, 1965.

6. Andrew Sparks, "Plastic Skin Reveals Secrets of Old Inn," *Atlanta Journal and Constitution Magazine*, November 13, 1966, 34.

7. Sparks, "Plastic Skin Reveals Secrets," 36.

8. Bouwman, *Traveler's Rest*, 42.

9. Bouwman, 214.

10. Traveler's Rest or Jarrett Manor, n.d., Historic Sites—Jarrett Manor, C 324113, RCB 13557, Georgia Historical Commission—Director's Office—Administrative Records, 061-01-001, Georgia Archives (hereafter, GHC Director's Office).

11. Billy Hawkins, interview by Hannah Eslinger, October 23, 2022.

12. Bouwman, *Traveler's Rest*, 77.

13. Vicki Bell Rozema, "Rivers, Roads, and Rails: The Influence of Transportation Needs and Internal Improvements on Cherokee Treaties and Removal from 1779 to 1838" (Master's thesis, University of Tennessee, 2007), 33.

14. Bouwman, *Traveler's Rest*, 76–77.

15. Bouwman, 227.

16. Bouwman, 215.

17. Bouwman, 92, 121.

18. Bouwman, 221.

19. Bouwman, 126.

20. Schroer, "Traveler's Rest"; G. Richard Wright and Kenneth H. Wheeler, "New Men in the Old South: Joseph E. Brown and His Associates in Georgia's Etowah Valley," *Georgia Historical Quarterly* 93, no. 4 (Winter 2009): 374; Bouwman, *Traveler's Rest*, 113.

21. Bouwman, *Traveler's Rest*, 110.

22. Bouwman, 111.

23. Bouwman, 112.

24. Bouwman, 126.

25. Bouwman, 121.

26. Bouwman, 131; "Devereaux Jarrett IV: 11 February 1785–9 February 1852," Family Search, accessed August 16, 2023, https://ancestors.familysearch.org/en/L7J7-WFV/devereaux-jarrett-iv-1785-1852.

27. Bouwman, *Traveler's Rest*, 138–139.

28. Bouwman, 181.

29. "High Spots in Georgia News," *Americus Times-Recorder*, November 5, 1920, 2.

30. "Jarret Manor Scene of Party in Honor of Roosevelt Victory," *Atlanta Journal*, November 29, 1932, 13.

31. M. L. St. John, "Georgia to Preserve Old Tavern of Revolutionary Fame," *Atlanta Journal*, July 4, 1955, 27.

32. Blythe McKay, "Mrs. Mary Jarrett White to Observe 90th Birthday in Macon While Ancestral Home Becomes State Shrine," *Macon Telegraph*, April 22, 1956, 21.

33. Mabel Ramsey to William Mitchell, January 28, 1966, Historic Sites—Jarrett Manor, C 324113, RCB 13557, GHC Director's Office.

34. William Mitchell to Mabel Ramsey, January 31, 1966, Historic Sites—Jarrett Manor, C 324113, rcb 13557, GHC Director's Office.

35. Bouwman, *Traveler's Rest*, 210.

36. Harold N. Cooledge Jr. to Georgia Historical Commission, July 10, 1968, 2, Historic Sites—Jarrett Manor, C 324113, RCB 13557, GHC Director's Office.

37. Bouwman, *Traveler's Rest*, 230, 231.

38. Mary Gregory Jewett, Report of Meeting at Historic Traveler's Rest, July 25, 1968, Historic Sites—Jarrett Manor, Georgia Historical Commission, RCB: 13557, Georgia Archives.

39. Notice of Intent to File for Federal Assistance with the United States Department of the Interior, June 2, 1971, Georgia Historical Commission, RCB: 33320, Georgia Archives.

40. Bouwman, *Traveler's Rest*, v.

Further Reading

Bouwman, Robert. *Traveler's Rest and the Tugaloo Crossroads*. Dahlonega: University of North Georgia University Press, 2015.

Cooksey, Elizabeth B. "Stephens County." *New Georgia Encyclopedia*, last modified July 9, 2022. https://www.georgiaencyclopedia.org/articles/counties-cities-neighborhoods/stephens-county/.

Lane, Mills, ed. *The Rambler in Georgia*. Bronx: Beehive Press, 1973.

Linley, John. *The Georgia Catalog: Historic American Buildings Survey; A Guide to the Architecture of the State*. Athens: University of Georgia Press, 1982.

CHAPTER 7

A. H. Stephens State Park

James Mitchum and Jennifer W. Dickey

Basic Information

PERIOD OF SIGNIFICANCE: 1845–1883
DATE ESTABLISHED AS A STATE PARK: 1933
ACREAGE: Park, 1,177 acres; historic site, 200 acres
LOCATION: 456 Alexander Street NW, Crawfordville, Ga. 30631, Taliaferro County

Established as a memorial state park in 1933, the former home of Alexander H. Stephens is a shrine to the Georgia politician who is most remembered for serving as the vice president of the Confederate States of America (CSA). Acquired by the Alexander H. Stephens Monumental Association not long after Stephens's death in 1883, the restored home and outbuildings in which Stephens lived in Crawfordville honor this controversial statesman who was known as "The Great Commoner" during his lifetime. An opponent of secession, Stephens helped draft Georgia's secession declaration once it became clear that the state would secede from the Union. Stephens was considered one of the most eloquent orators of his time, and his "Cornerstone Speech," delivered in Savannah in March 1861, helped form the foundation for the Lost Cause mythology and its white supremacist underpinnings that was the master narrative of the Civil War for more than a century.

Stephens's home was listed in the National Register of Historic Places in 1970 and became a National Historic Landmark in 1983. The site is significant as "a living image of certain aspects of the history of the Deep South prior to about 1900 as exemplified by one of the South's foremost

A. H. Stephens Liberty Hall main house.

antebellum political leaders." The house "is a significant architectural reflection—little changed from when he knew it—of Stephens's character and life."[1]

History of A. H. Stephens State Park

Alexander Stephens was born on February 11, 1812, on a farm in what was then Wilkes County but would later become Taliaferro County. The third child of Andrew and Margaret Stephens, Alexander inherited from his mother "a liking for books, and a turn for law."[2] He also inherited his mother's frail constitution. She died when Stephens was three months old. His father, who farmed and taught school, remarried two years later. Stephens had a difficult relationship with his stepmother, Matilda Lindsey, but he adored his father, after whom he "patterned his own conduct." In a letter to his half brother, Linton, Stephens wrote, "The principles and precepts he taught me have been my guiding-star through life. Even now the thought often occurs to me: I wonder what my father thinks of this?" Andrew instilled in his son and his students the virtues of "sobriety, morality, industry, energy, and honor."[3]

Stephens's frail health allowed him to be excused from many of the more arduous tasks on the farm, and at the age of twelve, he became "entranced" with books and reading after enrolling in a Sunday school class. The death of his father in May 1826 followed a week later by the death of his stepmother left Stephens and his siblings orphans. Alexander and his brother and sister were sent to live with their mother's brother, Aaron Grier, while his half siblings, including Linton, went to live with Matilda's family. Stephens's uncle had an extensive library in which young Alexander immersed himself.[4] He attended school but only sporadically until Charles C. Mills, superintendent of the Sunday school that Stephens attended, offered to pay for Stephens to attend the academy in Washington, Georgia, run by Presbyterian minister Alexander Hamilton Webster. Stephens accepted Mills's offer, and in July 1827 he moved to Washington and took up residence with Webster. It was Stephens's great admiration for Webster that led him to adopt the middle name Hamilton.[5]

Webster had high hopes for Stephens and encouraged him to think about going into the ministry, an idea that appealed to Stephens and that he planned to pursue. Webster's unexpected death in late 1827 nearly derailed Stephens's plans, but several of Webster's friends stepped in to help Stephens finish the school year and supported his effort to enroll at Franklin College, predecessor to the University of Georgia.[6] Sixteen-year-old Stephens arrived in Athens in August 1828, where he soon abandoned plans to go into the ministry and instead pursued the study of Greek, Latin, and other courses that were considered the standard of "New England classicism." Stephens honed his oratorical skills as the president of the Phi Kappa Society and graduated in 1832 at the top of his class.[7]

At the age of twenty, Stephens embarked on what would be a short-lived teaching career, first at a school in Madison, Georgia, and then as a tutor on a plantation in Liberty County near Sunbury. He found teaching to be unrewarding, however, and after eighteen months Stephens returned to the area where he was born, now Taliaferro County, and began to study law at the courthouse in the new county seat of Crawfordville. He moved into the home of his stepmother's brother-in-law, Williamson Bird, and immersed himself in reading a set of law books that he acquired from a local lawyer. In July 1834, Stephens sailed through the oral examinations and was admitted to the Georgia Bar. During his first year as a practicing lawyer, Stephens made $400 and developed a friendship with another lawyer, Robert Toombs from Washington, Georgia, that would become one of the most important relationships in Stephens's life.[8]

Stephens's political life began when he was elected to the Georgia General Assembly in 1836, where he served until 1841. In 1842 he was elected to the Georgia Senate, and in 1843, he was elected to the U.S. House of Representatives, where he remained until 1859. Home base for Stephens during this time was Crawfordville. Although he began acquiring land in and around Crawfordville, he continued to board at the home of Williamson Bird. Stephens purchased the "old homestead," as he called the land that had once belonged to his father; he also acquired enslaved people to work that land. Following the death of Bird in 1843 and Bird's wife in 1845, Stephens acquired the ten-acre Bird property as well. He now owned more than five thousand acres and at least ten enslaved people.[9] Stephens referred to his newly acquired home as Bachelor's Hall.[10]

Among his fellow representatives in the U.S. House were Robert Toombs, who represented Georgia's eighth district from 1845 to 1853, and Abraham Lincoln, who represented the seventh district of Illinois between 1847 and 1849. Stephens and Toombs were dear friends from their days on the circuit court and their time in the Georgia House of Representatives, and they led Georgia's congressional team in support of the Compromise of 1850. Stephens and Lincoln, both members of the Whig Party, became acquainted during Lincoln's one term in the House.

Although they held differing views on many issues, Stephens and Lincoln "acquired a sincere, lifelong mutual respect for each other."[11] The two were an odd pair, to be sure. The tall (six feet four), gangly Lincoln towered over the diminutive Stephens, who became known as "Little Aleck" because of his small size (five feet seven and less than one hundred pounds). Lincoln admired Stephens's oratory skills, and following Stephens's delivery of a speech in protest against the Polk administration's efforts to seize Mexican territory, Lincoln proclaimed Stephens's speech to be "the very best speech, of an hour's length" that he had ever heard.[12]

Among the issues upon which Stephens and Lincoln disagreed were the right of a state to secede from the Union and the peculiar institution of slavery. Although Stephens believed that states should not secede from the Union, he steadfastly believed that they had the right to do so. He also believed that white people were superior to Black people, an argument that he made most clearly and publicly in March 1861 in his Cornerstone Speech.[13] Lincoln was opposed to slavery and believed it to be a "monstrous injustice," although he struggled with what should be done about it, and he did not believe in racial equality.[14] Lincoln's view on secession was unequivocal—it was unconstitutional for a state to withdraw from the Union. As he wrote to Stephens in 1860, "Only unanimous consent of all the States can dissolve the Union."[15] Both men, wrote Stephens, had "an earnest desire to preserve and maintain the Union."[16]

Stephens and Lincoln discussed their differences of opinion on these two matters of great importance in a series of letters between December 1860 and January 1861 as Georgia politicians wrestled with what to do about secession. Stephens lamented the rush toward secession among the "people . . . run mad" who he claimed were "wild with passion and frenzy, doing they know not what." For him, the U.S. Constitution may have been a "leaky boat," but it was reparable, and remaining in the Union represented the best way forward for maintaining the institution of slavery.[17] As someone who knew and corresponded with Lincoln, Stephens did not believe that Lincoln's election foretold the end of slavery in the United States, as did many of his peers. However, he recognized that he was among the minority and "that Lincoln's election would unleash an uncontrollable 'whirlwind' leading toward secession and civil war." Having retired from the House of Representatives in 1859, Stephens spent the next year touring the state and arguing for the preservation of the Union and slavery, both of which he believed could best be done by supporting Democratic candidate Stephen A. Douglas.[18]

A week after Lincoln was declared the winner of the election, Stephens continued to oppose secession publicly. In a speech to the state legislature, Stephens argued that the election of Lincoln was constitutional and was not a reason to secede from the Union. Until the Constitution was violated, said Stephens, "let us be found to the last moment standing on the deck with the Constitution of the United States wavering over our heads. Let the fanatics of the North break down the Constitution." Stephens reminded his audience of the virtues of the U.S. government under which "Georgia had prospered mightily," and he advocated an appeal to the people of Georgia to select delegates to attend a convention to determine whether the state should secede. Although he hoped that cooler heads would prevail and Georgia would remain in the Union, "I shall bow to the will of the people," concluded Stephens.[19]

On January 2, 1861, Stephens's called-for election was held, and delegates were chosen to attend the Georgia Secession Convention beginning January 16, 1861. At the convention, Stephens, who was elected to serve as a delegate, was asked to serve as president of the gathering. Feeling discouraged and defeated, he declined the honor. During the convention, he spoke only briefly to remind his fellow delegates of his arguments against secession.[20] The die was cast, however, and Stephens knew it. By January 19, the immediate secessionists achieved their objective by a vote of 208 to 89, and Georgia officially seceded from the Union. The next step was to draft a new state constitution, a process that was completed in March following the creation of the new Confederate Constitution in Montgomery in February 1861.[21]

Despite his opposition to Georgia's secession, Stephens was selected to attend the Constitutional Convention in Montgomery, and he played a key role in writing the Confederate Constitution. His name was floated briefly as a candidate for the president of the Confederate States, a position that went to Jefferson Davis, before Stephens was eventually nominated to be the vice president. The hope was that appointing Stephens, an avowed Unionist, to this high-level position in the new government would generate support for the new nation from among the proponents of cooperation with the United States.[22]

As the vice president of the Confederate States of America, Stephens pledged to uphold and advocate for the new nation and its constitution. It was with this in mind that he traveled to Savannah in March 1861 to make a speech in front a crowd of several thousand people at the Athenaeum. Speaking extemporaneously, Stephens began his defense for the creation of a new nation by explaining that the new constitution "secures all our ancient rights, franchises, and liberties." He continued, "All the essentials of the old constitution, which have endeared it to the hearts of the American people, have been preserved and perpetuated," adding, "Some changes have been made." He clarified some of the more mundane details of the new constitution, such as the role that cabinet secretaries would play, the term of the president, and the delegation of internal improvements to state and local governments and then launched into a discussion of slavery.

The new Confederate Constitution "put to rest, forever, all the agitating questions relating to our peculiar institution—African slavery as it exists amongst us—the proper status of the negro in our form of civilization. This was the immediate cause of the late rupture and present revolution," stated Stephens.[23] Reminding the audience that the U.S. Constitution was based "upon the assumption of the equality of the races," which he considered to be an error, he continued as follows: "Our new government is founded upon exactly the opposite idea; its foundations are laid, its cornerstone rests, upon the great truth that the negro is not equal to the white man; that slavery—subordination to the superior race—is his natural and moral condition."[24]

This declaration was met with a round of applause, and Stephens continued with his defense of white supremacy and the virtues of the new constitution that he had helped write in Montgomery the month before.[25] Stephens's speech, which he delivered without notes, was transcribed in real time by a reporter from the *Savannah Republican* and was first printed in that paper on March 23, 1861. By the time the Confederate Army began shelling the United States military garrison at Fort Sumter in the port of Charleston, South Carolina, on April 12, 1861, the speech had been reprinted in more than two hundred newspapers around the world. While most southern newspapers applauded Stephens's speech and celebrated the idea of "A White Man's Government," northern papers, such as the *New York Post*, characterized it as "the Confederate 'manifesto'" that made clear that "slavery [was] the basis of the new Confederacy."[26]

Jefferson Davis, meanwhile, was displeased with his vice president's proclamations, which changed the focus from "state versus national sovereignty" to slavery and white supremacy and clarified for foreign governments the true nature of the Confederate States. According to the *New York Daily Tribune*, the speech "was of incalculable value to us," as it galvanized abolitionists and moderates across the country and around the world.[27]

Stephens would spend the rest of his life claiming that his remarks in Savannah were taken out of context and misconstrued, but there was no retracting the words that the audience heard and that were reported in the *Savannah Republican*. The relationship between Stephens and Davis, which had already been strained, became more tenuous. Davis ceased relying on Stephens as an adviser, and the vice president found himself on the outside of the CSA administration that he had helped create. Stephens continued to carry out his vice presidential duties as president of the

Senate, but he largely disagreed with Davis's policies on everything from taxes to conscription. He often retreated from the Confederate capital of Richmond to his plantation in Crawfordville, where he had left things in the hands of Harry Goodyear, an enslaved worker who managed operations, and George Bristow, a young lawyer whom Stephens had trained and who had taken up residence at the plantation.[28]

Stephens began calling his plantation home Liberty Hall in 1860, claiming that "I do as I please here and expect my guests to do the same."[29] While Stephens's guests may have done as they pleased, the thirty to thirty-five enslaved people who lived and worked on his plantation did not. For the duration of the time that Stephens owned the plantation, he employed the labor of enslaved people to tend his fields and livestock and cook his meals. Among the people who waited on Stephens and tended to his needs and those of his guests was Eliza, whom Stephens purchased at auction in the 1840s when she was a child. Eliza had been trained as a cook, and she fulfilled that role at Stephens's home.

Around 1852, Eliza married Harry Goodyear, who lived on a nearby plantation. The next year, Stephens purchased Harry, who came to serve as the de facto overseer on Stephens's plantation. Stephens entrusted Harry with the management of the plantation, and Harry continued in that role after emancipation. Harry and Eliza built a two-story house on the land adjacent to Stephens's home, and they lived there, along with their five children, until their deaths. Their daughter, Dora, cared for Stephens as he became increasingly disabled in his later years.[30]

In the aftermath of the war, Stephens was arrested at Liberty Hall on May 11, 1865, by U.S. troops and charged with treason. He was incarcerated at Fort Warren in Boston for five months, during which time he kept a diary in which he bemoaned the conditions of his imprisonment, most notably the cold and the food, and began his effort to rehabilitate his image by resituating his Cornerstone Speech. While he doubled down on his idea that the "African race" was inferior and that "slavery was, without doubt, the occasion of secession," he claimed that he believed that if the institution of slavery "was not the best, or could not be made the best, for both races . . . it ought to be abolished."[31]

Stephens was granted parole by President Andrew Johnson in October 1865 and returned to Georgia, where he briefly contemplated running for governor before putting his name forward as a candidate for the U.S. Senate in 1866. Despite a message from President Johnson stating that

Stephens running for the Senate would be "exceedingly impolitic," he ran and won by a large margin. However, the Senate refused to seat him, so Stephens returned to Liberty Hall and began work on his two-volume epic, *A Constitutional View of the Late War between the States*, a more than 1,400-page argument in defense of state's rights and secession, both of which he still believed to be sacrosanct. The first volume, published in 1868, sold more than 64,000 copies. The second volume, published two years later, sold only 20,000 copies. The books were poorly reviewed and quickly faded from view.

Stephens, meanwhile, continued hosting visitors and law pupils at Liberty Hall and dabbling in Georgia politics. Among the notable guests were Oliver Wendell Holmes and Henry Ward Beecher. He played matchmaker for his beloved half brother, Linton, with Mary Salter, the daughter of a Boston woman who had been his "guardian angel" while he was imprisoned in Fort Warren. Linton and Mary married in 1867. Stephens also suffered an injury from which he would never recover in February 1869. While walking around his plantation, he tried to open a metal gate that was off its hinges. The gate fell on top of him, injuring his hip, and for the rest of his life he had to rely on crutches or a "roller chair" to move around.[32]

The death of Linton in 1873 shook Stephens to his core, yet he was determined to remain active despite his injury and the loss of his half brother.[33] He once again ran for Congress and was elected to serve as the U.S. Representative from the eighth district, an office he held from 1873 to 1882. His many ailments during this time dictated that he take a variety of medications, including large doses of morphine for pain.[34] Around 1875, he carried out a major renovation at Liberty Hall. A visitor that year explained that Stephens had "swept away" the old house and replaced it with a "larger, more stylish residence." The new two-story house had a large, central hall that was flanked by four rooms on each floor. He had preserved his library behind the house—a space in which he offered instruction to young men who aspired to be lawyers.[35]

Stephens resigned from Congress in November 1882 after he was elected governor of Georgia, an office he held until his death on March 4, 1883. Upon his death, the *Atlanta Constitution* declared, "A Life of Duty Finished," noting, "By the death of Alexander H. Stephens, Georgia loses one of her most illustrious and patriotic sons, and the union loses one of its most liberal and enlightened statesmen, and humanity at large loses a faithful friend and earnest and faithful counselor."[36] Thousands lined up

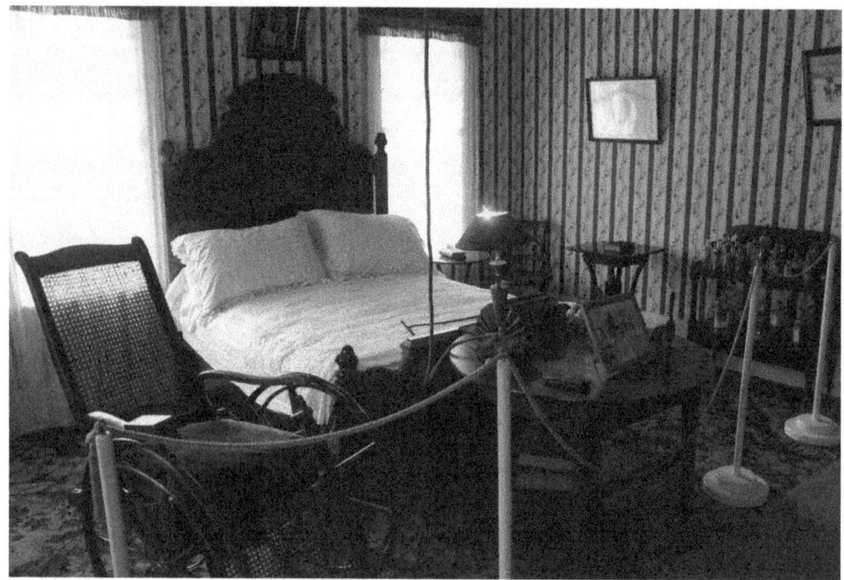

A. H. Stephens's bedroom at Liberty Hall.

to see "The Great Commoner" as he lay in state in the Georgia Capitol, and thousands attended his funeral. Newspapers across the country reported his death, and he was generally characterized, even in northern papers, as having "filled a most conspicuous place in the political history of the last thirty years." The *Philadelphia Times* noted that his home in Crawfordville "ever presented the most hospitable welcome to the friend or stranger, and he was venerated in Georgia," adding that "the whole country will cherish his memory with profound respect."[37] In his will, Stephens stated that "Eliza Stephens, widow of Harry Stephens, is to have a home in the house she now occupies as long as she may feel disposed to, free from rent or charge."[38]

Stephens was interred initially in a vault in Atlanta's Oakland Cemetery, but his body was moved to the front lawn of Liberty Hall next to that of his half brother, Linton, two years later. Meanwhile, the Alexander Stephens Monumental Association began raising money to create a monument that would be placed at the gravesite on the front lawn. A decade after Stephens's death, the monument, which was topped with a life-size statue of Stephens, was erected. Thousands attended the unveiling.[39]

Liberty Hall continued to serve as a residence and then a boarding house for several years after Stephens's death. Eliza Stephens lived in the two-story home adjacent to Liberty Hall until her death in 1917. Eliza's daughter, Dora, continued to live in the home until she died in 1931. Stephens's niece, Mary Corry Holden, resided in the main house for several years along with other family members. However, the Stephens Monumental Association, led by Holden, envisioned a permanent shrine to Stephens that went beyond a statue on the front lawn. The association worked with the United Daughters of the Confederacy (UDC) to acquire the property and briefly operated a school, the Alexander H. Stephens Institute, which they hoped would become affiliated with the University of Georgia, on property adjacent to the site. Unable to secure enough funding to maintain the school, in 1933 Holden appealed to state government leaders to take over the site as a memorial park. Holden's appeal was successful, and in 1933 the Monumental Association donated the house and twelve acres to the state.

Between 1933 and 1935, workers from the Civilian Conservation Corps (CCC) restored the house to its 1875 appearance. Holden also assisted with

A. H. Stephens monument and grave site in front of Liberty Hall.

the return to the property of many of Stephens's furnishings and personal effects.[40] The CCC workers also built recreational facilities on additional land acquired by the state through the National Park Service Recreation Demonstration Program. Under the auspices of the Georgia Department of Natural Resources (DNR), the Alexander Stephens Memorial Park was dedicated on July 18, 1935, in a ceremony in which "Lost Cause beliefs and rituals saturated the day's events."[41]

Holden, who was also an active member of the UDC, remained involved in activities at Liberty Hall up until her death in 1944. Her last wish, granted by Governor Ellis Arnall, was that she be allowed to "lie in state" in Liberty Hall the evening before her burial.[42] Less than a decade later, the UDC oversaw the erection of a Confederate Museum on the site of the former home of Eliza and Harry Stephens. The museum opened in October 1952 with Governor Herman Talmadge as the featured speaker.[43]

For the next several decades, the site received UDC support and maintenance and experienced robust visitation. Schools throughout the area often brought students to the site for field trips.[44] Sponsored by the UDC and coordinated with the state superintendent of schools, annual essay contests were held based on various themes of Alexander Stephens's public life. Winners were recognized during ceremonies at Liberty Hall.[45] An attempt to close the recreational park facilities at the site in 1975 amid a state budget crisis met with a great outcry from the residents of Taliaferro County. The state reconsidered, and the site remained open. In 1992, the Department of Natural Resources carried out restoration work at Liberty Hall, a project for which the DNR received an award for "Outstanding Restoration of a Residential Structure" from the Georgia Trust for Historic Preservation.[46]

While veneration of Stephens continued in Georgia for many decades, on the national stage he was less well remembered. In 1981, historian John Brumgardt wrote that Stephens "was an unattractive, self-centered, often caustic individual who considered himself superior, evidenced a habitually condescending nature, and had a penchant for acid sarcasm and overstatement which was sometimes imprudent." Brumgardt further noted that "historians have seen Stephens as a detriment to the South."[47] While other Confederate leaders were celebrated, Stephens became a scapegoat for many of the CSA's failings. While his views on the constitutional issues of state's rights and secession supported the rise of the Lost Cause mythology that long obscured the true history of the Civil War's origins, his views on race relations fueled the fire of white supremacy that dominated life in the American South well into the twentieth century. However abominable his beliefs may be, Stephens was an important figure who played a significant role in the history of Georgia. His former home in Crawfordville should be a place to learn about this complicated figure.

Touring the Site

Tours of Liberty Hall begin at the Civil War (formerly Confederate) Museum, located where Eliza and Harry Stephens's house once stood. The museum features an array of artifacts, including one of Alexander H. Stephens's wheelchairs, as well as a variety of Civil War and Confederate memorabilia. Perhaps the most important artifact is one unrelated to Stephens or the war—a stoneware jug made by David Drake, the enslaved man known as Dave the Potter. Drake (ca. 1800–1870s), who was enslaved in Edgefield, South Carolina, became famous for his jugs, which feature alkaline glazes and short inscriptions of poetry as well as the name "Dave." Drake's jugs have become prized possessions at leading art museums around the country in recent years.[48]

Civil War Museum at Liberty Hall.

While the museum is self-guided, the tour of Stephens's home is led by a docent. Visitors must check in at the Civil War Museum to arrange for the tour of the house and outbuildings. The house is furnished much as it was in the latter years of Stephens's life, when he was confined to a wheelchair and reliant on a vast array of medications to get through each day. Among the most impressive spaces is Stephens's library connected to the rear of the house via a breezeway. This was where Stephens ran his tutorial sessions for aspiring young lawyers for many years.

Behind the house is a collection of outbuildings including the gas house, the wood house, the wash house, and a reconstructed cabin that represents the home of Eliza and Harry Stephens. In the back corner of the fenced area behind the house is the grave of Rio, one of Stephens's dogs.

Stephens and his half brother, Linton, are buried next to the statue of Stephens on the front lawn. Erected in 1893, the statue heralds Stephens as "The Great Commoner" and the author of *A Constitutional View of the Late War between the States.*

Overall, Stephens is interpreted as a brilliant and beloved politician with almost no reference to his political views beyond his opposition to secession. The basis of his opposition, that he believed the institution of

A. H. Stephens's library at Liberty Hall.

Reconstructed cottage of Eliza and Harry Stephens at Liberty Hall.

slavery was best protected under the U.S. Constitution, is not discussed, nor are his beliefs in racial inequality, which he described as the "cornerstone" of the Confederate government. At a time when the state of Georgia is contemplating replacing the statue of Stephens that represents Georgia in the U.S. Capitol with a statue of Braves baseball great Henry Aaron, a more nuanced and critical perspective on Stephens is surely warranted at Liberty Hall.

Adjacent to Liberty Hall is the Crawfordville Baptist Church, and in the cemetery located east of the church are the graves of Harry, Eliza, and Dora Stephens. The three graves are inside a low, stone wall on the southwest side of the road that runs through the center of the cemetery. The plot includes the marked graves of Harry, Eliza, and Dora, as well as a number of other graves designated by fieldstones.

Notes

1. William R. Mitchell Jr., "Liberty Hall," National Register of Historic Places Nomination Form (Washington, D.C.: U.S. Department of the Interior, National Park Service, 1970), section 8.

2. Alexander Stephens, *Recollections of Alexander H. Stephens: His Diary Kept When a Prisoner* (New York: Doubleday, 1910), 3.

3. Thomas E. Schott, *Alexander H. Stephens of Georgia: A Biography* (Baton Rouge: Louisiana State University Press, 1988), 5–7.

4. Robert Grier Stephens Jr., "The Background and Boyhood of Alexander H. Stephens," *Georgia Review* 9, no. 4 (Winter 1955): 392–394.

5. R. G. Stephens, "Background and Boyhood," 396.

6. Schott, *Recollections of Alexander H. Stephens*, 12–14.

7. Schott, 15–16.

8. Schott, 25–28.

9. Schott, 45, 65.

10. Martha Norwood, *Liberty Hall: Taliaferro County, Georgia; A History of the Structures Known as Liberty Hall and Their Owners from 1827 to the Present* (Atlanta: Georgia Department of Natural Resources, 1977), 11.

11. Jamil Zinaldin, "Before the Flood: Alexander H. Stephens and Abraham Lincoln," *Saporta Report*, last modified November 25, 2013, https://saportareport.com/before-the-flood-alexander-h-stephens-and-abraham-lincoln/uncategorized/nge/#:~:text=Lincoln%20served%20one%20term%20in,on%20the%20morality%20of%20slavery.

12. Schott, *Recollections of Alexander H. Stephens*, 81.

13. Chad Morgan, "Alexander Stephens," *New Georgia Encyclopedia*, last modified June 6, 2017, *https://www.georgiaencyclopedia.org/articles/government-politics/alexander-stephens-1812-1883/.*

14. "Lincoln on Slavery," Lincoln Home, National Park Service, accessed August 31, 2023, https://www.nps.gov/liho/learn/historyculture/slavery.htm.

15. Zinaldin, "Before the Flood."

16. Schott, *Recollections of Alexander H. Stephens*, 310.

17. Zinaldin, "Before the Flood."

18. Keith S. Hébert, *Cornerstone of the Confederacy: Alexander Stephens and the Speech That Defined the Lost Cause* (Knoxville: University of Tennessee Press, 2021), 24–25.

19. Schott, *Recollections of Alexander H. Stephens*, 308.

20. Schott, 320–321.

21. George Justice, "Georgia Secession Convention of 1861," *New Georgia Encyclopedia*, last modified Jun 6, 2017, https://www.georgiaencyclopedia.org/articles/government-politics/georgia-secession-convention-of-1861/.

22. Morgan, "Alexander Stephens."

23. Hébert, *Cornerstone of the Confederacy*, 222–223.

24. Alexander H. Stephens, "Cornerstone Speech," American Battlefield Trust, accessed August 31, 2023, https://www.battlefields.org/learn/primary-sources/cornerstone-speech.

25. Hébert, *Cornerstone of the Confederacy*, 223.

26. Hébert, 54.

27. Schott, *Recollections of Alexander H. Stephens*, 334–335.

28. Schott, 341.

29. Norwood, *Liberty Hall*, 11.

30. Norwood.

31. Myrta Lockett Avary, ed., *Recollections of Alexander H. Stephens: His Diary Kept When a Prisoner at Fort Warren, Boston Harbour, 1865* (New York: Doubleday, Page, 1919), 199.

32. Schott, *Recollections of Alexander H. Stephens*, 482–483.

33. Schott, 490–492.

34. Schott, 503.

35. "Liberty Hall," *Savannah Morning News*, October 16, 1875.

36. "Stephens Dead," *Atlanta Constitution*, March 4, 1883, 3.

37. "Death of Alexander H. Stephens," *Philadelphia Times*, March 5, 1883, 2.

38. "Stephens's Last Will," *Atlanta Constitution*, April 10, 1883, 4.

39. "Stephens," *Atlanta Constitution*, May 14, 1893, 14.

40. "Historic Residence of Stephens Is Restored as Southern Shrine," *Atlanta Journal Constitution*, July 26, 1936, 2.

41. Hébert, *Cornerstone of the Confederacy*, 166–167.

42. "Arnall Grants Dying Wish of Mrs. Holden," *Atlanta Constitution*, January 25, 1944.

43. Eugene Anderson, "Around the Circle," *Macon Telegraph*, October 17, 1952.

44. "Bruce Pupils Take Trip to Liberty Hall," *Macon News*, May 31, 1958.

45. "Essay Contest Planned on Alexander H. Stephens," *Macon Telegraph*, December 9, 1945, 3.

46. Certificate for "Outstanding Restoration of a Residential Structure," Georgia Trust for Historic Preservation, March 4, 1992.

47. John R. Brumgardt, "The Confederate Career of Alexander H. Stephens: The Case Reopened," *Civil War History* 27, no. 1 (1981): 65.

48. Jori Finkel, "The Enslaved Artist Whose Pottery Was an Act of Resistance," *New York Times*, last updated June 18, 2021, https://www.nytimes.com/2021/06/17/arts/design/-enslaved-potter-david-drake-museum.html.

Further Reading

Cooksey, Elizabeth B. "Taliaferro County." *New Georgia Encyclopedia*, last modified July 8, 2022. https://www.georgiaencyclopedia.org/articles/counties-cities-neighborhoods/taliaferro-county/.

Davis, William C. *The Union That Shaped the Confederacy: Robert Toombs and Alexander H. Stephens*. Lawrence: University Press of Kansas, 2001.

Georgia State Parks & Historic Sites Division. "A. H. Stephens State Historic Park." A. H. Stephens State Park, Department of Natural Resources Division. Accessed September 16, 2022. https://gastateparks.org.

Hébert, Keith S. *Cornerstone of the Confederacy: Alexander Stephens and the Speech That Defined the Lost Cause*. Knoxville: University of Tennessee Press, 2021.

Meyers, Christopher C. *The Empire State of the South: Georgia History in Documents and Essays*. Macon: Mercer University Press, 2018.

Morgan, Chad. "Alexander Stephens." *New Georgia Encyclopedia*," last modified June 6, 2017. Accessed September 10, 2022. https://www.georgiaencyclopedia.org/articles/government-politics/alexander-stephens-1812-1883/.

Richardson, Ramsey E. *Little Aleck: A Life of Alexander Stephens*. New York: Grosset and Dunlap, 1932.

Schott, Thomas E. *Alexander H. Stephens of Georgia: A Biography*. Baton Rouge: Louisiana State University Press, 1988.

Thomas, Emory M. *The Confederate Nation, 1861–1865*. New York: Harper Perennial, 2011.

CHAPTER 8

Pickett's Mill Battlefield

Jennifer W. Dickey

Basic Information

PERIOD OF SIGNIFICANCE: May 27, 1864

DATE ESTABLISHED AS A STATE HISTORIC SITE: 1974

ACREAGE: Currently 765 acres

LOCATION: 4432 Mount Tabor Church Road, Dallas, Ga. 30157, Paulding County

Pickett's Mill Battlefield in Paulding County was the scene of ferocious fighting between U.S. troops and Confederate troops in May 1864. Part of U.S. general William T. Sherman's Campaign for Atlanta, the battle at Pickett's Mill was a decisive Confederate victory at a time when the outcome of the Civil War still hung in the balance. Sherman began his invasion of Georgia from Chattanooga with around a hundred thousand troops with the objective of capturing Atlanta, an important transportation and supply hub for the Confederates. Opposing Sherman's army was the Confederate Army of Tennessee under the command of General Joseph E. Johnston, who commanded around sixty thousand troops. Sherman repeatedly flanked Johnston's army along the route of the Western and Atlantic Railroad for two weeks, forcing Johnston to fall back over and over and establish a new defensive position. In mid-May, Sherman changed his strategy and headed west and south away from the railroad and toward the crossroads town of Dallas in Paulding County. Here, U.S. and Confederate forces clashed in three bloody battles over a four-day period between May 25 and May 28 at New Hope Church, Pickett's Mill, and Dallas.

Site of the mill on Pickett's Mill Creek at Pickett's Mill Battlefield.

The battle at Pickett's Mill, which took place on May 27, proved to be both a strategic and tactical blunder by Sherman. Sherman's army far outnumbered that of Confederate general Joseph Johnston at Pickett's Mill, yet the Confederates were able to claim victory in the battle as U.S. troops retreated. U.S. casualties exceeded those of the Confederates at Pickett's Mill by more than three to one.[1] Writing about the battle twenty-four years later, U.S. lieutenant Ambrose Bierce described it as "a needless defeat" in an article titled "The Crime at Pickett's Mill."[2] Bierce predicted the battle was "foredoomed to oblivion."

Ironically, the site of the battle is today considered one of the most intact Civil War battlefields in the country, and the battle is studied by U.S. Army leaders as a prime example of a tactical failure.[3] The site was listed on the National Register of Historic Places in 1973, in spite of being the site of one of the "little known and least recorded battles of General William T. Sherman's Atlanta Campaign." The site's significance lay in its "integrity" and the fact that it was "still basically in the same condition as it was at the time of the battle," according to the National Park Service.[4] Acquired by the state in the 1970s, Pickett's Mill Battlefield opened to the public in 1990.

History of Pickett's Mill Battlefield

In the spring of 1864, the United States and the Confederate States of America (CSA) were beginning the third year of fighting the war that would determine the viability of the U.S. Constitution and the great question as to whether states, once members of the United States of America, were entitled to withdraw from the Union. For U.S. president Abraham Lincoln, the answer was unequivocal—secession was unconstitutional—and by 1864, he believed, so should be slavery.[5] For CSA president Jefferson Davis, peace could only be achieved by the United States recognizing the independence of the CSA and acknowledging the right of Southerners to continue to enslave African Americans. Following U.S. general Ulysses Grant's appointment of General William T. Sherman as head of the Military Division of the Mississippi in the spring of 1864, Sherman began his campaign at the head of three armies—Army of the Cumberland, Army of the Tennessee, and Army of the Ohio—with a total of over a hundred thousand troops. The stakes were high as Sherman began his Atlanta campaign in May 1864 as Lincoln was locked into a reelection battle against a peace candidate, George McClellan. Sherman's capture of Atlanta on September 2, 1864, shifted the odds in Lincoln's favor, but the march from Chattanooga to Atlanta was neither swift nor decisive.[6] Along the way Sherman's army suffered significant losses. Among the most inglorious of those losses was the Battle of Pickett's Mill.

Sherman's strategy in Georgia was to capture and control the Western and Atlantic Railroad that linked Chattanooga and Atlanta. In the first few weeks of May, Sherman succeeded in doing this through a series of flanking maneuvers that forced General Johnston to retreat repeatedly. At Allatoona Pass, however, Johnston dug in, and Sherman, realizing that the Confederate position was unassailable, veered southwest away from the railroad and toward the town of Dallas. Each man was given twenty days of rations as they began their march away from the railroad and into Paulding County.[7]

The landscape through which the U.S. soldiers marched was hilly and heavily wooded. The few roads that punctuated this sparsely populated area were narrow dirt tracks. Progress was slow, and while Sherman's army marched south, Johnston ordered his troops to move toward Dallas as well. The Confederate troops arrived in the area first and built earthworks at New Hope Church, where they dug in to face the advancing U.S. troops. On May 25, U.S. soldiers "were severely mauled in front of the Confederate earthworks by infantry and artillery fire." Although skirmishing continued into May 26, Sherman recognized the futility of the attack and withdrew his forces with a plan to reconcentrate his efforts on the Confederate right flank at a place known as Pickett's Mill.[8]

One of the ten counties created from Cherokee County by the Georgia state legislature in 1832, Paulding County had a population of just over seven thousand in 1864. The presence of two gold veins through the county led to the distribution of the former Cherokee lands in forty-acre gold lots in the 1832 gold lottery. However, gold mining in newly created Paulding County proved to be disappointing, and the county developed slowly. The hilly terrain and poor, rocky soil of Paulding County also proved poorly suited to cotton agriculture. In his 1849 *Statistics of the State of Georgia*, George White reported that "the roads are neglected, and many of them are very bad." He also wrote that there were "some very fine lands in this county, especially on Pumpkin Vine [*sic*], Euharlee, Tallapoosa, and Racoon creeks, adapted to corn, wheat and tobacco."[9]

It was on a tributary to Pumpkinvine Creek, known as Pickett's Mill Creek, that Malachi Pickett first acquired land in what was still Cherokee County in the early 1830s. By 1860, Pickett had increased his landholdings along Pumpkinvine Creek, and his sons, Benjamin, James, and Francis, owned adjacent farms. The Pickett family also owned and operated a gristmill on Pickett's Mill Creek.[10] By 1860, Malachi's farm was valued at $3,500, and Benajmin's farm was valued at $2,000, making them among the more well-off farmers in the area. Benjamin enlisted in the Confederate Army of Tennessee in March 1862. He was killed at the Battle of Chickamauga on September 19, 1863, and left behind his wife, Martha, four children, and an enslaved man named Martin.[11]

The Pickett family and their neighbors along Pumpkinvine and Pickett's Mill Creeks had fled their homes by the time U.S. troops arrived in the area in May 1864. Following the battle at New Hope Church, the Confederates, who were more familiar with the terrain, moved quickly toward the Pumpkinvine Creek area and began constructing fortifications atop a ridge on the Pickett farm. Northwest of the Confederate earthworks, U.S.

troops gathered following a five-hour march in hot weather through difficult terrain. Sherman's plan was to flank the Confederates on their right, but poor communication and even worse execution led the U.S. troops into a slaughter. About an hour before the fighting began, as he was scanning the battlefield and moving his troops into position, General Oliver Howard sent a note back to his commanding officer, General George Thomas, in which he wrote, "No person can appreciate the difficulty of moving over this ground unless he can see it." He added, "Am now turning the enemy's right flank, I think."[12]

Howard's message reflects almost everything that was about to go wrong for the U.S. forces. The difficult terrain and a lack of understanding of the Confederate positions combined with the hesitation by Howard to commit an adequate number of troops to the ensuing attack doomed the U.S. effort. Howard ordered Brigadier General William B. Hazen to lead the attack with his brigade of 1,500 men. Ambrose Bierce, Hazen's topographical engineer, later wrote that "after a march of less than a mile an hour and a further delay of three hours at the end of it to acquaint the enemy of our intention to surprise him, our single shrunken brigade of fifteen hundred men was sent forward without support to double up the army of General Johnston." Describing Hazen's reaction to receiving Howard's orders, Bierce added, "Only by a look which I knew how to read did he betray his sense of the criminal blunder."[13]

The battle began around 4:30 p.m. Hazen's brigade advanced and pushed through a group of dismounted Confederate cavalrymen only to find themselves in a deep, heavily wooded ravine below the entrenched infantrymen of Confederate general Patrick Cleburne. Hazen's brigade split, and while one group fought in a skirmish in a cornfield near the right flank of the Confederate line, the other attempted to fight their way up the steep slope of the ravine, which was covered with "almost impassable tangles of underwood" and topped by "breastworks [temporary fortifications] constructed at leisure and manned with two divisions of [Confederate] troops," according to Bierce. "In less than one minute the trim battalions had become simply a swarm of men struggling through the undergrowth of the forest," wrote Bierce. The terrain caused a breakdown of military formation, and as the troops clawed their way up the hill, they were met with a barrage of bullets from the Confederates. The result was a bloodbath in which hundreds of U.S. soldiers were killed in less than thirty minutes.[14]

The ravine at Pickett's Mill Battlefield.

Although the Confederate lines were spread out and paper thin, they had a tremendous advantage in terms of position. They were also dug in, either in shallow entrenchments or behind fallen logs, and they merely had to hold their line while the U.S. troops tried to climb a heavily wooded, slippery, steep hill. In the aftermath, Bierce described the pile of fallen corpses along the "dead-line," the point of closest advance by U.S. soldiers to the Confederate line, noting that "of the hundreds of corpses within twenty paces of the Confederate line," fewer than "a third were within fifteen paces, and not one within ten." The battle would continue for an additional five hours as U.S. troops retreated, reformed, and attacked again. The last assault by the Confederates took place after dark as U.S. soldiers tried to evacuate their wounded and retreat from the ravine.

Overall casualties on the U.S. side totaled around fifteen hundred, nearly half of which "fell killed and wounded in Hazen's brigade in less than thirty minutes of actual fighting," according to Bierce.[15] Confederate major James Ratchford reported that a single volley by Confederate general Patrick Cleburne's division "left seven-hundred-and-seventy Yankees to be buried in one pit," adding that "a pyramid of human skulls could have been erected" at the site. Upon passing through the battlefield at the end of the war, Ratchford "saw the trees imbedded with shot and shell" and "wondered how it was possible for any human being to get out of that battle alive."[16]

On the morning of May 28, 1864, after sunrise, Confederate captain Samuel Foster wrote, "We have to pass over the dead Yanks of the battle field of yesterday; and here I beheld that which I cannot describe; and which I hope to never see again, dead men meet the eye in every direction, and in one place I stoped [*sic*] and counted 50 dead men in a circle of 30 ft. of me." On the U.S. side, William Oliphant wrote, "The field looked as though a great blue carpet had been spread over the ground. Dead men were everywhere; they lay in solid lines just as they fell and in many places were in heaps." Confederate troops began gathering up weapons from the dead U.S. soldiers, reportedly collecting over a thousand rifles, and then buried the soldiers in mass graves near where they had fallen on the battlefield.[17] Most of the U.S. soldiers killed would later be exhumed and moved to the U.S. National Cemetery in Marietta, leaving behind shallow pits that are still visible today.[18]

In his memoirs, Sherman explained that his "objective" during the Atlanta campaign was always the railroad, not any of the small towns along the way between Chickamauga and Atlanta. He writes that "a continual battle was in progress by strong skirmish-lines, taking advantage of every species of cover, and both parties fortifying each night by rifle-trenches, with head-logs, many of which grew to be as formidable as first-class works of defense. Occasionally one party or the other would make a dash in the nature of a sally, but usually it sustained a repulse with great loss of life." In spite of this slow progress, wrote Sherman, "substantially in the month of May, we had steadily driven our antagonist from the strong positions of Resaca, Cassville, Allatoona, and Dallas; had advanced our lines in strong, compact order from Chattanooga to Big Shanty, nearly a hundred miles of difficult country as was ever fought over by civilized armies; and thus stood prepared to go on, anxious to fight, and confident of success." According to Sherman, it was "impossible to state accurately our loss of life and men in any one separate battle; for the fighting was continuous, almost daily, among trees and bushes, on ground where one could rarely see a hundred yards ahead."[19] Never does Sherman mention the battle at Pickett's Mill.

Following the "criminal blunder" at Pickett's Mill, fighting erupted around the county seat of Dallas on May 28, and the two sides continued to skirmish for another three days before Sherman began moving his army back toward the Western and Atlantic Railroad on June 1. Skirmishing continued in and around Marietta throughout the month of June. On June 27, Johnston's Confederates won another battle, this one at Kennesaw Mountain; however, the Confederate victories on the battlefields did not stop Sherman's advance toward Atlanta. Sherman continued maneuvering around Johnston's flank, forcing the Confederates to fall back. In mid-July, CSA president Jefferson Davis, who had become exasperated with Johnston's retreats, replaced Johnston with General John Bell Hood. While Hood proved more aggressive than Johnston, he failed to win a decisive victory on the battlefield, and by the end of August, Sherman's army had surrounded Atlanta and cut off Hood's supply routes. Hood abandoned the city on September 1, and on September 2 Sherman marched into the city before sending a telegram to President Lincoln announcing, "Atlanta is ours, and fairly won."[20]

Although Confederate victories at New Hope Church, Pickett's Mill, and Kennesaw Mountain had cost the U.S. Army a great deal of blood and treasure, they had little impact on the overall military or political situation. Sherman ultimately captured Atlanta, and Abraham Lincoln was reelected president in November 1864. That same month, Sherman began his March to the Sea, which ended when he captured Savannah on December 21, 1864. By spring of 1865, the war was over. In Paulding County, the families that had farmed the land that was the site of the horrific battle on May 27, 1864, returned to their farms. Although the Pickett gristmill had been destroyed by U.S. troops during the battle, members of the Pickett family still owned land in and around the area, including Malachi Pickett, who owned 440 acres along Pumpkinvine Creek, and Martha Pickett, who owned 166 acres within the battlefield site.[21]

Over the next few years, much of the land that today comprises the battlefield changed hands several times before being acquired by the North Georgia Timberland Company in the early 1950s. By 1952, the timber company owned 395 acres of land that constituted the "core" of the battlefield property. Twenty years earlier, the battlefield site was mapped by Atlanta historian Wilbur Kurtz and Atlanta real estate developer and Civil War relic hunter Beverly Dubose Jr., although Kurtz and Dubose kept their efforts secret. Historian Philip Secrist began exploring the site in the 1950s and published an article about the battlefield in May 1971. By this time, the timber company, now known as Georgia Kraft Company, had logged the land and was ready to sell it. Secrist and a group of investors acquired almost five hundred acres from Georgia Kraft, and in 1973 the newly created Georgia Heritage Trust acquired the property from Secrist's group.

Over the next decade, the state acquired additional acreage around its original acquisition area to increase the size of the site to 765 acres. The state conducted surveys and archaeological excavations of the site and identified surviving features such as trenches, roadbeds, gravesites, and the locations of houses and the gristmill.[22] After almost two decades of study and preparation, during which time a visitor center was constructed, the state opened the site to the public in May 1990.[23]

Pickett's Mill Battlefield today offers visitors a glimpse into the past where they can visit the site of an event that once seemed "foredoomed to oblivion." The relative remoteness of the site throughout much of the twentieth century and ownership for several decades by a corporate entity that made minimal changes to the land has resulted in an evocative landscape. The tree canopy is quite different from what existed in 1864 in terms of age and species, but the basic landscape features remain much as they were at the time of the battle. Described as a "criminal blunder" by Ambrose Bierce, the Battle of Pickett's Mill is among the U.S. Army's favorite battlefields at which to conduct geographical tactical analysis. "It's a textbook case of tactical failure," according to interpretive ranger John Hoomes.[24] That it was a Confederate victory is inconsequential in the broader context of the outcome of the Civil War, but there are lessons to be learned from the site and the battle.

Touring the Site

The Pickett's Mill Battlefield State Historic Site is often described as "one of the best-preserved Civil War battlefields in the nation"; however, it is perhaps better described as one of the best "restored" battlefields.[25] The site was farmed for many years after the battle, and in the mid-twentieth century the site was logged by a timber company. However, by the time the site opened to the public in 1990, the trees and undergrowth were similar to what had been there in 1864, according to site superintendent Jeff Dean, who stated, "What you see now is what the soldiers saw 126 years ago, even to the old road sites."[26] The state manages the acreage to reflect conditions at the time of the battle, including maintaining several open fields in which fighting occurred that in 1864 were wheatfields or corn fields. Periodic burning of certain wooded areas keeps the undergrowth at a level that is reflective of what the soldiers would have encountered during the battle. The battlefield has no monuments or memorials and limited interpretive panels. Visitors should familiarize themselves with the events of the battle by watching the film *The Battle of Pickett's Mill* and touring the exhibit prior to exploring the trails that wind throughout the site.

The 3,724-square-foot visitor center includes offices, a research library, a theater, and exhibit space. The research library contains a rich collection of Civil War–related publications, including a complete set of the 128-volume *The War of the Rebellion: A Compilation of the Official Records of the Union and Confederate Armies*. The film shown in the visitor center is also available on the website (https://gastateparks.org/PickettsMillBattlefield). The exhibit explains the strategy and tactics employed in the battle and features an array of artifacts, including a U.S. flag finial, which was discovered at the bottom of the ravine in the 1960s.

In 2002 a log cabin once located on Old Stilesboro Road in Paulding County that dates to the 1850s was moved to the site and restored to its

Finial from a U.S. flag found in the ravine at Pickett's Mill Battlefield.

Prather Cabin at Pickett's Mill Battlefield.

1860s appearance. The cabin, donated by the Prather family, and its attendant outbuildings are representative of the types of farmsteads in which the Pickett family and other farmers in the area would have lived at the time of the battle. The cabin is used for living history demonstrations related to life on the home front during the Civil War.

Staff offer other programs at the site, including demonstrations of weapons and games from the nineteenth century. Picnic tables are located next to the demonstration area behind the museum. A wooden platform next to the demonstration area offers an overlook toward the ravine. Just below the platform are two trenches that were the temporary graves of U.S. soldiers who were disinterred and then reinterred in the U.S. National Cemetery in Marietta in 1866.

The main attraction of the site, however, is the 6.5 miles of hiking trails that traverse the ridge upon which the Confederate troops positioned themselves as well as the bottom of the ravine where U.S. troops were killed by the hundreds. Individual trails range in length from 0.5 miles to the Prather Cabin to 3 miles to the Brand House site. While the trail to

Trail above the ravine at Pickett's Mill Battlefield.

the Prather Cabin is relatively flat and an easy walk, the remaining trails are more difficult as they wind through the battlefield site. Visitors should expect to encounter narrow trails with uneven terrain and steep descents and climbs. The experience is immersive and will prompt visitors to reflect on the tragedy that unfolded here.

Notes

1. Roy Morris Jr., "The Crime at Pickett's Mill," Warfare History Network, April 2012, accessed August 21, 2023, https://warfarehistorynetwork.com/article/the-crime-at-picketts-mill/.

2. Ambrose Bierce, "The Crime at Pickett's Mill," American Battlefield Trust, accessed August 21, 2023, https://www.battlefields.org/learn/primary-sources/crime-picketts-mill.

3. John Hoomes, interview by Jennifer Dickey, August 26, 2023.

4. Jean K. Buckley, "Pickett's Mill Battlefield Site," National Register of Historic Places Nomination Form (Washington, D.C.: U.S. Department of the Interior, National Park Service, 1973), section 8.

5. James M. McPherson, *Battle Cry of Freedom* (New York: Ballantine Books, 1988), 699; "Abraham Lincoln and Emancipation," Library of Congress, accessed August 21, 2023, https://www.loc.gov/collections/abraham-lincoln-papers/articles-and-essays/abraham-lincoln-and-emancipation/.

6. "The Atlanta Campaign: A Strategic Overview," American Battlefield Trust, accessed August 21, 2023, https://www.battlefields.org/learn/articles/atlanta-campaign.

7. Brad Butkovich, *The Battle of Pickett's Mill: Along the Dead Line* (Charleston: History Press, 2013), 21.

8. "New Hope Church," American Battlefield Trust, accessed August 21, 2023, https://www.battlefields.org/learn/civil-war/battles/new-hope-church.

9. George White, *Statistics of the State of Georgia* (Savannah: W. Thorne Williams, 1849), 466.

10. Morton R. McInvale, *The Battle of Pickett's Mill: Foredoomed to Oblivion* (Atlanta: Georgia Department of Natural Resources, 1977), 20–22.

11. McInvale, 17, 25.

12. Butkovich, *Battle of Pickett's Mill*, 89.

13. Bierce, "Crime at Pickett's Mill."

14. Bierce.

15. Bierce.

16. W. A. Foster Jr. and Thomas Allan Scott, *Paulding County: Its People and Places*, vol. 1 (Roswell, Ga.: W. H. Wolfe, 1983), 129–130.

17. Butkovich, *Battle of Pickett's Mill*, 151–153.

18. John Hoomes interview.

19. William T. Sherman, *Memoirs of General William T. Sherman* (New York: Library of America, 1990), 514–515.

20. McPherson, *Battle Cry of Freedom*, 774.

21. McInvale, *Battle of Pickett's Mill*, 141–142.

22. Butkovich, *Battle of Pickett's Mill*, 162.

23. Bob Harrell, "2,000 Men Died during the 1864 Pickett's Mill Battle," *Atlanta Constitution*, May 23, 1990, 55.

24. Hoomes, interview.

25. "Pickett's Mill Battlefield," Georgia Department of Natural Resources, State Parks & Historic Sites, accessed August 23, 2023, https://gastateparks.org/PickettsMillBattlefield.

26. Harrell, "2,000 Men Died," 55.

Further Reading

Bierce, Ambrose. *Ambrose Bierce's Civil War: Annotated Warbler Classics Edition*. Edited by William McCann. New York: Warbler Press, 2019.

Bonds, Russell S. *War Like the Thunderbolt: The Battle and Burning of Atlanta*. Yardley, Pa.: Westholme, 2009.

Brown, Barry L., and Gordon R. Elwell. *Crossroads of Conflict: A Guide to Civil War Sites in Georgia*. Athens: University of Georgia Press, 2010.

Butkovich, Brad. *The Battle of Pickett's Mill: Along the Dead-Line*. Charleston: History Press, 2013.

Croon, Janet Elizabeth. *The War outside My Window: The Civil War Diary of LeRoy Wiley Gresham, 1860–1865*. El Dorado Hills, Calif.: Savas Beatie, 2018.

Foster, W. A. *Paulding County: Its People and Places*. Vol. 1. Roswell, Ga.: W. H. Wolfe Associates, 1983.

Fowler, John D. "Civil War in Georgia." *New Georgia Encyclopedia*, last modified August 24, 2020. https://www.georgiaencyclopedia.org/articles/history-archaeology/civil-war-in-georgia-overview/.

Hyun, Jun Suk. "Battle of Pickett's Mill." *New Georgia Encyclopedia*, last modified July 2, 2020. https://www.georgiaencyclopedia.org/articles/history-archaeology/battle-of-picketts-mill/.

Inscoe, John C., ed. *The Civil War in Georgia: A New Georgia Encyclopedia Companion*. Athens: University of Georgia Press, 2011.

Joslyn, Mauriel P., ed. *A Meteor Shining Brightly: Essays on Major General Patrick R. Cleburne*. Macon, Ga.: Mercer University Press, 1998.

McInvale, Morton R. *The Battle of Pickett's Mill: Foredoomed to Oblivion*. London: Forgotten Books, 2018.

McPherson, James M. *Battle Cry of Freedom: The Civil War Era*. Oxford: Oxford University Press, 1988.

McPherson, James M. *The War That Forged a Nation: Why the Civil War Still Matters*. Oxford: Oxford University Press, 2015.

Sherman, William T. *Memoirs of General W. T. Sherman*. New York: Library of America, 1990.

CHAPTER 9

Roosevelt's Little White House

Jennifer W. Dickey, Katelyn Gregory, and Seth Rodie

Basic Information

PERIOD OF SIGNIFICANCE: 1924–1945

DATE ESTABLISHED AS A STATE HISTORIC SITE: 1948

ACREAGE: 163 acres

LOCATION: 401 Little White House Road, Warm Springs, Ga. 31830, Meriwether County

One of Georgia's most visited state historic sites is Roosevelt's Little White House. Located in the small west-central Georgia town of Warm Springs, the Little White House serves as a memorial to the nation's thirty-second president as well as an "unofficial transitional capital in the South's historical process of modernization."[1] It was at Warm Springs in 1924 that Franklin D. Roosevelt regained the confidence and courage necessary to resume his political career following a bout with polio that left him partially paralyzed. The warm waters of the springs in what was a failing nineteenth-century resort facility rejuvenated Roosevelt and became, for him, a refuge to which he would retreat over the next two decades to rest and recover his strength as he led the United States through the crises of the Great Depression and World War II. The little house in the piney woods remains today much as it was on the day that Roosevelt died while sitting for a portrait in the living room. The house and nearby historic pools, where Roosevelt swam his way back into national politics, are part of a National Historic Landmark District that includes the Roosevelt Warm Springs Institute for Rehabilitation. The site "has dual significance in U.S. History. Not only does it commemorate a major humanitarian

Main House at Roosevelt's Little White House.

endeavor, the Warm Springs Foundation, but it is also strongly related to the career of President Franklin D. Roosevelt (1933–1945), the key figure in the creation of the foundation."[2]

The state opened a new museum in 2004 on the grounds of the Little White House that provides historical context for the symbiotic relationship between Roosevelt and the section of rural Georgia that helped shape his presidency. The historic pools at the rehabilitation center have also been preserved and are open to the public, although they are no longer filled with water.

History of the Little White House

The development of Warm Springs into a resort town began in the early 1800s following the forced removal of the Creek Indians, who had long inhabited the area. Creek land was redistributed through a land lottery in 1827. Originally claimed by "orphans from Putnam and Baldwin counties" in a program designed to give "'unfortunates' a financial start in life," the land that became Warm Springs was developed as a resort by David Rose in the 1830s.[3] Rose recognized the rejuvenating potential of the naturally warm spring water, and he built accommodations at the springs for up to two hundred guests.

The property changed hands in 1844 and again in 1848 when Columbus businessman John Mustian purchased the fledgling resort, which by this time had several cottages scattered around the springs. Mustian built a hotel at the site, which burned in 1869. Mustian's grandson, Charles Davis, took over the property and built another hotel with bathhouses at the site in 1874. After a fire destroyed that hotel in 1889, Davis rebuilt again.[4] The Meriwether Inn, which opened in 1893, was a forty-six-room, three-story, rambling, Queen Anne style building with turrets and wraparound porches and featured two small indoor pools and a large outdoor pool, all filled with the eighty-eight-degree mineral water that bubbled up from the ground. The resort facility also included fifteen cottages that were available for guests during the summer season. In 1896, the town of Bullochsville, which had developed around the resort, was incorporated.

For a few years, the Meriwether Inn seemed to thrive, but by the 1920s, the resort had fallen on hard times. Davis had leased the resort to Thomas Loyless, a newspaper editor from Columbus, Georgia, who struggled to make ends meet. During a chance encounter in New York City between Loyless and George Foster Peabody, also a native of Columbus, Loyless mentioned to Peabody that a young man named Louis Joseph had recovered from the aftereffects of polio by swimming in the waters at the resort. Peabody shared Joseph's story with his friend Franklin D. Roosevelt, who had been desperately seeking a cure for the paralysis that had plagued him since his 1921 bout with polio. Roosevelt was intrigued, and in early October 1924 he and his wife, Eleanor, his personal secretary, Marguerite (Missy) LeHand, and his valet, Irvin McDuffie, arrived in the town that would soon change its name to Warm Springs.[5]

By the time of Roosevelt's arrival, the Meriwether Inn was well past its prime, and Roosevelt thought it was a fire trap, so he and his entourage elected to stay in one of the adjacent cottages. Roosevelt met with the twenty-six-year-old Joseph, who had been paralyzed from the waist down by polio, much as Roosevelt had been. Joseph had spent two years at the resort, and "he seemed to have swum himself back to health." In Joseph, Roosevelt saw, perhaps for the first time in three years, real hope that he might recover the use of his legs. On October 4, 1924, Roosevelt took his first swim in the warm water of the resort. The experience was transformative, and soon Roosevelt found that he could stand and walk with ease in four feet of the warm, buoyant spring water.[6]

Roosevelt remained at the resort for seventeen days, during which he spent several hours a day swimming and exercising in the pool. Eleanor returned to New York, while Missy LeHand remained with Roosevelt in Warm Springs. This unusual arrangement of his "work wife," as LeHand was sometimes known, being by Roosevelt's side while his "home wife" pursued other interests had been in place since 1920, when LeHand came to work for Roosevelt at Eleanor's request. Renowned for her secretarial skills, LeHand served as Roosevelt's personal secretary for twenty-one years until she suffered a stroke in 1941.[7]

Roosevelt's stay at the resort, where he had the place virtually to himself, was newsworthy. The *Brooklyn Daily Eagle* reported, "Through learning to live the life of a merman and spending the bulk of his day in hot water, Franklin D. Roosevelt, Democratic leader, is regaining his health." Roosevelt was "getting back the vigor that made him a political leader," the paper reported, noting, "His admirers were stunned when word came that he had been stricken in the epidemic of infantile paralysis which swept New York State in 1921." He had been "transformed from a stalwart man in the prime of life to an almost helpless cripple," according to the *Eagle*, but this "new and strange treatment . . . he hoped, would make him a new man." Speaking with a reporter, Roosevelt stated: "I've been greatly helped, and I've only been here two weeks. This leg (indicating the right one) I hadn't been able to move for three years. I can use it a little now. The other is much better, too." Recalling that he had spent the better part of the past three years on a houseboat in Florida trying to recuperate, Roosevelt noted that the waters along the Florida coast "were too full of sharks." "I've turned fish-man," said Roosevelt as he explained that the doctors theorized that exercising his atrophied muscles in the warm water would "build up" the nerves and muscles in his legs. The reporter noted that "there was something more than physical mending in his attitude," adding that Roosevelt described the place as "a mental tonic."[8]

Two months after Roosevelt's first visit to Warm Springs, Thomas Loyless wrote in a column for the *Macon Telegraph* that he was convinced, after becoming "well acquainted" with Roosevelt during his sojourn at Warm Springs in October, that Roosevelt combined "all the qualities and advantages needed in the next Democratic standard-bearer." Loyless indicated that Roosevelt planned to return in April to Warm Springs, where he was "getting back the use of his legs" through therapy at the resort and encouraged "up-standing Georgians" to come to Warm Springs to meet Roosevelt.[9] Loyless's motives were not purely political. As the proprietor of the Meriwether Inn, he had a vested interest in promoting the benefits of the "healing waters" of Warm Springs. Nevertheless, this enthusiastic endorsement of Roosevelt as the future of the Democratic Party heralded a comeback of sorts. It seemed that the career of this former New York State senator and vice presidential candidate, which had been derailed by polio, was about to get back on track.

As anticipated, Roosevelt returned to Warm Springs on April 1, 1925, and remained at the resort until May 15. In the meantime, much had changed at the site, which was now being heralded as a "health resort." Loyless, with financial backing from George Peabody, had bought the Warm Springs resort and had begun promoting the healing properties of its warm mineral waters.[10] During Roosevelt's stay in the spring of 1925, a dozen other polio patients arrived at the site to begin the same therapy that Louis Joseph and Roosevelt had undertaken. For six weeks in the spring of 1925 Roosevelt swam and exercised several times a day in the warm, soothing waters. In the afternoons, he would often go for a drive into the surrounding countryside, where he began to make the acquaintance of local farmers.

A year later, Roosevelt returned for a five-week stay beginning March 27. It was during this visit in the spring of 1926 that newspapers began reporting that Roosevelt was planning to purchase the resort, a welcome development that would "assure the completion of the project that was set underway by George Foster Peabody and Thomas W. Loyless." Loyless had died in March 1926, and Peabody was eager to sell to Roosevelt, who had ideas about developing the resort on a larger scale.[11] By late April 1926, newspapers in Georgia and New York were reporting that Roosevelt had acquired the Warm Springs resort along with several thousand acres of land from Peabody for an undisclosed sum.[12] The amount was later revealed to be $195,000, which constituted a sizeable investment for Roosevelt, whose net worth at the time was around $275,000.[13]

Roosevelt soon announced ambitious plans for the development of a club and colony at what he anticipated would be "a pleasure resort of national appeal" and "a health resort for utilizing the curative powers of the waters." The pleasure resort and health resort were to be operated as separate entities. The resort was to be known as Georgia Warm Springs and would "become known throughout the country as a recreational center of unrivaled natural beauty and peopled by a colony . . . composed of the families of leaders in the social, cultural and business life of the nation." Roosevelt planned for a three-phased development beginning with improvements to the Warm Springs baths and swimming pools, followed by the construction of a health resort to "accommodate patients suffering with infantile paralysis and kindred afflictions which have been relieved by the waters here." Finally, Roosevelt planned to develop a "cottage colony around a magnificent country club" complete with a golf course, a shooting preserve, and bridle paths for horseback riding.[14]

Roosevelt's plans for a year-round pleasure resort with national appeal never came to fruition, but his efforts to develop a therapeutic resort were more successful. He returned to Warm Springs for seven weeks in the fall of 1926 and spent almost six months spread out across four separate visits at the site in 1927. During that time, he shifted his focus from creating a profit-making resort to creating the Georgia Warm Springs Foundation, Inc., of which he was president. He began soliciting donations for the foundation from his wealthy friends. Among those who contributed were Edsel Ford, who provided money to build an indoor pool that made the facility useable year-round.[15] The expanded pool facility, which included both indoor and outdoor pools as well as changing rooms, would become the centerpiece of the rehabilitation facility.

Throughout 1927 and 1928, Roosevelt devoted much of his time to his own hydrotherapy and developing the foundation, but he also increased his engagement in the political arena. When New York governor Al Smith, the Democratic nominee for president in 1928, asked Roosevelt to run in the New York gubernatorial election of 1928, Roosevelt at first refused, citing his work developing his foundation in Warm Springs. Eventually, however, Roosevelt agreed to run, and he was elected to succeed Smith as the forty-fourth governor of New York in November 1928.

Roosevelt's victory in New York and his reelection as governor in 1930, combined with his efforts to mediate the impact of the Great Depression in New York, made him the leading Democratic candidate for president. In the presidential election of 1932, Roosevelt handily defeated

The historic pools at Warm Springs.

incumbent Herbert Hoover in what proved to be a referendum on Hoover's ineffective economic policies. The residents of Warm Springs and Meriwether County rejoiced over Roosevelt's victory. At the Warm Springs Foundation, "the routine of baths, exercises and rest periods went forward as usual, but there seemed to be a happier spirit at the bath house as the patients splashed about in the same pool where Roosevelt [had] spent many hours."[16]

During his time in office as governor, Roosevelt had managed eleven trips to Warm Springs, where he stayed in a cottage that he had built for himself at the resort in 1926. He engaged the services of architect Henry Toombs, a native Georgian and graduate of the University of Pennsylvania who had worked for the renowned firm of McKim, Mead, and White in New York, to design not only a cottage for himself but also the pools and bathhouses as well as other buildings for the foundation. In 1931 Toombs began work on another cottage for Roosevelt that was somewhat removed from the cluster of residential cottages that made up the foundation complex. This six-room cottage, located on a hillside southeast of the main resort facilities, would become known as the Little White House. Here, Roosevelt would reside whenever he visited Warm Springs from 1932 until his death in 1945.

Throughout his twelve years as president of the United States, Roosevelt visited Warm Springs sixteen times. The challenges he faced as president were unprecedented—mitigating the economic calamity of the Great Depression followed by engagement in the global catastrophe of World War II. While his stays in Warm Springs became shorter and less frequent, they still seemed to rejuvenate the president. Each year, with the exception of 1936 and 1942, Roosevelt presided over a grand Thanksgiving dinner held in Georgia Hall, a building designed by Toombs that upon its completion in 1933 became the centerpiece of the Warm Springs Foundation.[17] In November 1933, under the headline "All Roads Leading to Warm Springs," the *West Point News* reported: "Leaders in the world of statesmanship, science, commerce, and industry, heralded and unheralded" had visited the president in Warm Springs as he prepared for his usual Thanksgiving Day feast. Following his usual custom, Roosevelt sat "at the head of the big table at the Foundation, surrounded by his Warm Springs friends." Roosevelt appeared at the dinner, not as the president of the United States, but as the "friend and comrade of the patients at the Foundation," casting aside his "executive mantle," if only for a day.[18]

Fundraising for the Warm Springs Foundation remained a challenge, especially with Roosevelt's attentions diverted by his responsibilities as president. However, in late 1933, one of his advisers suggested that a series of balls be held across the country on the president's birthday, January 30, to raise money for the foundation. More than six thousand fundraising balls were held in January 1934, during which Roosevelt spoke via radio, not as president, but as "the representative on this occasion of the hundreds of thousands of crippled children in our country." The balls raised over $1 million after expenses, and the success of the effort inspired Roosevelt to continue the Birthday Ball tradition.[19]

In 1937, Roosevelt agreed to the creation of a new organization, the National Foundation for Infantile Paralysis (NFIP), which became the umbrella organization under which fundraising activities would be conducted to benefit polio patients. The new foundation supported rehabilitation efforts at Warm Springs as well as research efforts aimed at devising improved treatment programs and, ultimately, a vaccine. Actor and comedian Eddie Cantor, a friend of Roosevelt's, suggested that radio celebrities should appeal to their audiences to send in dimes to support the foundation in what became known as the March of Dimes campaign. In honor of Roosevelt's involvement in the March of Dimes, the Roosevelt dime, which replaced the Mercury dime, was introduced the year after Roosevelt's death on what would have been his sixty-fourth birthday in January 1946.[20]

As Roosevelt attempted to steer the nation through the Great Depression, he sought counsel far and wide for solutions to the economic collapse. When he was in Warm Springs, he took daily drives into the countryside and talked to area farmers about their needs. He also experienced firsthand one of the challenges that faced rural folk across the country—the lack of affordable electricity. When Roosevelt received an electrical bill for his cottage that was four times what he paid for electricity at his much larger home in Hyde Park, New York, he embarked on a quest to help facilitate the delivery of affordable electricity in rural areas. He created the Rural Electrification Administration (REA) by executive order in May 1935, which provided financing to state and local governments to support the development of electrical power supplies and distribution systems in rural areas. The next year the president signed the Rural Electrification Act of 1936, which expanded the programs begun under the REA.[21]

Roosevelt's last visit to the Little White House was in April 1945. He had, in November 1944, been elected to a fourth term as president, and as he began his twelfth year in office, he was in failing health. Dr. Howard Bruenn, a naval officer who had been assigned to be the president's physician in 1944, traveled with Roosevelt. Bruenn had accompanied the president to Yalta for the conference with Churchill and Stalin in February 1945, and when the president left for a two-week stay at the Little White House, Bruenn was aboard the train. Also accompanying the president to Warm Springs were his cousins, Laura Delano and Margaret Suckley, as well as Grace Tully, Roosevelt's personal secretary, and his dog, Fala. When the train arrived at Warm Springs on March 30, the station attendant noted that Roosevelt "was the worst looking man I ever saw who was still alive."[22] However, the attendant and the members of the president's entourage all assumed that a couple of weeks in the warm air and rejuvenating waters of Warm Springs would revitalize Roosevelt as had happened on previous occasions.

The pace at Warm Springs proved beneficial for Roosevelt, and while he attended to his presidential duties as needed, he also spent a great deal of time with his guests. The entourage expanded on April 9, when Roosevelt's former mistress, Lucy Mercer Rutherfurd, and her friend, Elizabeth Shoumatoff, arrived from South Carolina. Eleanor's discovery of Roosevelt's affair with Lucy Mercer in 1918 had nearly destroyed the Roosevelts' marriage. At the time, Franklin promised Eleanor that he would end the affair and never see Mercer again. Mercer married Winthrop Rutherford in 1920, but she and Roosevelt continued to meet periodically throughout his time as president. His daughter, Anna, would arrange for Rutherford to come to the White House for lunch or dinner when Eleanor was away, and she had made arrangements for Rutherford to visit her father in Warm Springs in April 1945.

Roosevelt and his female companions spent several days relaxing at his cottage and driving around the countryside near Warm Springs. Shoumatoff, a renowned portrait painter, began work on a portrait of Roosevelt for Rutherford's daughter, Barbara. On the afternoon of April 12, the women chatted with Roosevelt while Shoumatoff painted, when suddenly Roosevelt complained of a terrific headache and then slumped forward. Suckley summoned Dr. Bruenn, who immediately realized that the president had suffered a cerebral hemorrhage. As efforts to revive Roosevelt commenced, Rutherford and Shoumatoff, recognizing the severity of the situation and that Eleanor would surely be summoned to the scene, packed their bags and returned to South Carolina. Roosevelt was declared dead later that afternoon in his bedroom in the Little White House.[23]

The death of Roosevelt sent shock waves through the nation and the world. For the residents of Warm Springs, where Roosevelt had come to relax and recover for more than two decades, the news hit especially hard. "We had lost our very best friend," recalled Suzanne Pike, one of the children who had been treated at the Warms Springs Foundation.[24] Eleanor attended the swearing in of vice president Harry Truman as president and then flew to Warm Springs, arriving around midnight. The next day she accompanied her husband's body on the long, mournful train ride back to Washington, D.C. Following a funeral service in the East Room of the White House, Roosevelt was buried on the grounds of his Hyde Park estate.[25]

With Roosevelt's death, ownership of the Little White House and other property in the area where Roosevelt had operated an experimental farm transferred to the Georgia Warm Springs Foundation according to the terms of Roosevelt's will. As early as 1930, Roosevelt and the leaders of the foundation, who were concerned about the foundation's reliance on Roosevelt as the principal fundraiser, had taken out a $560,000 life insurance policy on Roosevelt. That policy paid the full amount to the foundation upon the president's death. However, maintenance of the Little White House, which the leadership of the foundation as well as political leaders of the state agreed needed to be preserved, would be a burden to the foundation and outside of its principal mission.

The state created a new entity, the Franklin D. Roosevelt Warm Springs Memorial Commission, to which the foundation transferred ownership of the Little White House in 1947. The purpose of the commission was to maintain the house as "a national shrine in memory of a man who was devoted to the alleviation of the suffering of mankind."[26] Some two thousand people descended on the town of Warm Springs on Wednesday, June 25, 1947, for the ceremonial transfer of title. Among the dignitaries was Georgia governor M. E. Thompson, who accepted the deed from foundation president Basil O'Connor.[27] In his public remarks, former Secretary of the Navy Josephus Daniels, under whom Roosevelt had served as assistant secretary from 1913 to 1920, stated, "What we have to guard, we are determined to guard well—both the memory and the premises!"[28] Commission chair Ivan Allen, who would later be instrumental in saving the Chief Vann House, spoke as well, and a hundred army and navy fighter planes performed an aerial salute. The block-long, downtown business district was decorated with bunting for the occasion. The cottage, which had been preserved in the state that it was in at Roosevelt's death, was open to the public for the day, and then it was to be closed for repairs to enable the building to accommodate the anticipated crowds of visitors that were expected at this new "national shrine."[29]

The work necessary to allow the Little White House to host the public included replacing the wooden deck on the back of the house, where Roosevelt often sat while working, with a concrete and steel structure of the same shape and size, construction of an administration building with room to display artifacts, and creation of a paved parking lot with space for two hundred vehicles. The grounds were "cleared and beautified," and a road was constructed to connect Georgia Hall at the rehabilitation center to the Little White House parking lot. Ivan Allen explained that the books, ship models, bric-a-brac, and glassware of which Roosevelt had been most fond were all put back in place and "securely wired down," and the bed in which Roosevelt died had been insured for $10,000.[30] Apparently Roosevelt's home at Hyde Park, which he had willed to the federal government as the site for his presidential library and which had been opened to the public, had "all but been carted away by an army, hungry for mementoes of Roosevelt," and the thousands of visitors had created substantial "wear and tear" on the building. The Warm Springs Memorial Commission was determined that the Little White House would not suffer the same fate; therefore, the underpinnings of the house had been reinforced "to withstand the steady pounding of millions of visitors," and the artifacts had been "riveted in place with copper wiring—every picture, every ship, every curio."[31]

The Little White House opened to the public on October 28, 1948. *Georgia Progress*, a publication of the State Agricultural and Industrial Development Board, reported: "In the legacy of the Little White House and the acres around it, Georgia has had the good fortune to inherit something of international interest and affection with Mt. Vernon and the Hermitage as the home of a great President, and the Warm Springs Foundation beside it will continue to give hope and help to the handicapped. Truly, President Roosevelt built his house in the woods . . . and the world has beat a path to his door." Noting that while Roosevelt's Hyde Park home would draw thousands of visitors, only at the Little White House and adjacent foundation could people "fully understand and appreciate the man." The *Macon News* reported that while the site was closed for repairs and upgrades, two million people drove by to peer over the fence to look at the house and anticipated that the site would become "one of the nation's most famous tourist attractions."[32]

While the Little White House did not become one of the most visited historic sites in the nation, it did draw more than a hundred thousand visitors a year throughout the late 1940s and into the early 1950s. The Memorial Commission acquired additional land, including much of the land that had constituted Roosevelt's experimental farm, by 1952.[33] Included in the 4,050 acres owned by the commission was Dowdell's Knob, the highest point of the Pine Mountain Range in the area and a favorite spot of Roosevelt's for picnics and pondering world affairs. This area is today part of the 9,000-acre F. D. Roosevelt State Park, a recreation area with hiking, camping, swimming, and horseback riding facilities.

The Little White House facilities were expanded in the early 1960s after Georgia Mustian Wilkins, who had long owned a summer house within walking distance of Roosevelt's cottage, willed her property to the Memorial Commission. Wilkins's house was remodeled by the commission into a museum at a cost of $75,000. Wilkins and Roosevelt had been close friends, and she had shared Roosevelt's "great concern for the welfare of their fellow men." The addition of Wilkins's house to the Little White House facilities allowed for expanded exhibitions and space for a theater where visitors could watch a film that featured rarely seen footage of Roosevelt swimming and frolicking in the pools with other polio patients.[34]

For the next two decades, the Little White House continued to operate under the auspices of the Memorial Commission and attracted between 135,000 and 150,000 visitors a year, but in 1980, a special task force appointed by Governor George Busbee recommended major changes at both the historic site and the adjacent rehabilitation facility. Joining the conversation was the National Park Service, which determined that Warm Springs would be an ideal location for a national memorial to former president Franklin D. Roosevelt. Tangled up in the mix was a lawsuit filed by the Warm Springs Foundation, which was opposed to the state's plans to close the hospital and rehabilitation center. The foundation had sold the hospital facility to the state in 1974 after securing an agreement that the state would continue to operate the facility for at least ten years; however, Governor Busbee had decided to void the contract and close the center in an effort to cut costs. By July, a resolution to the crisis was reached. The state agreed to renovate the hospital facilities and operate the former polio hospital/rehabilitation center as a vocational rehabilitation center. The National Park Service designated the entire facility, including the hospital, cottages, historic pools, and Roosevelt's Little White House, as a National Historic Landmark District, placing it among the list of the nation's most important historic places. The historic pools, which had not been used regularly since the 1960s, were transferred to the Department of Natural Resources, as was the Little White House, where they joined the list of state historic sites under DNR management.[35]

In the twenty-first century, a significant upgrade to the facilities at the Little White House site was the addition of a new museum, which opened in 2004. The facility includes a seventy-five-seat theater and expanded exhibitions about Roosevelt's time in Georgia. The state provided $2.5 million toward the construction of the museum, and that amount was matched by private and corporate donations. With the opening of the eleven-thousand-square-foot facility, the former museum in the Wilkins home was renovated to serve as administrative offices for DNR staff.[36] Although the addition of the museum enhanced the interpretive program at the site, the Little White House and its adjacent buildings remain the main draw for visitors. Combined with the historic pools, located 1.4 miles away at the entrance to the rehabilitation center, visitors can get a glimpse into the life of the nation's longest-serving president and leading advocate for the disabled. Most visitors find the modesty and simplicity of Roosevelt's home to be surprising, but it was here, surrounded by the piney woods and rural folk of Georgia, that Roosevelt seemed happiest. The site remains the most famous and most visited of the state's historic sites.

Touring the Site

Roosevelt's Little White House State Historic Site includes two main locations—the Little White House property and the Historic Pools. The Little White House location includes a visitor center with a museum, theater, gift shop, and restrooms. The museum is the best place to begin a visit to the site as the exhibit provides contextual information about Roosevelt's life and his political career. *Little White House*, a fifteen-minute film narrated by Walter Cronkite (also available on the website at https://gastateparks.org/LittleWhiteHouse), offers a good overview of Roosevelt's time as president and also his time at Warm Springs. Among the notable objects on display in the exhibit is one of the automobiles that was adapted so that it could be driven by Roosevelt using hand controls. Hundreds of additional artifacts tell the story of his life and times. Along one wall near the end of the exhibit is a display of almost one hundred hand-carved walking canes that were gifts to the president from his many admirers.

Museum exhibit at Roosevelt's Little White House.

Canes given to President Roosevelt displayed in the Little White House Museum.

Visitors exit the exhibit space onto the grounds and follow a walkway that diverges in two directions. One path follows the route toward the former museum at Mustian Place along the Walk of Flags & Stones, which features the flag and a representative stone from each of the fifty states as well as Washington, D.C. The other path leads toward the Little White House itself. Visitors walk through the "bump gate," which was designed to swing open when bumped by a car and is flanked by sentry posts. Two additional buildings, a servant's cottage and a guest cottage, are just beyond the bump gate.

The Little White House is down the slope past the cottages. Visitors enter the house through the kitchen on the right side of the building. Among the highlights in this area is a note written on the wall by Daisy Bonner, the president's cook, stating, "Daisy Bonner cook the 1st meal and the last one in this cottage for the President Roosevelt." The kitchen, like the rest of the cottage, is simple and functional. The house is furnished as it was at the time of Roosevelt's death. The tour is self-guided with interpretive signage throughout and is augmented by the presence of an interpretive

Kitchen of the Little White House.

Living Room at the Little White House where President Roosevelt was sitting when he suffered a stroke on April 12, 1945.

ranger who answers questions and points out interesting details, such as the scratches on the front door glass made by Fala, Roosevelt's dog. Much of the furniture in the house was made at Val-Kill Industries, a small arts and crafts industrial enterprise established by Eleanor Roosevelt at the family's Hyde Farm estate in New York.

Visitors exit the site through the Legacy exhibit, which features the "Unfinished Portrait" by Elizabeth Shoumatoff for which Roosevelt was sitting at the time of his fatal stroke. A hallway leads from the Legacy exhibit to the gift shop.

The Historic Pools, located off the Roosevelt Highway a little over a mile away from the Little White House, are well worth a visit. The site includes an exhibit on the history of polio and its treatment, but the main attraction is the pool complex. Visitors can walk around and into the network of empty pools and feel the warm water that bubbles up from the springs at a fountain located in one of the pools. A ranger is on site to answer questions, but the tour of the exhibit and the pools is self-guided.

Although not part of the Little White House State Historic Site, several historic buildings from the Roosevelt era are still in existence at the Roosevelt Warm Springs Institute for Rehabilitation, which is located up the hill from the Historic Pools. Among the notable buildings is Georgia Hall, which was the centerpiece of the facility. Designed by architect Henry Toombs and constructed in 1933, Georgia Hall once housed offices for the Warm Springs Foundation and a large dining room. A small exhibit about the history of the Warm Springs Foundation is on display in the Georgia Hall history alcove. The Roosevelt Warm Springs Institute for Rehabilitation, a residential campus for students with disabilities, is now operated by the Georgia Vocational Rehabilitation Agency.

Notes

1. Sally Stein, "FDR, Disability, and Politics: A View from the South," *Public Historian* 27, no. 2, 83.

2. James H. Charleton, "Warm Springs Historic District," National Register of Historic Places Nomination Form (Washington, D.C.: U.S. Department of the Interior, National Park Service, 1980), section 8.

3. F. Martin Harmon, *The Warm Springs Story: Legacy and Legend* (Macon, Ga.: Mercer University Press, 2014), 26–27.

4. Harmon, 33.

5. Theo Lippman, *The Squire of Warm Springs: FDR in Georgia, 1924–1945* (Chicago: Playboy Press Paperbacks, 1978), 32.

6. Lippman, 34–35.

7. Doris Kearns Goodwin, *No Ordinary Time: Franklin & Elanor Roosevelt: The Home Front in World War II* (New York: Simon & Schuster, 1994), 20–21.

8. "Always in Hot Water, Franklin D. Roosevelt Is Making a Comeback," *Brooklyn Daily Eagle*, November 6, 1924, 2.

9. Thomas Loyless, "As Loyless Sees It," *Macon Telegraph*, December 18, 1924, 4.

10. Thomas Loyless, "As Loyless Sees It," *Macon Telegraph*, March 28, 1925, 4.

11. "Mr. Roosevelt and Warm Springs," *Macon Daily Telegraph*, April 20, 1926, 4.

12. "Franklin D. Roosevelt Negotiating to Buy Warm Springs Property," *Atlanta Constitution*, April 22, 1926, 6; "Franklin D. Roosevelt Purchases Big Estate," *Ithaca Journal*, April 27, 1926, 1.

13. Lippman, *Squire of Warm Springs*, 42.

14. Paul Stevenson, "Big Development at Warm Springs Will Be Rushed," *Atlanta Constitution*, May 9, 1926, 11, 14.

15. Lippman, *Squire of Warm Springs*, 51–52.

16. "Neighbors at Warm Springs Rejoice over Great Victory," *Atlanta Constitution*, November 9, 1932, 11.

17. James H. Charleton, "Warm Springs Historic District."

18. "All Roads Leading to Warm Springs," *West Point News*, November 30, 1933, 5.

19. Lippman, *Squire of Warm Springs*, 204–205.

20. "Dime," United States Mint, accessed June 21, 2023, https://www.usmint.gov/coins/coin-medal-programs/circulating-coins/dime.

21. "Rural Electrification Administration (REA) (1935)," Living New Deal, accessed June 21, 2023, https://livingnewdeal.org/glossary/rural-electrification-administration-rea-1935/.

22. Goodwin, *No Ordinary Time*, 598.

23. Goodwin, 601–603.

24. Becky Marshall and Jim Couch, producers, *Presidential Portrait: FDR at Warm Springs*, Georgia Department of Natural Resources, 2004, accessed June 21, 2023, https://www.youtube.com/watch?v=BhkbZCEoDWw&t=4s.

25. Goodwin, *No Ordinary Time*, 614.

26. Paul Simmons, "Little Bit of Georgia, A Memorial to FDR," *Atlanta Constitution*, June 25, 1947, 1.

27. "Warm Springs Dedicated as a National Shrine," *Elmira Star-Gazette*, June 25, 1947, 3.

28. Qus Bernd, "Little White House," *Macon News*, November 23, 1948, 4.

29. "Warm Springs Dedicated as a National Shrine," 3.

30. "Little White House to Open," *Macon News*, August 11, 1948, 6.

31. Bill Boring, "FDR Shrine Is Protected," *Atlanta Constitution*, October 7, 1948, 7.

32. "Little White House Opens," *Georgia Progress* (State Agricultural and Industrial Development Board) 5, no. 4 (October 28, 1948): 2; "Warm Springs Best Memorial to FDR," *Macon News*, December 2, 1948, 8.

33. "Last of FDR's Georgia Land Sold to State," *Macon News*, August 3, 1952, 5.

34. "Friend of FDR Is Honored on Anniversary of His Birth," *Macon News*, January 30, 1961, 16.

35. Brenda Rusell, "20 Years Later, Waters of Warm Springs Are Available for Patients," *Atlanta Constitution*, July 7, 1980, 29.

36. "Little White House Gets Museum-Quality Makeover," *Atlanta Constitution*, April 11, 2004, K1.

Further Reading

Cooksley, Elizabeth B. "Meriwether County." *New Georgia Encyclopedia*, last modified July 12, 2022. https://www.georgiaencyclopedia.org/articles/counties-cities-neighborhoods/meriwether-county/.

Goodwin, Doris Kearns. *No Ordinary Time: Franklin & Eleanor Roosevelt: The Home Front in World War II.* New York: Simon & Schuster, 2008.

Harmon, F. Martin. *The Warm Springs Story: Legacy and Legend.* Macon, Ga.: Mercer University Press, 2014.

Lippman, Theo. *The Squire of Warm Springs: FDR in Georgia, 1924–1945*. Chicago: Playboy Press Paperbacks, 1978.
Mazzari, Louis. "New Deal." *New Georgia Encyclopedia*, last modified August 12, 2020, https://www.georgiaencyclopedia.org/articles/history-archaeology/new-deal/.
Polak, Sara. *FDR in American Memory: Roosevelt and the Making of an Icon*. Baltimore: Johns Hopkins University Press, 2021.

CHAPTER 10

Jarrell Plantation

Nathaniel Perkins and Jennifer W. Dickey

Basic Information

PERIOD OF SIGNIFICANCE: 1847 to 1968

DATE ESTABLISHED AS A STATE HISTORIC SITE: 1976

ACREAGE: 200 acres

LOCATION: 711 Jarrell Plantation Road, Juliette, Ga. 31046, Jones County

The Jarrell Plantation in rural Jones County was the home of three generations of the John Fitz Jarrell family between the mid-nineteenth and the mid-twentieth centuries. Despite being located fewer than twenty miles from the city of Macon, Georgia, the plantation appears largely untouched by modern civilization. Listed in the National Register of Historic Places in 1973 as an excellent example of "19th and 20th century agrarianism," this "self-sustaining farm complex" provides an immersive experience.[1] The dwelling houses and outbuildings have been preserved, along with the collection of tools and the landscape in and around the buildings, and illustrate more than one hundred years of development of agriculture in the Georgia Piedmont region. From ginning cotton to establishing a lumber mill, the Jarrell family adapted the farm's operations to accommodate changing circumstances. The plantation was maintained by the children and grandchildren of the founder, John Fitz Jarrell, until the 1970s, when it was given to the state of Georgia to be preserved as a state historic site.

House built by John Fitz Jarrell in 1847 at Jarrell Plantation.

History of Jarrell Plantation

The area in which Jarrell Plantation is located, Jones County, is near the geographic center of Georgia and, like much of what would become the state of Georgia, was occupied by Creek Indians at the time of European settlement. In an effort to relieve debts incurred by the Indians to white traders, the Creeks ceded large swaths of land to Georgia in 1773 and 1790, but white settlers continued to push the frontier westward across Georgia. What is today Jones County was ceded to the United States by the Treaty of Washington in 1805.[2] The state legislature created Baldwin County and in June 1806 passed legislation to have the new territory surveyed and distributed to white settlers in 202½-acre lots through a land lottery in 1807. The state legislature further divided Baldwin County in December 1807, creating four additional counties, including Jones County. In 1808, the town of Clinton was established as the county seat.[3] Following the Creek War of 1813–1814, the Creek Indians were forced into a series of treaties that ceded their territory in Georgia to the United States.[4] As the Creeks were pushed westward, white settlers began to flood into the former Creek territory, including Jones County.

Although no one from the Jarrell family claimed land in Jones County in the 1807 land lottery, the family, headed by Blake Fitz Jarrell, seems to have arrived in Jones County in the 1820s from North Carolina. Blake and his wife, the former Zilphia Dunaway, brought with them six or seven of their nine children, including their oldest son, John Fitz, as well as perhaps five enslaved people.[5] In 1832, John Fitz Jarrell married Elizabeth Middlebrooks, the daughter of a wealthy local landowner, and by 1840, the couple had four children. Jarrell's household also included seven enslaved people.[6] According to family tradition, the John Fitz Jarrell family settled on the land that is today Jarrell Plantation in 1847, although tax records indicate that Jarrell did not acquire the land until 1850. Nevertheless, Jarrell built a four-room, timber-framed house on 7.5 acres of land—a house that became known as the 1847 house.[7] This was the beginning of the development of the farm that is known today as the Jarrell Plantation.

In his 1855 *Historical Collections of Georgia*, George White described Jones County as "hilly" and noted that "the soil, though much worn, is productive." Extracts from the 1850 census revealed that the total free population of the county was 3,945, and the enslaved population was 6,279. The county had 405 farms and 15 manufacturing establishments. The value of real estate in the county was almost $1.4 million, while the value of personal estate, namely enslaved people, was $3.5 million.[8]

In spite of the poor soil, Jarrell grew cotton on his farm, and in antebellum Georgia, cotton cultivation relied upon an enslaved labor force. By the eve of the Civil War, according to the 1860 census, the John Fitz Jarrell family included three children under the age of seventeen still living at home. Jarrell's list of property included thirty-nine enslaved people. The value of Jarrell's real estate holdings at this time was $3,640, while the value of his "personal property," the enslaved people, was reported as $20,400.[9] Although Jarrell Plantation appeared to be a modest operation with the unpainted, four-room house as its centerpiece, Jarrell's landholdings by this time, around six hundred acres, and his slaveholdings put him among the "planter aristocracy" in Georgia.[10]

Cotton, while an important cash crop for Georgia farmers, was a notoriously volatile commodity. In an effort to reduce the risk of relying on the cotton market, Jarrell diversified his crops and was generally more progressive than many farmers in the area in terms of the production of foodstuff and livestock. The U.S. agricultural census of 1860 indicates that Jarrell owned 140 swine, 30 cattle, and 10 milk cows. His farm produced substantial amounts of wheat, corn, oats, potatoes, hay, and butter, in addition to thirty bales (four hundred pounds each) of cotton. The cotton had been ginned in the Jarrell cotton gin, a facility that not only allowed Jarrell to process his own crops but also to do the same for his neighbors. In addition to farming, Jarrell operated a blacksmith shop, where he manufactured the tools and implements he needed to run his farm. According to one of his grandchildren, Jarrell was an "expert wheelwright, carpenter, a good farmer, blacksmith, mason, weaver and tanner."[11] Jarrell employed his skills and resources, including his children and the enslaved people who lived on his farm, to create an operation that was resilient and less susceptible to the vagaries of the market than were the farms of many of his neighbors. His diversification also helped him survive the great catastrophe of the Civil War.

Jarrell himself, at the age of fifty-one, was too old to enlist in the Confederate Army when the war broke out in 1861; however, two of his sons did enlist—John Randolph (who joined the Confederate Army in Texas) and Anderson Joseph (who joined the Army of Tennessee as a chaplain). Although both sons survived the war, the Jarrell family experienced great loss. Oldest son Levi Williamson died of illness in June 1861, as did Jarrell's wife, the former Elizabeth Middlebrooks, and daughter Elizabeth in October 1864. Soon after the deaths of his wife and daughter, U.S. troops arrived in Jones County. The *Macon Telegraph & Confederate* reported that one-third of the county seat of Clinton was reduced to ashes by Sherman's army and that "the whole country around is one wide waste of destruction." Jarrell's plantation was not spared as raiders from Sherman's army "plundered Jarrell Plantation" during the week of November 19–25, 1864. The raiders burned the ginhouse as well as more than three hundred bushels of wheat and took with them all the livestock except for an aged horse. The 1847 house and remaining outbuildings were spared, and the raiders left behind an army mule, which would be beneficial to Jarrell in the aftermath of the war.[12]

Not one to dwell on his losses, Jarrell got back to work as soon as Sherman and his troops cleared the area. He also remarried in December 1864, a mere two months after the death of Elizabeth Middlebrooks. Jarrell's second wife, the former Nancy James, was the widow of William

Jackson James, a Confederate soldier who died in December 1862. Nancy brought with her into the Jarrell household two children from her previous marriage. She and John Jarrell would have seven children of their own, and it was their second son, Benjamin Richard Jarrell, who would perpetuate the family farm following his father's death in 1884.[13]

The emancipation of John Fitz Jarrell's enslaved workforce, which had increased to forty-two people during the course of the war, brought with it a significant change for both the formerly enslaved people and the Jarrell family. While many of the formerly enslaved workers might have wanted to leave the plantation, they may not have had the wealth to do so. As a result, instead of leaving, some were relegated to working as tenant farmers or sharecroppers on the plantation. These workers were often in perpetual debt and trapped in what was essentially a system of peonage not far removed from their former condition of enslavement. Sharecroppers were subject to the whim of the landowners in terms of what crops to plant and how much, if any, profit they might reap from their labor. However, they did have far more social independence than they had when they were enslaved. Ultimately, although sharecroppers and tenant farmers found it difficult to build wealth, they were no longer in bondage and were free to leave, which many did in the 1910s and 1920s as the Great Migration from agricultural work in the American South to industrial labor in urban areas throughout the country began.[14]

Jarrell reported fourteen farmhands in the 1870 agricultural census. With a reduced workforce, Jarrell continued farming, although the value of his farm and his productivity decreased significantly. He reduced the amount of acreage in cultivation, although he did not sell any of his land. Jarrell reported sixteen cattle and sixteen swine in 1874. He began cultivating cane, from which he produced syrup, in addition to continuing to produce wheat, corn, and sweet potatoes, although at dramatically lower levels than he had in 1860. Although the Jarrell family was less prosperous than they had been before the war, they were still able to eke out a living. However, the death of John Fitz Jarrell on August 4, 1884, at age seventy-four would bring about changes to the farm, although those changes were not immediate.

Jarrell's wife, Nancy, inherited 368 acres of the farm, and she bought the remainder of the property that had belonged to her husband, keeping the Jarrell landholdings intact. At the time of John Fitz's death, Nancy was living in the 1847 house along with her two children from her first marriage and the surviving six children from her marriage to Jarrell. The eldest surviving son of the Jarrell marriage, Benjamin Richard, known as Dick, had worked on the farm all his life. However, three years following his father's death, Dick, age twenty, left the farm to attend Mercer University in Macon. Dick graduated from Mercer in 1891 and began teaching, first in Jones County and then in Abbeville, Georgia, a small town in Wilcox County located about seventy miles south of Macon. In December 1891, Dick married Mary Elizabeth "Mamie" Vanzandt, a Jones County resident, before embarking on teaching assignments in Social Circle and Plains.[15]

Dick and Mamie, along with their infant son, Benjamin Jr., returned to the Jarrell farm in the mid-1890s, and Dick began developing a new industry on the family farm—a lumber mill. While his father had cut and sawed timber to meet his own needs and occasionally that of his neighbors, Dick developed a sawmill operation that would provide a source of income for his family. He purchased a sawmill, a cotton gin, and a steam engine in 1895. He used the sawmill to cut lumber with which he rebuilt the ginhouse that had been destroyed during the Civil War. Dick and Mamie had a second child in early 1895, Willie Lee, and in 1896 he bought from his mother a four-acre piece of land and constructed a dwelling house for his growing family.

The new house was even simpler than the 1847 house, with a kitchen and dining room in the rear connected by a small porch to the two front rooms that served as a family room and sleeping area. Like the 1847 house, the new house was unpainted. In 1899, Dick began operating a gristmill where he ground corn for the public. By the turn of the century, Dick Jarrell's industrial operations—the sawmill, cotton gin, and gristmill—were the main sources of income for the family. Farming continued mostly with the food crops and livestock needed to sustain the family. In 1901, Dick, Mamie, and their four children left the farm and moved to Macon. He continued operating the sawmill, which he relocated to the small town of Kathleen in Houston County, about twenty-six miles south of Macon. However, three years later, Dick and his family returned to the farm, where he resumed his assorted industrial enterprises.[16]

By 1905, Dick and Mamie had six children of their own, and Dick had been appointed guardian of his brother Robert Lee's four children after his brother's death. Dick's mother, Nancy, still lived in the 1847 house along with her daughter, Mattie, who had operated a post office out of the

House built by Richard Jarrell in 1895 at Jarrell Plantation.

house for several years up until 1903.[17] Mattie left the farm for a brief time but returned in 1905 to help care for Robert Lee's children, who resided with their grandmother in the 1847 house. Dick expanded his landholdings in 1905, acquiring from his mother the twelve acres of land that separated their two houses.[18]

As Dick and Mamie's family grew—they would ultimately have twelve children, nine of whom would live to adulthood—so did Dick's industrial enterprises. He bought a larger steam engine in 1905 and a new boiler in 1910. He grew sugar cane and after 1914 began the steam-powered production of cane syrup. Like his father, Dick was a man of many talents. He manufactured coffins and wagon wheels. He built a bridge over Falling Creek and a school and a church in nearby communities. On his own farm, he and his sons built a blacksmith shop and workshop and a barn between 1912 and 1913. All of the children were engaged in the various enterprises on Jarrell Plantation, from skimming and cooking the cane syrup to tending the garden and the livestock.[19]

With the death of Dick's mother, Nancy, in 1911, her remaining landholdings were divided among her four surviving children. Mattie, who had lived with and cared for her mother as she aged, received the 1847 house, its furnishings, and the thirty-acre tract of land upon which the house sat.

Syrup furnace at Jarrell Plantation.

Dick bought out the remaining interests of his siblings. He also inherited the bulk of the farm equipment, but by the 1920s the Jarrell family was doing little farming beyond what was necessary for subsistence. Instead, Jarrell expanded his other operations, buying a new cane mill and planer and constructing a new engine house, evaporator house, and cane mill and planer shed between 1916 and 1918. Perhaps most significant of all was the construction of a new dwelling house that would be completed in 1920. Work began on the new house on Christmas Day in 1916 when Dick and his sons began cutting the timber from which they would build the house. The framing of the house was completed in 1918. Construction paused when the two oldest sons left to fight in World War I, although Dick put a roof over the frame while his sons were away. He and his sons completed construction of the two-story, five-thousand-square-foot house in 1920.[20]

Although Dick and Mamie continued to live on the farm until their deaths in early 1958, most of their children left the farm within a decade of the completion of the new house. By 1930, only their second son, Willie

Lee, remained on the farm. Although he had hoped to attend Georgia Tech and study engineering, Willie Lee, who never married, continued the family tradition of living and working on the Jarrell farm. Reflecting on his fate in 1976 at age eighty-one, Willie Lee speculated that if his father had the money, "I reckon he would have sent us on to school." Instead, only three of the Jarrell children, all girls, attended college. Willie Lee, who was the sole member of the family still living on the farm when his parents died, continued to farm until the 1960s, albeit at a reduced scale. The many industrial enterprises were scaled back, and he planted mainly what he needed for his own subsistence. He cited "lack of finance" as the problem that faced him as well as most farmers, stating, "I can't remember hiring anyone to help. At the last, I wouldn't have but just a few acres in row crops, six or eight acres in hay."[21]

Around 1968, the nine surviving Jarrell children began contemplating what to do with their land. They could not bear the thought of selling the farm on which members of their family had lived for three generations. Most of the buildings remained intact, including the original 1847 dwelling house built by John Fitz Jarrell even before he acquired title to the land. At first the siblings contemplated trying to find "some wealthy person to buy it and let him charge admission for people to see it," said Willie Lee, but then a cousin put them in touch with Mary Gregory Jewett, executive director of the Georgia Historical Commission. Jewett came to see the property and "she liked it," according to Willie Lee.[22]

To say that Jewett "liked it" would be a gross understatement. She was so besotted with the farm during her initial visit to the property in October 1968 that she invited members of the Senate Business, Trade, and Commerce Committee to visit the site, and they were equally as impressed. Jewett began negotiations with the family, who expressed an interest in donating 7.5 acres of land, which included all of the extant buildings other than the 1920 house, to the state with the provision that the state would preserve the buildings and landscape and open the site to the public as a state historic site. Enthusiasm was high on both sides, and soon the state began surveying the land. However, the effort was almost derailed following the election in 1970 of Jimmy Carter as governor of Georgia. After taking office in 1971, Carter's reorganization of state government eliminated the Georgia Historical Commission, folding its responsibilities into a new unit called the Historic Preservation Section within the Department of Natural Resources. Soon thereafter, he created the Georgia Heritage

Trust, which was charged with preserving the "historic and natural remnants of the state's past." Although the Jarrell family was donating the land to the state, there was a substantial amount of deferred maintenance that would have to be undertaken before the site could be opened to the public. Not until the state legislature agreed to fund the trust was it able to move forward with the land acquisition process.[23]

Carter, himself a farmer, was enthusiastic about the site as well, and he toured the farm as a guest of Willie Lee Jarrell in 1973. The deal was finally sealed on January 4, 1974, in Carter's office in the State Capitol. Jewett was delighted by the acquisition and stated, "There has never been a situation just like this where a family has held together all of its possessions . . . all of its knowledge and has made it available to the State." While several other sites that had been held by a single family over multiple generations would come into the state's possession through the Georgia Heritage Trust (Wormsloe, Traveler's Rest, and Hofwyl-Broadfield), none of them included such a complete collection of buildings and equipment as did Jarrell Plantation. The site opened to the public on January 3, 1976, following two years of work to make repairs to the buildings and develop an interpretive program for the site.[24] After years of tending the farm and protecting everything on it, Willie Lee Jarrell's dream that the whole place should be preserved and "be in a museum" came true. Commenting on the transition of the farm to state ownership, Willie Lee stated, "It doesn't belong to anyone. It belongs to posterity."[25]

Touring the Site

Jarrell Plantation is located near the town of Juliette in a remote area surrounded by the Piedmont National Wildlife Refuge. Signage for the site is minimal, so visitors should pay close attention when traveling to the site. There is ample parking in front of the visitor center, which was added to the site in 1989. The 1920 house, which is located just north of the historic site, is still owned by Jarrell descendants and is not part of the state-owned property.

Unlike plantations in such places as Louisiana's River Road, the quarters for the enslaved workers on Jarrell Plantation were not organized in rows away from the main house. The main house, of course, was the modest 1847 house, which is located near the back of the property. The enslaved people, and later the tenant farmers, lived in five or six cabins scattered about the property. The chimney ruins of one such cabin, the home of Reason Jarrell and his wife Martha prior to emancipation, are visible in between the parking lot and the visitor center.

The visitor center offers a film about the Jarrell family, including information about the enslaved people who helped make the plantation successful, as well as several small exhibits and a gift shop. Visitors walk through the visitor center to access the main pathway that wends its way through the seven-acre farm. Along the way, visitors encounter the many buildings that illustrate the evolution of the Jarrell homestead from a small farm to a full-blown, industrial enterprise. The experience is almost like walking back in time as the first buildings encountered tend to be more recent, dating to the 1910s. The barn, built in 1912–1913, is flanked by a garden. Just beyond the chicken coop and smokehouse is the 1895 house, which was built by Dick Jarrell when he first returned to the farm.

The path continues to the back of the property, where the 1847 house and its collection of outbuildings that date to the John Fitz Jarrell period are still standing. The path from the oldest section of the farm snakes through the woods and down the hill to the heart of the industrial operations.

The staff and volunteers offer living history experiences, such as an annual syrup-making day, during which cane juice is cooked in the original

Ruins of the home of enslaved couple Reason and Martha Jarrell at Jarrell Plantation.

Chicken coop (left), smokehouse (center), and 1895 house (right) at Jarrell Plantation.

Cotton gin, sawmill, and gristmill complex at Jarrell Plantation.

kettles and is available for purchase at the end of the day. The syrup-making event includes other living history components, such as butter churning, spinning, weaving, blacksmithing, and woodstove cooking. Evening lantern tours that feature voices from the past are offered in October, and Christmas Traditions house tours are offered in December.

Although budget cuts have kept the plantation from living up to its potential as a full-time living history site, the interpretive program is rich, and the original buildings and artifacts at the site provide a degree of authenticity that is unparalleled throughout the state. As stated in the National Register nomination, "The buildings are not great architectural specimens; their merit is in representing the typical Georgia farm building from the earliest days almost to the present."[26] Half a century after the family gifted their family farm to the state, it remains as a remarkable time capsule of the three generations of Jarrell family members who lived and worked here.

Notes

1. Carole A. Summers, "Jarrell Plantation," National Register of Historic Places Nomination Form (Washington, D.C.: U.S. Department of the Interior, National Park Service, 1973), section 8.

2. National Park Service, "Creek Land Cessions," Ocmulgee Mounds, accessed September 11, 2023, https://www.nps.gov/ocmu/learn/historyculture/upload/Accessible-Creek-Land-Cessions.pdf.

3. Victoria Reeves Gunn, *Jarrell Plantation: A History* (Atlanta: Department of Natural Resources, 1974), http://dlg.galileo.usg.edu/do:dlg_ggpd_s-ga-bn200-pp6-bm1-b1974-bj2.

4. "The Creek War of 1813–1814," American Battlefield Trust, accessed September 11, 2023, https://www.battlefields.org/learn/articles/creek-war-1813-1814; National Park Service, "Creek Land Cessions."

5. Gunn, *Jarrell Plantation*, 152–157.

6. Gunn, 153.

7. Gunn, 18–19, 37–38.

8. George White, *Historical Collections of Georgia* (New York: Pudney & Russell, 1855), 505.

9. Gunn, *Jarrell Plantation*, 154–155.

10. Gunn, 22.

11. Gunn, 23–24.

12. Morton R. McInvale, *Jarrell Plantation: A Piedmont Heritage* (Atlanta: Georgia Department of Natural Resources, 1988), 13–14.

13. McInvale, 15–16.

14. James C. Giesen, "Sharecropping," *New Georgia Encyclopedia*, last modified September 28, 2020, https://www.georgiaencyclopedia.org/articles/history-archaeology/sharecropping/; Frederick A. Bode, "Tenant Farming," *New Georgia Encyclopedia*, last

modified September 25, 2020, https://www.georgiaencyclopedia.org/articles/history-archaeology/tenant-farming/; "The Great Migration, 1910 to 1970," U.S. Census Bureau, last updated September 12, 2012, https://www.census.gov/dataviz/visualizations/020/.

15. Gunn, *Jarrell Plantation*, 26.

16. McInvale, *Jarrell Plantation*, 19–21.

17. Gunn, *Jarrell Plantation*, 214.

18. McInvale, *Jarrell Plantation*, 21–22.

19. McInvale, 25–26.

20. McInvale, 27–28.

21. Jane Oppy, "Plantation Owner Says He Never Liked Farming," *Macon News*, January 19, 1976, 11.

22. Margaret Shannon, "129 Years on One Family's Farm," *Atlanta Constitution*, January 11, 1976, SM12.

23. Caleb Pirtle III, "The Sacred Trust of Georgia," *Southern Living*, December 1974, 79, 81–84.

24. "Jarrell Plantation," *Macon News*, December 26, 1975.

25. Roger Ann Jones, "They Gave Away Their Bit of History," *Macon News*, January 4, 1974, B1.

26. Summers, "Jarrell Plantation."

Further Reading

Bailey, Anne J. "Sherman's March to the Sea." *New Georgia Encyclopedia*, last modified September 30, 2020. https://www.georgiaencyclopedia.org/articles/history-archaeology/shermans-march-to-the-sea/.

Bragg, William Harris. "Jones County." *New Georgia Encyclopedia*, last modified July 12, 2022. https://www.georgiaencyclopedia.org/articles/counties-cities-neighborhoods/jones-county/.

Bode, Frederick A. "Tenant Farming." *New Georgia Encyclopedia*, last modified September 25, 2020. https://www.georgiaencyclopedia.org/articles/history-archaeology/tenant-farming/.

Craig, Robert M. "Jarrell Plantation." *sah Archipedia*, ed. Gabrielle Esperdy and Karen Kingsley. Charlottesville: University of Virginia Press, 2012. Accessed September 7, 2023. https://sah-archipedia.org/buildings/GA-01-169-0016.

Giesen, James. "Sharecropping." *New Georgia Encyclopedia*, last modified September 29, 2020. https://www.georgiaencyclopedia.org/articles/history-archaeology/sharecropping/.

Gunn, Victoria Reeves. *Jarrell Plantation: A History*. Atlanta: Georgia Department of Natural Resources, Historic Preservation Section, 1974. http://dlg.galileo.usg.edu/ggpd/docs/1974/ga/n200_pp6/m1/1974/j2.con/1.pdf.

Williams, Carolyn White. *History of Jones County, Georgia, for One Hundred Years, Specifically 1807–1907*. Macon, Ga.: J. W. Burke, 1957; rpt., Fernandina Beach, Fla.: Wolfe, 2003.

REGION 3

Coastal Plains

The region between the fall line and the coast, known as the Coastal Plains, makes up almost half of Georgia's surface area but only boasts one state historic site—Kolomoki Mounds. Covered by sea water until approximately eleven thousand years ago, the Coastal Plains were for centuries dominated by an ecosystem of longleaf pine and wire grass. Two sites formerly owned and operated by the state—the Jefferson Davis Memorial Historic Site in Fitzgerald and the Lapham-Patterson House Historic Site in Thomasville—are located within this area but are no longer part of the state system. The Davis site is today owned and operated by Irwin County, while the Lapham-Patterson House, still owned by the state, is maintained and operated by the Thomasville History Center. Within this vast geographic area are more than a dozen state parks, including Kolomoki Mounds State Park, which includes the prehistoric mound site that is among the oldest and most well-preserved such sites in Georgia. Although embedded within a state park, Kolomoki Mounds is considered to be one of the sixteen historic sites in the state system.

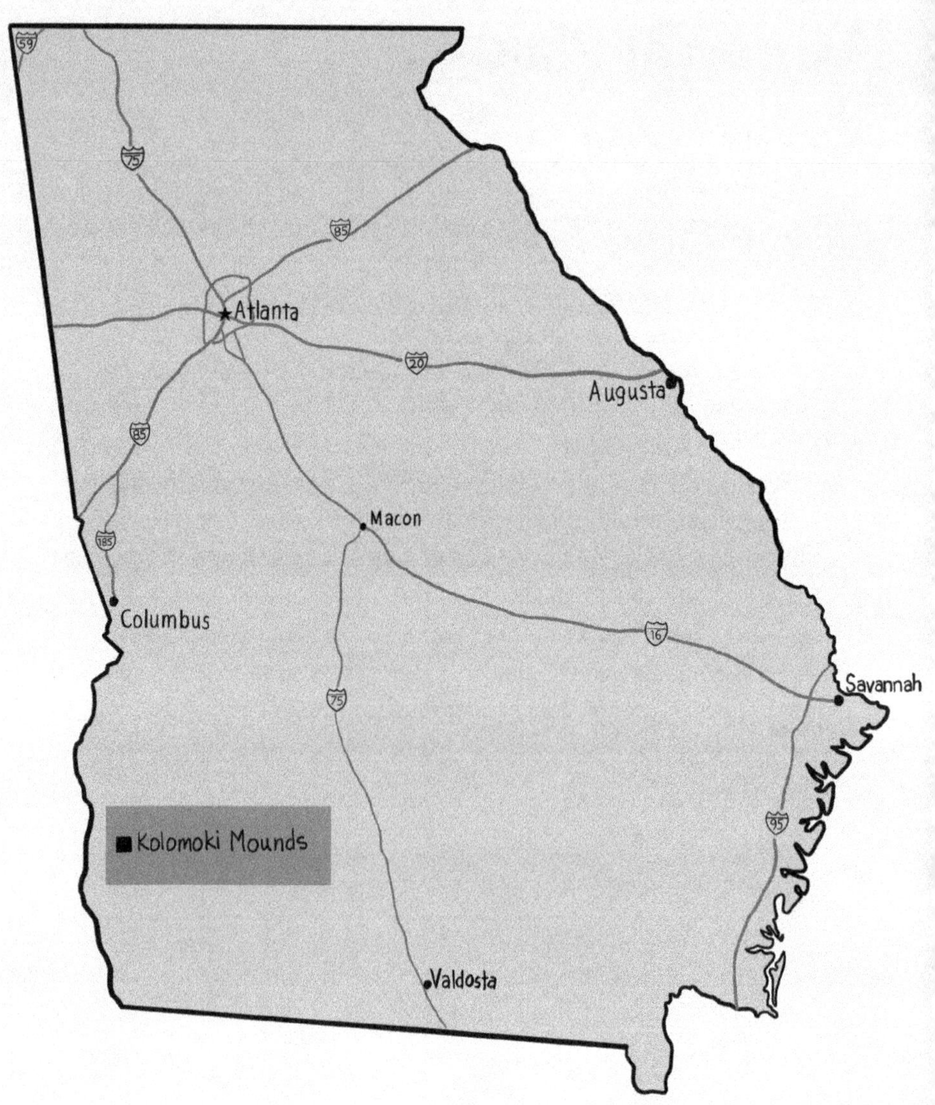
59
75
85
Atlanta
20
Augusta
85
Macon
185
Columbus
16
Savannah
75
95
Kolomoki Mounds
Valdosta

CHAPTER 11

Kolomoki Mounds

Jennifer W. Dickey

Basic Information

PERIOD OF SIGNIFICANCE: 200–900 CE

DATE OPENED TO THE PUBLIC: 1950

ACREAGE: Park, 1,293 acres; historic site, 286 acres

LOCATION: 205 Indian Mounds Road, Blakely, Ga. 39823, Early County

Kolomoki Mounds, located in southwest Georgia near the town of Blakely, is one of Georgia's oldest and largest prehistoric mound sites. Occupied for over five hundred years during the Middle and Late Woodland periods and taking its name from an eighteenth-century waterway that was named after a nearby Creek Indian settlement, Kolomoki was acquired by the state in 1938. The mounds were described in 1945 by Dr. Frank Setzler of the Smithsonian Institution as "the largest and best-preserved monument in the southeast."[1] Archaeologist Thomas J. Pluckhahn labeled Kolomoki "a site without equals."[2] The 286-acre mound complex was declared a National Historic Landmark in 1964 as a site "found to possess exceptional value in commemorating and illustrating the history of the United States."[3] The history commemorated at Kolomoki Mounds, however, predates that of the United States by as much as sixteen hundred years, and the more recent understanding of this prehistoric site has been controversial. From the first explorations by archaeologists in the nineteenth century to recent surveys conducted in the twenty-first century, the story of the inhabitants of this site has evolved dramatically. As the anchor

Mound D (left), plaza (center), and A (right) at Kolomoki Mounds.

for the Kolomoki Mounds State Park, the prehistoric mound site provides a glimpse into the ancient cultures that existed in this area as well as a case study of how those cultures have been analyzed and interpreted.

History of Kolomoki Mounds

The Woodland period (1000 BCE to 1000 CE) of prehistory in North America was a period of change as Native peoples transitioned from a hunter-gatherer existence to a more sedentary lifestyle that included permanent settlements, an increase in horticulture, increased pottery production, and mound building. Although many of these activities began in the Late Archaic period, they expanded and improved during the Early Woodland subperiod (1000 to 300 BCE) and peaked in the Middle Woodland subperiod (300 BCE to 600 CE), the time during which the Kolomoki settlement reached its zenith.[4] Pluckhahn has concluded that at its peak, Kolomoki was "one of the most populous settlements north of Mexico."[5]

Written accounts of the Kolomoki Mounds date back to the nineteenth century when George White, drawing on a publication four years earlier by A. J. Pickett, noted the "ancient works" located six miles north of Blakely on the plantation of Judge George Mercier. Quoting from Pickett's *History of Alabama and Georgia*, White described a mound complex dominated by a "large sacrificial mound, seventy feet in height, and six hundred feet in circumference," that was "covered with large forest trees, from four to five hundred years old." According to White, a shaft had "been sunk in the centre to the depth of sixty feet, and at its lower portion a bed of human bones, five feet in thickness, and in a perfectly decomposed state, was passed." Two additional "sacrificial mounds" were noted, each thirty feet high, as well as a wall enclosing the mounds and a series of twenty-foot earthen watchtowers.[6]

White's account of the shaft into the large mound, now known as Mound A, in which human bones were discovered, appears to be a fiction according to Smithsonian archaeologist Edward Palmer, who conducted limited excavations at the site in 1884.[7] In his report following his investigation, Palmer reported that the "digger of the shaft" into Mound A, Lisbon Everett, stated that White's statement "was entirely false for not a trace of bone was seen nor did he go below 57 feet."[8] The ancient mound site, known as the Mercier Mound throughout much of the nineteenth century, was heavily farmed by George Mercier, who acquired the land in the 1830s, and his descendants, who owned the land until 1907. During the Mercier period of ownership, George's son, Augustus, who inherited the property upon the death of his father in 1868, allowed numerous investigations of the site. Pluckhahn notes that these investigations, while "poorly controlled and inadequately reported, nevertheless described important features that were subsequently lost to agriculture and erosion," most notably the enclosure walls that had largely disappeared by the time more extensive surveys began in the mid-twentieth century.[9]

Following the death of Augustus Mercier in 1892, his second wife retained ownership until 1911, when she sold the property to J. E. Mansfield. Mansfield operated a gristmill on the site but was forced to sell to pay his mortgage in 1928. The property was owned by the estate of E. Hilton until 1936, when Dr. C. C. Harrold, president of the newly created Society for Georgia Archaeology (SGA), purchased 280 acres of land that included the mounds and surrounding acreage of what had once been the prehistoric settlement. Harrold, a physician by trade and an amateur archaeologist, acquired the site with the intention of having it declared a national monument and selling it to the National Park Service (NPS).[10] In 1936, NPS assistant archaeologist H. Summerfield Day visited the site and described it as "practically a virgin site archeologically. The only work done was a small pit sunk in the top of Mound #1 during the nineteenth century, and some surface collections of pottery and flints made within the last year." Day strongly recommended that the site be declared a national monument and be given to the NPS for development "as a fine display of an Indian settlement."[11]

Although the NPS declined to acquire Kolomoki, Harrold's campaign for the preservation of the site caught the interest of local officials and led to a visit in 1937 by J. L. Valliant, affiliated with the museum at the University of Pennsylvania. Following four days on-site, Valliant concluded that Kolomoki "was a large and important town and that it was occupied for a long period." He noted the existence of "ten or twelve mounds" as well as the "remains of two and probably three 'Walls,'" confirming the existence of the enclosure walls noted in the nineteenth century. Local excitement about the site increased in the wake of Valliant's report, and when his efforts to get the NPS to acquire the property failed, Harrold sold the property at cost to the Early County Rotary Club, which deeded the land to the Georgia Department of Natural Resources in 1938 for use as a state park.[12] Not long thereafter, Charles Elliott, director of state parks, in a speech to the SGA, congratulated "the citizens of Blakely and Early County for the addition of Kolomoki to the State Park System," adding that "care will be taken to prevent recreational developments from interfering with archaeological features." Elliott suggested that the state would follow the advice of Jesse Jennings, superintendent of the NPS Ocmulgee National Monument near Macon, and delay archaeological investigation of Kolomoki for a few years "until archaeological technique is improved and the pre-history of the southeast is better understood." Elliott promised that the state would "protect the archaeological features of the area as an intriguing sort of 'not to be opened 'til Christmas' package."[13]

Jennings, who had visited the site several months earlier, noted the presence of Swift Creek pottery sherds at Kolomoki and opined that the site "would seem to be a relatively early manifestation," adding that "the Swift Creek pottery type, which at Kolomoki comprises 90 percent of the surface wares, is one of the earlier cultures of the Southeast." Excavations at a site in Macon five years earlier by the Works Progress

Administration had led to the identification of what became known as the Swift Creek culture, which referred to cultural groups in Georgia that manufactured a distinctive type of pottery from around 20 BCE to 800 CE. Although not much was known about this period in 1938, Jennings recognized enough similarities between the sherds found at Kolomoki and those found at the Swift Creek mound site in Bibb County to conclude that Kolomoki, which he considered to be a large and complex site, likely dated to the Woodland period.[14]

Despite the suggestion from Jennings and the promise of Elliott to delay archaeological work at the site, the implementation of the development plan for the recreation area at the site necessitated a series of ad hoc archaeological surveys beginning in 1940 as Civilian Conservation Corps (CCC) workers began building an access road across the property. Archaeologists Charles Fairbanks and Robert Wauchope began surveying the site, conducting surface collections and test pits on the proposed route of the road, and Fairbanks excavated earthworks that would be inundated following the construction of a dam on Little Kolomoki Creek to create a recreational lake.[15] After the discovery of a house site along the route of the road, Fairbanks suggested that the road be raised in order to preserve the house site.

In his final report, issued in 1941, Fairbanks noted that the CCC "had destroyed two mounds" and altered the shape of others with no documentation. "If this sort of protection continues," he wrote, "it is obvious that little or nothing of the site will remain in a few years." Fairbanks concluded that although Kolomoki was "a mess from the stratigraphic point," the site showed evidence of "a large Swift Creek occupation," adding, "The village is extensive," and "There was little evidence of anything really but Swift Creek," seeming to confirm Jennings's assessment of the Woodland period occupation at the site.[16] The ongoing destruction stalled in 1941 as the United States became involved in World War II. The CCC camp was closed, and work was discontinued until 1948. Fairbanks's observation about the "stratigraphic mess" of the site, a recognition that the appearance of artifacts in clearly delineated layers was not obvious, would prove to be significant when excavations resumed after the war.

Three years after the end of the war, work resumed on the recreational facilities and on the archaeological investigations. The state hired a young archaeologist, William H. Sears, who was a U.S. Marine veteran, graduate student at the University of Michigan, and instructor at the University of Georgia School of Archaeology. Over the next five seasons, Sears would lead teams of archaeologists and graduate students as they excavated areas around Mound A and Mounds B, C, D, E, and F. The most extensive excavations were conducted on Mounds D and E between 1949 and 1951. Both mounds contained numerous burials (seventy-seven in Mound D and four in Mound E) along with an abundant array of distinctive pottery. The larger of the two burial mounds, Mound D, was a conical-shaped mound, twenty feet high and nearly one hundred feet in diameter, believed to be the burial mound of a leader.[17] Mound E, also conical in shape, was eleven feet high and over eighty feet in diameter, making it the third largest mound, after mounds A and D, at Kolomoki. A temporary museum structure was erected around the excavated section of Mound E and opened to the public in 1950.[18] The effect was that visitors could walk into the half-excavated mound and see the human remains, along with fifty-four pottery items, in situ.[19]

In his final report summarizing his five years of excavations, issued in 1956, Sears identified the ceramics as Swift Creek and Weeden Island

Visitor center/museum and Mound E at Kolomoki Mounds.

types, but he "declined to accept the growing consensus that these were Woodland pottery types." Instead, Sears attributed the ceramics to the much later Mississippian period. Owing in part to the "stratigraphic mess" that he had encountered and in part to the presence of the enormous Mound A, which Sears believed to be beyond the capabilities of the earlier Woodland cultures, Sears inverted the timeline of the pottery findings and proclaimed that Kolomoki was a Mississippian-era site that reached its peak of power and population around 1200 CE. Sears's misidentification of the site's period of significance, which was off by more than five hundred years, created what came to be known in the archaeological field as "the Kolomoki problem."[20] As historian Charles Trowell explained, Sears's reversal of chronological periods was the equivalent of "placing Roman civilization before Classical Greek or the American Civil War before the American Revolution."[21]

Although many archaeologists disagreed with Sears, few of them publicly refuted him. Charles Fairbanks, who had published in 1954 a basic chronology of Kolomoki based on work that he and Robert Wauchope had done in 1946, wrote a review of Sears's report in which he questioned Sears's chronology, but Sears ignored him. Joseph Caldwell, who, like Sears, was working under the supervision of University of Georgia archaeologist A. R. Kelly, wrote several critiques of Sears's work, but none of them were ever published. Stephen Williams cited Caldwell in a "carefully worded refutation" of Sears's final report and stated that "Sears's dating of the Kolomoki complex was too late," yet Sears refused to engage in the debate. Even as archaeological reports of other large temple mounds that followed the Kolomoki pattern and dated to the Woodland period began to emerge in the 1980s, Sears held fast to his chronology for the site.[22]

Not until 1992 did Sears admit his mistake. In an article entitled "*Mea Culpa*," which appeared in the summer 1992 issue of *Southeastern Archaeology*, Sears admitted that he "was wrong about the sequence (*mea culpa*), an error which has contributed to the difficulty of perceiving real relationships."[23] He also admitted that he had ignored radiocarbon dates, a relatively new technology in the early 1950s, for Mounds D and E, which put the dates of the mounds at 30 CE and 170 BCE, ± 300, respectively.[24] In the meantime, Sears's flawed chronology had formed the basis for the DNR's interpretation of the site. The exhibits in the museum facility, which was expanded in 1966, situated Kolomoki in the Mississippian period (800 to 1600 CE), and explained that the massive Mound A, which rose to a height of 56 feet and was 325 by 200 feet wide at the base, was likely "used for Indian religious rites in the 12th and 13th centuries."[25] The Georgia Historical Commission had installed a marker at the site indicating the same and, for more than forty years, had distributed brochures that claimed, "The first Indian settlement at this site took place some time in the twelfth century, 1100–1200 A.D."[26]

The discrepancy in the dates caused by Sears's confused chronology was not the only problem at Kolomoki. As archaeological excavations wound down and the development of the recreational facilities increased in the 1950s, tens of thousands of visitors bypassed the small museum in favor of the lake and camping facilities. The *Early County News* reported that high school football teams were holding practice on the village plaza at the base of Mound A in 1953. In 1960, the Blakely Bobcats used the park for their preseason training camp. The plaza served as a practice field, and Mound A was used as a "fitness course to build leg muscles."[27]

Such activities were detrimental to the archaeological resources at the site, but the most devastating event occurred in March 1974 when thieves broke into the museum and stole 129 objects, including several stone axes and arrowheads and the entire collection of rare effigy vessels and clay bowls that were on display. Although the street value of the stolen items was estimated at $400,000, they were, in fact, priceless. The objects, which constituted the entire collection of the museum, were unique to the site and could not be replaced. Devoid of artifacts that constituted its interpretive exhibits, and clearly in need of rethinking site security, the museum closed temporarily. Four years later, twelve of the clay pots were recovered at the home of an amateur collector in North Miami. In 1996, two pots were discovered in St. Petersburg in the possession of a man whose mother had bought them at a flea market. Eventually, sixteen Kolomoki pots were recovered and returned to the site.[28]

The publication by Sears of his *"Mea Culpa"* in 1992 seemed to resolve the Kolomoki problem, and archaeologists, who had for four decades shied away from engaging with the site, began reexamining the complex. Among the leaders in this new exploration was Thomas J. Pluckhahn, whose dissertation, *Kolomoki: Settlement, Ceremony, and Status in the Deep South, A.D. 350 to 750*, was published in 2003 by the University of Alabama Press. Pluckhahn's research provided new insights into the main period of occupation at Kolomoki and teased out a history of the site from what he hypothesized was the site's founding in 350 CE through its abandonment around 750 CE.

Pluckhahn focused on what he termed the village sites rather than the mounds in an effort to understand how and where the people lived. He identified four phases of settlement between 350 and 750, with each phase approximately one hundred years in duration. During phases 1 and 2, Pluckhahn concluded that Kolomoki had a permanent population exceeding 400 people, with another 125 temporary seasonal residents, and began serving as a ceremonial site.[29] While mound building began during phase 1, it was in phase 2, 450–550, that the major mound building occurred, including the monumental Mound A, which Pluckhahn calculated required over ten thousand person-days, or 200 people working for about fifty days, to complete.[30] The ceremonial importance of the site increased in phase 2 and then began to decline in phase 3, as reflected in the decline of mound construction and a reduction in the population between 550 and the abandonment of the site in 750. Pluckhahn suggests that the "tension between the communal themes of the ritual and the semi-exclusive control of its practice," which occurred in conjunction with the stratification of society in the latter part of phase 2, led to the eventual demise of Kolomoki as a permanent settlement.[31]

Whether Pluckhahn's conclusions were correct was less important than the fact that the publication of his book moved Kolomoki back into "its role as a key site in an understanding of the Woodland period in Southeastern archaeology," according to archaeologist Frank T. Schnell, who reviewed Pluckhahn's book for *American Antiquity* in 2006.[32] Indeed, Pluckhahn would revisit the site and his conclusions several times over the next decade and would revise his chronology to include a first phase of settlement that likely began between 80 and 300 CE during which a vacant ceremonial center evolved into a residential community.[33] While the formal arrangement of mounds began in phase 2 between 490 and 650 CE, it was likely during phase 3, which began around 670, that the village "expanded to a discontinuous oval nearly a kilometer across," and Mound A was completed. Pluckhahn also revised his estimate of the labor required to build Mound A, which he describes as "probably the largest extant Woodland period mound in eastern North America," to "90,000 earthmoving days, enough to occupy a 200-person workforce for well over a year." The final phase of occupation began around 715 CE, but the settlement was more dispersed. The site was abandoned altogether in the late 800s following a period of below-average rainfall between 811 and 891 that may have precipitated a population crash in the area.[34] The site was reoccupied briefly in the late Mississippian period, but only by "one or two households,"

Mound A from the plaza at Kolomoki Mounds.

according to Pluckhahn. What had been a major ceremonial and residential center in the Woodland period "was reduced to a small satellite farmstead of a Lamar period chiefdom centered elsewhere."[35]

Pluckhahn's ongoing engagement at Kolomoki has led to new understandings of the development and decline of this prehistoric site. More importantly, as Schnell noted in 2006, Pluckhahn's work has led to the reemergence of this remarkable complex as one of the preeminent Woodland-era sites in the southeastern United States. No longer do the Blakely Bobcats use the plaza in front of Mound A as a training field. The state historical marker at the entrance was updated by the Georgia Historical Society in 2019 to reflect the consensus narrative of Kolomoki as a Middle and Late Woodland period site, and exhibit panels throughout the park have been updated as well. While the recreation area continues to host far more visitors than do the mounds and museum, the story encountered by those visitors who do stop to visit the museum and climb the steps up Mound A is much richer and complete than ever before. Although there is still much that is unknown about the people who lived at this site in ancient times, their story is slowly beginning to emerge.

Touring the Site

Visitors to the historic site should stop at the visitor center to pick up a map of the site. The visitor center contains a gift shop, an exhibit gallery, and, prior to 2024, a cutaway view of Mound E. The Department of Natural Resources (DNR) is working with the Muscogee (Creek) tribe to repatriate the funerary objects previously on display in the exhibit gallery, under the terms of the Native American Graves Protection and Repatriation Act (NAGPRA). As part of the agreement between the DNR and the tribe, access to Mound E has been permanently closed. The state archaeologist has removed NAGPRA-affiliated items from the exhibit gallery until tribal consultation can determine the long-term plans for those pieces. However, the exhibit gallery remains open to the public.[36]

The walls of the hallway leading into the museum exhibit gallery feature timelines of world culture and of the Kolomoki excavations, which provide a useful context for understanding the site and the evolution of its interpretation. Displays in the exhibit gallery provide additional information on the people who lived at Kolomoki and their culture. The exhibit is evolving as the tribal consultations continue.

In front of the museum is a seating area and a model wattle-and-daub house that park rangers use for educational programs. Interpretive panels provide an overview of the site and details about the dwellings and lifestyle of its prehistoric residents.

The greatest attraction, however, is the mounds, eight of which are still visible. Although Mound E is now partially enclosed in the museum, the remaining mounds are scattered across the landscape. Visitors can walk across the field from the museum to Mound D, the second largest of the mounds at Kolomoki. More than seventy burials and a vast array of burial objects were found in Mound D during excavations in the 1950s.

Beyond Mound D lies the plaza that links to Mound A, the largest of the mounds at Kolomoki. Rectangular in shape, the base of Mound A is bigger than two football fields and is made up of more than two million basket

Education area and wattle-and-daub house at Kolomoki Mounds.

loads of dirt. Steps on the west side of this fifty-six-foot-high mound enable visitors to climb to the top, from which they can look out over the vast expanse of the main plaza of this Woodland-era site. During its peak period (490–670 CE), the plaza would have been surrounded by wattle-and-daub dwellings much like the reconstructed house located near the visitor center. Like the other mounds at Kolomoki, Mound A was capped by a layer of red clay. Mounds B and C flank Mound A to the north and the south.

The much smaller Mounds F, G, and H are located across the access road from the main site and are easy to miss if not for the signs indicating their location. The Mercier family cemetery is located atop Mound G. Interpretive panels located throughout the site offer information on the Kolomoki settlement during the Woodland period.

View from atop Mound A at Kolomoki Mounds.

Mercier family burials on Mound G at Kolomoki Mounds.

Notes

1. "Kolomoki Mounds Are Described as Largest and Best," *Macon Telegraph*, May 11, 1945, 5.

2. Thomas J. Pluckhahn, "Fifty Years since Sears: Deconstructing the Domestic Sphere at Kolomoki," *Southeastern Archaeology* 19, no. 2 (Winter 2000): 154.

3. "President Kennedy's Birthplace Heads Latest National Historic Landmark List," National Park Service, July 19, 1964.

4. Thomas J. Pluckhahn, "Woodland Period," *New Georgia Encyclopedia*, last modified June 8, 2017, https://www.georgiaencyclopedia.org/articles/history-archaeology/woodland-period-overview/.

5. Thomas J. Pluckhahn, "Kolomoki Mounds," *New Georgia Encyclopedia*, last modified September 1, 2020, https://www.georgiaencyclopedia.org/articles/history-archaeology/kolomoki-mounds/.

6. George White, *Historical Collections of Georgia* (New York: Pudney & Russell, 1855), 425.

7. Thomas J. Pluckhahn, *Kolomoki: Settlement, Ceremony, and Status in the Deep South, A.D. 350 to 750* (Tuscaloosa: University of Alabama Press, 2003), 56.

8. C. T. Trowell, "A Kolomoki Chronicle: History of a Plantation, A State Park, and the Archaeological Search for Kolomoki's Prehistory," *Early Georgia* 26, no. 1 (Athens: Society for Georgia Archaeology, 1998), 23.

9. Pluckhahn, *Kolomoki: Settlement*, 4.

10. Trowell, "Kolomoki Chronicle," 29–30.

11. H. Summerfield Day, "Report on Inspection of Kolomoki" (Washington, D.C.: National Park Service, May 11, 1936).

12. Trowell, "Kolomoki Chronicle," 32–33.

13. Trowell, 34.

14. Trowell, 35.

15. Pluckhahn, *Kolomoki: Settlement*, 48–49.

16. Trowell, "Kolomoki Chronicle," 41.

17. "Trails at Kolomoki Mounds State Park," Georgia Department of Natural Resources, Division of State Parks & Historic Sites, accessed September 6, 2023, https://gastateparks.org/KolomokiMounds/Trails#:~:text=Mound%20E,be%20used%20in%20the%20afterlife.

18. "Kolomoki Mounds Park to Be Opened Thursday," *Columbus Ledger-Enquirer*, July 26, 1950, 10.

19. Tim Brawner, "An Overview of the Kolomoki Mound Site, Early County, Georgia," *Central States Archaeological Journal* 61, no. 1 (January 2014): 33–35; "1,150 Indian Pottery in Georgia Mound," *Atlanta Journal*, July 24, 1949, 20.

20. Pluckhahn, *Kolomoki: Settlement*, 5.

21. Trowell, "Kolomoki Chronicle," 62.

22. Trowell, 66.

23. Willam Sears, "*Mea Culpa*," *Southeastern Archaeology* 11, no. 1 (Summer 1992): 66.

24. Sears, 67.

25. Amelia Barksdale, "Kolomoki Mounds to Be Dedicated Next Week," *Columbus (Ga.) Ledger*, July 12, 1966, 11.

26. "Kolomoki Indian Mound-A," Georgia Department of State Parks, n.d.

27. Trowell, "Kolomoki Chronicle," 51.

28. "Georgia Theft Robs World of Unique Legacy," *Atlanta Journal*, September 19, 1999, 70.

29. Pluckhahn, *Kolomoki: Settlement*, 191.

30. Pluckhahn, 198.

31. Pluckhahn, 211–214.

32. Frank T. Schnell, "Review of *Kolomoki: Settlement, Ceremony, and Status in the Deep South, A.D. 350 to 750*," *American Antiquity* 71, no. 3, 2006, 592.

33. Thomas Pluckhahn, Martin Menz, Shaun E. West, and Neill J. Wallis, "A New History of Community Formation and Change at Kolomoki (9ER1), *American Antiquity* 83, no. 2 (April 2018): 332.

34. Pluckhahn et al., 337–338.

35. Pluckhahn, *Kolomoki: Settlement*, 220.

36. Valarie Ikhwan, email to Jennifer Dickey, April 22, 2024.

Further Reading

Milanich, Jerald T. *The Archaeology of Precolumbian Florida*. Gainesville: University Press of Florida, 1994.

Pluckhahn, Thomas J. *Kolomoki: Settlement, Ceremony, and Status in the Deep South, A.D. 350 to 750*. Tuscaloosa: University of Alabama Press, 2003.

Pluckhahn, Thomas J. "Kolomoki Mounds." *New Georgia Encyclopedia*, last modified September 1, 2020. https://www.georgiaencyclopedia.org/articles/history-archaeology/kolomoki-mounds/.

Pluckhahn, Thomas J. "Woodland Period." *New Georgia Encyclopedia*, last modified June 8, 2017. https://www.georgiaencyclopedia.org/articles/history-archaeology/woodland-period-overview/.

Sears, William H. *Excavations at Kolomoki: Final Report*. Athens: University of Georgia Press, 1956.

Smith, Betty A. "Swift Creek Culture." *New Georgia Encyclopedia*, last modified January 9, 2014. https://www.georgiaencyclopedia.org/articles/history-archaeology/swift-creek-culture/.

Steinen, Karl T. "Weeden Island Culture." *New Georgia Encyclopedia*, last modified January 9, 2014. https://www.georgiaencyclopedia.org/articles/history-archaeology/weeden-island-culture/.

Williams, Mark, and Daniel T. Elliot, eds. *A World Engraved: Archaeology of the Swift Creek Culture*. Tuscaloosa: University of Alabama Press, 1998.

REGION 4

The Coast

The Coast includes the area along the Atlantic coast once known as "the debatable land" because of its location between the English colony of South Carolina and the Spanish colony of Florida. It was along this coast that English settlement of the Georgia colony began in the 1730s. Among the five state historic sites in this region are two plantations—Wormsloe and Hofwyl-Broadfield—as well as three forts—Fort McAllister, Fort Morris, and Fort King George. Fort King George, located in Darien, recognizes the earliest attempt by the English to establish a toehold along the coast of what would become the Georgia colony, while Wormsloe dates back to the 1733 arrival of James Oglethorpe and the English settlers who carved out the last of the original thirteen English colonies on the North American mainland. The earthworks at Fort Morris represent the only American Revolutionary War site in the state system, while the earthworks at Fort McAllister date to the Civil War period. The southernmost site in the state system, Hofwyl-Broadfield Plantation, tells the story of over 160 years and five generations of family ownership of a former rice plantation.

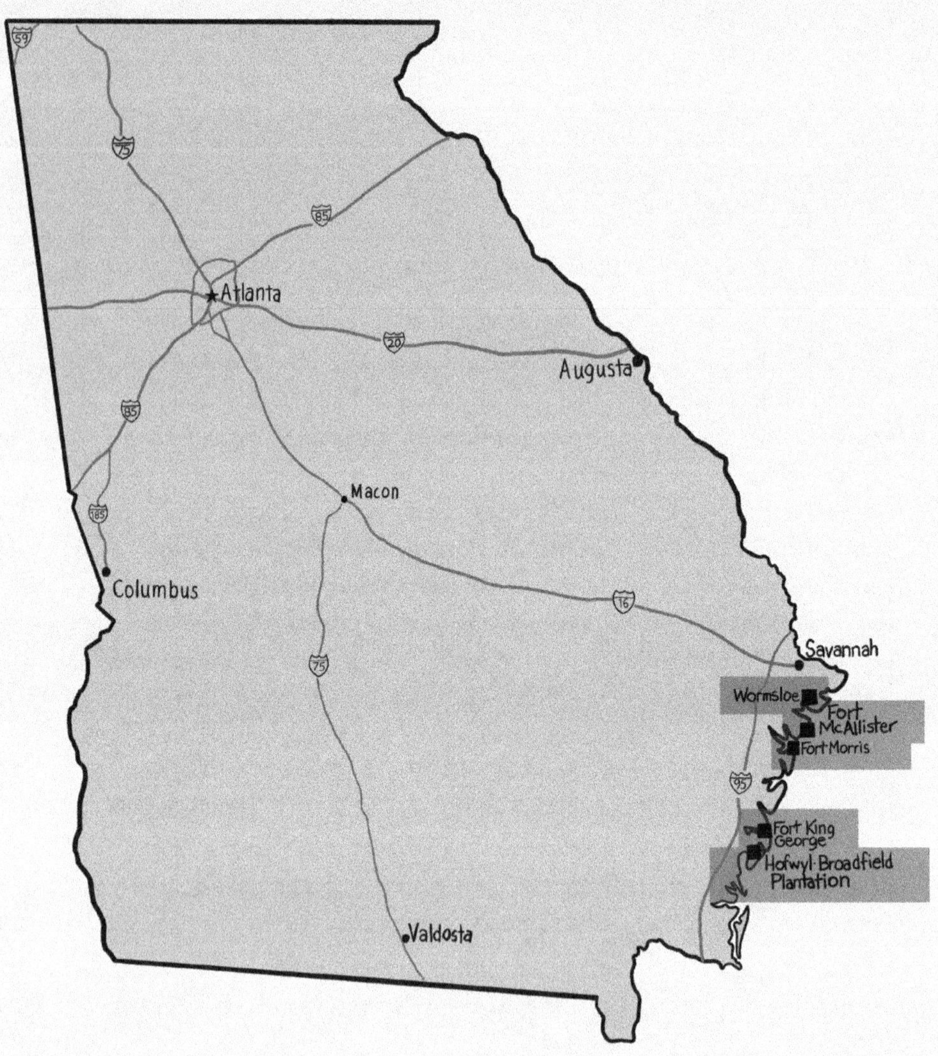

59
75
85
Atlanta
20
Augusta
85
Macon
185
Columbus
16
75
Savannah
Wormsloe
Fort McAllister
Fort Morris
95
Fort King George
Hofwyl-Broadfield Plantation
Valdosta

CHAPTER 12

Wormsloe

Kari Ramos-Suarez and Jennifer W. Dickey

Basic Information

PERIOD OF SIGNIFICANCE: 1736–1973

DATE ESTABLISHED AS A STATE HISTORIC SITE: 1973

ACREAGE: 1,233 acres

LOCATION: 7601 Skidaway Road, Savannah, Ga. 31406, Chatham County

Wormsloe is a site of great beauty that dates back to the early years of the Georgia colony. It has been described by historian Paul S. Sutter as "one of the most significant historical, archaeological, and natural sites in Georgia."[1] Established in 1736 by Noble Jones, Wormsloe (originally spelled Wormslow) is located approximately ten miles from downtown Savannah. The property remained in the Jones/De Renne/Barrow family for over 230 years before it was acquired by the state in 1973. Listed in the National Register of Historic Places in 1973, Wormsloe is significant because it was "established by an original English colonist and still owned by the same family over 200 years later." According to historian Marilyn Pennington, Wormsloe reflected "two facets of its first owner: a feeling of tradition and an acute appreciation for a new potential."[2]

The site includes the oldest known tabby ruins of any estate in Georgia, Civil War–era Confederate earthworks, and the main attraction, a one-and-a-half-mile live-oak-lined avenue planted in the 1890s by Noble Jones's descendant Wymberley Jones De Renne. A museum and the nature trails are open seven days a week, and the site hosts live colonial-era reenactments during special events throughout the year.

Live oak allée at Wormsloe.

History of Wormsloe

The arrival in February 1733 of James Oglethorpe and 114 colonists at what would become the site of the city of Savannah marks the beginning of British settlement in the Georgia colony. This new British colony, the first in North America in five decades, had its origins as a charitable endeavor. It was to be a place where the "worthy poor" of England could get a chance to redeem themselves through hard work and become farmers and merchants. King George II granted a charter to Oglethorpe and twenty other trustees to establish the colony, which would be located between British South Carolina and Spanish Florida and would serve as a military buffer while providing economic opportunities for the colonists. To prevent the development of a plantation economy based on the labor of enslaved workers, the trustees prohibited slavery in the new colony.[3]

Among the colonists who sailed with Oglethorpe on the ship *Anne* was Noble Jones, identified as a carpenter on *Anne*'s passenger list, along with his wife, Sarah, and their two children, Mary and Noble Wimberly. In addition to his carpentry skills, Jones was a self-trained doctor. He also was a skilled surveyor, draftsman, and builder, all of which would serve him well as he embarked on his new life in the Georgia colony.[4]

The trustees employed Jones as a surveyor to help lay out the city of Savannah on a patch of land for which Oglethorpe had negotiated with the Yamacraw Indians who occupied the site when the colonists arrived. Jones was relieved of his duties as surveyor in 1737 because of negligence, a move he protested, claiming he was unable to fulfill his assigned duties because he lacked adequate helpers. Oglethorpe responded by giving him "the command of the Narrows," the area along the Skidaway River that bordered Wormsloe.[5]

Jones had been granted five hundred acres along the river in 1736. By that time, he had developed his intown lot and had sponsored the transport of at least ten indentured servants to Georgia as specified by the trustees, so Oglethorpe granted his application for the outlying plantation on the Isle of Hope, marking the beginnings of the "family's land stewardship" that would last well into the twentieth century.[6]

Although referred to as a plantation, Wormsloe served more as an experimental farm for Jones in the early years. It was also a defensive outpost against the Spanish for the fledgling Georgia colony. The land granted to Jones had earlier been inhabited by the Guale, a semi-nomadic Mississippian tribe, but the Guale were gone from the Georgia coast by the time the English arrived in Georgia. Jones would use the shell middens from the Guale period as a source for the oyster shells with which he made tabby, the building material he used to construct his fortified residence. Jones first constructed a wattle-and-daub hut on the site in which he lived while overseeing the construction of his tabby house.

Archaeologist William Kelso, who excavated the site in 1968–1969, noted that Jones must have had "a considerable labor force for the undertaking" of constructing the tabby house and speculated that Jones may have "used some of the ten 'marines' who had been placed under his command to guard the Narrows for the tabby work."[7] Upon completion, the fortified residence included a five-room house "surrounded by a tabby enclosure wall in the shape of a four-bastioned fort." Kelso estimated that the tabby enclosure was built between 1739 and 1744, that the house was expanded between 1750 and 1770, and that the final occupation period was 1800–1820.[8]

Marker at the site of Noble Jones's tabby house at Wormsloe.

From his fortified residence, Jones had a view of the salt marsh and the river. He would also clear a path to the Bethesda Orphan House, constructed on a five-hundred-acre plot of land granted to the preacher George Whitefield in 1738. Whitefield's orphan house, which he envisioned serving as "a place of literature and academical studies" for the colony's orphans, was a compound of several buildings, the most important of which was a "sixteen-room 'great house' built on elevated ground, with a ten-foot-wide piazza wrapping around all four sides." The Bethesda Orphan House became well known for its gardens, which renowned naturalist William Bartram described as "handsomely laid out and planted with oranges, pomegranates, figs, peaches, and other fruit trees." Although Whitefield's "great house" was destroyed by fire in 1773, operations at the school continued. It served as a school for children of the poor in the nineteenth century and is today the site of Bethesda Academy, a private boys' school.[9]

If Whitefield's "great house" was considered to be the "finest masonry structure" in Georgia, Jones's Wormsloe, which was far less grand, was "delightfully situated on a large tide salt creek," according to Bartram, who visited Wormsloe following his visit to Bethesda. Bartram noted that the houses in Georgia featured piazzas on one or more sides, likely referring to both Bethesda, which was surrounded by such a feature, and Wormsloe, which featured a piazza on one side.[10] Bartram also commented on the variety of fruit trees cultivated by Jones, essentially the same as those cultivated on neighboring Bethesda—"orange trees, pomegranates, figs, peaches & nectarins," as well as grapes and apricots.

Jones was known for experimenting with plants to see what might grow along the Georgia coast. His reputation for such experiments extended to his son, Noble Wimberly Jones, who received from Benjamin Franklin samples of rice from "Cochin China" and seeds from a Chinese tallow tree in 1772. Although historian Drew Swanson states that there is no evidence that rice was ever cultivated at Wormsloe, he does note that "a few mature specimens" of the Chinese tallow tree, considered an invasive species, can still be found at the site.[11]

As required by the trustees, Jones planted mulberry trees on Wormsloe in an effort to produce silk as a commercial crop, and his daughter, Mary, oversaw the silk operations. However, silk production in Georgia proved unprofitable, and by the beginning of the Revolutionary War, silk production had been largely discontinued.[12] Jones certainly produced corn and housed livestock on the plantation, and he may have produced indigo, a labor-intensive crop for which he would have used enslaved labor. The trustees had prohibited slavery in the Georgia colony upon its establishment in 1732, but that prohibition was revoked in 1751. Noble Jones had already begun acquiring enslaved workers prior to this date to help clear the land and work his fields on Wormsloe as well as on other properties in the area that he acquired beginning in the 1740s. At the time of his death in 1775, Noble Jones's estate included around fifty enslaved people.

Jones had served the colony in numerous capacities by the time of his death on the eve of the American Revolution. He had helped survey the land lots for Savannah and commanded a force of marines who guarded the inland waterways around Savannah during the War of Jenkins' Ear (1739–1748) between England and Spain. He served as a member of the Royal Council and became a judge of the General Court. He also worked as a doctor and trained his son in the practice of medicine. During the tumultuous decade leading up to the Revolutionary War, Jones remained "a staunch loyalist." Considered the "Loyalist leader of the colony," Jones was the president of the Upper House of the Assembly while his son, Noble

Wimberly, who was a leader of the Patriots and known as "The Morning Star of Liberty," served as speaker of the House of Commons. Jones and his son reportedly "never permitted political differences to intrude into family harmony and affection." The father and son practiced medicine together, and Noble Wimberly would come to consider medicine his true profession following the Revolutionary War.[13]

Upon his death in 1775, Noble Jones left Wormsloe to his daughter, Mary, who maintained a residence in downtown Savannah. Little is known about the period of Mary's ownership, which overlapped with the American Revolution (1775–1783), although Kelso speculates that she divided her time between her house in town and Wormsloe, noting that Wormsloe was likely not a substantial working plantation during this time. A sketch of the mouth of the Savannah River by Archibald Campbell from 1780 shows the house and "a small section of cleared land, perhaps a garden or a small, cultivated field."[14] Of note in Archibald's sketch is the thick forest on the property and the continued clear line of sight to the Bethesda Orphan House.[15]

Upon Mary's death in 1795, Wormsloe passed to her brother, Noble Wimberly, who by this time was well established on his plantation, Lambeth, located on the Little Ogeechee River. Born around 1723, Noble Wimberly was ten years old when his family came to Georgia. He had worked closely with his father developing Wormsloe, but upon marrying Sarah Davis in 1755, he moved to Lambeth and began developing that plantation. He was a leader of the Patriots during the Revolutionary War, serving in the state legislature as well as the Continental Congress. He was a protégé of Dr. Benjamin Rush while serving in the Continental Congress in Philadelphia, and he continued to practice medicine upon his return to Savannah in 1783. Following a five-year stint in Charleston, Noble Wimberly returned to Savannah and took up residence at Lambeth.[16] He and Sarah would outlive all but one of their fourteen children, George, to whom he transferred ownership of Wormsloe in 1804. Noble Wimberly Jones died a year later.[17]

Like his father and grandfather, George Jones was trained as a physician, but unlike his father, he did not pursue a career in medicine. He was active in public life in Savannah, serving as a judge and twice as the mayor of Savannah. He also made a fortune in banking and promoting railroads and canals.[18] By the time he inherited Wormsloe, George was splitting his time between Savannah and his two plantations, Poplar Grove and

Newton, where he had his main residence. For the first two decades of his ownership, he periodically raised cotton on Wormsloe under the supervision of an overseer and then leased the property to a widow named Ann Reid. The terms of the lease indicate that there were only twenty acres of cultivated land on Wormsloe and that the buildings, including the tabby house, were "in something less than good repair," notes Kelso. George's situation would change in 1825 when his principal residence at Newton burned. He relocated to Wormsloe, and after a brief period in his grandfather's tabby house, he decided to build a larger, more modern residence on the property. This new residence, a two-story, timber-framed building constructed on a tabby foundation made from materials salvaged from the original tabby house, would become the principal residence of George and his descendants at Wormsloe.[19]

Tabby ruins from which George Jones quarried materials for his new house in the 1820s at Wormsloe.

George Jones began planting sea island cotton at Wormsloe, and he used the services of enslaved workers to cultivate the crops. Sea island cotton would remain the main crop on the plantation for the next five decades.[20] At the time of his death in 1838, Jones owned over nine thousand acres and 137 enslaved people who worked on his multiple plantations.[21] In addition to managing his plantations, George traveled frequently to Philadelphia, and it was there that he met Eliza Smith, who became his third wife in 1822. George's first two wives, Mary Gibbons and Sarah Fenwick, predeceased him, as did his son by his first wife. George left Wormsloe, now the principal family residence, to Eliza upon his death in 1838. Eliza relied on her son, George Frederick Tilghman Jones, born in 1827, to help manage Wormsloe following her husband's death, and ownership of the plantation passed to him after Eliza's death in 1857.[22]

George Frederick married Mary Wallace Nuttall in 1851. The couple would have four children—Wymberley (1853), Everard (1857), Letitia (1860), and Kentwyn (1862). George had a keen interest in history, and between 1844 and 1861 he amassed a collection of over thirteen hundred books, which he kept in a library at Wormsloe. During the Civil War, U.S. troops destroyed most of his collection on Georgia history, considered among the best in the state.[23] The family fled inland after the war began, first to the Blue Ridge Mountains and then to the Carolinas. Wormsloe, meanwhile, was occupied by Confederate troops who built earthworks on the southern tip of the plantation overlooking the Moon River. Known as Fort Wymberly, the fortifications were more than twenty feet high and one hundred yards long. The earthworks are still visible today.[24]

The Confederate troops fled Wormsloe as Sherman's Army descended on Savannah in December 1864. U.S. cavalry troops ransacked the plantation, burned all the cotton, and confiscated the horses and mules. Although U.S. troops made off with some of the furnishings and the family silver and destroyed most of George's books, the main house was largely unscathed. Part of the plantation fell within the boundaries of General Sherman's Special Field Order 15, which ceded "abandoned lands" along the coast to formerly enslaved people in forty-acre tracts. Although he had played no role in the Confederate government and had not served in the Confederate Army, George was a wealthy planter, and his property holdings, which exceeded $20,000, exempted him from the general amnesty issued by President Andrew Johnson at the conclusion of the war. Wormsloe was briefly under U.S. government control until George received a presidential pardon in August 1865 and was able to reclaim the plantation.[25]

Following the war, George would change the family surname to De Renne. George had a cousin, also named George Jones, who lived in Savannah, and he apparently became annoyed at the confusion caused by having two George Joneses in the city.[26] He began using an alternative name, George Wymberley Jones, and in 1866 he had his name legally changed to George Wymberley Jones De Renne, adopting a variation of his grandmother's name as his surname.[27] He also changed the name of the plantation from Wormslow to Wormsloe. He expanded the home that his father had built and increased his landholdings to include additional acreage north of Wormsloe.

During the early Reconstruction years (1865–1868), De Renne and his family traveled to Europe and rented the bulk of Wormsloe's cotton fields to white northern investors who grew sea island cotton on the plantation. He later experimented with sharecropping on Wormsloe until around 1871, when he decided that cotton was no longer a profitable enterprise for the plantation. At that point, he began leasing smaller parcels to a group of Black tenants and continued to do so until his death in 1880.[28]

Under the terms of De Renne's will, Wormsloe was left to his wife for the remainder of her life (she died in 1887) and then passed to his daughter, Letitia. Following Letitia's death in 1890, ownership of Wormsloe transferred to George and Mary's oldest son, Wymberley Jones De Renne. Wymberley, who had spent much of his life in Europe, was a graduate of the Columbia Law School, but he never practiced law. He married Laura Norris in 1880 and soon thereafter tried his hand as a cattle rancher in Texas. He abandoned ranching in 1884 and moved to Biarritz, France. By the time he returned to Wormsloe to claim his inheritance in 1893, he and Laura had three children. He spent the remainder of his life at the estate rebuilding his father's book collection and beautifying the home and grounds.[29]

Among the construction projects that Wymberley undertook was the construction of a fireproof library building in 1907 to house his book collection.[30] He also began operating a commercial dairy on the property, and in 1891, in honor of his son's tenth birthday, he created a new entry road to the plantation, which he lined with four hundred live oak trees, creating the iconic oak allée through which visitors still enter the property today. In 1913, Wymberley added the concrete archway that marks the entrance to the property.[31]

Laura died in 1913, so upon Wymberley's death in 1916, Wormsloe was left to his three children—son Wymberley Wormsloe (W. W. De Renne) and daughters Elfrida and Audrey. The two sisters sold their shares to their brother in 1917. W. W. and his wife, Augusta, continued building the book collection and beautifying the grounds, creating formal gardens that would become a popular tourist attraction in the late 1920s. By that time, W. W. had lost most of his inheritance and had mortgaged the property in an effort to stay afloat. His sister, Elfrida De Renne Barrow, bought the mortgage in 1930. She leased the home to her brother for the next eight years until he moved to Athens to oversee the transfer of the Wormsloe library to the University of Georgia.

Following her brother's departure, Elfrida and her husband, Craig Barrow, a renowned physician, moved to Wormsloe. They made modifications to the main house, stripping it of its Victorian ornamentation, and in 1951 created the nonprofit Wormsloe Foundation, which had as its purpose "the promotion of historical research and the publication of the results thereof; the restoration, preservation, and maintenance of historical sites and documents and the conduct of an educational program in the study of history in the State of Georgia, and in states adjoining thereto."[32] Elfrida transferred the bulk of the plantation to the foundation in 1961 in an effort to reduce future estate taxes and help facilitate preservation of the estate. The Barrows retained ownership of forty-five acres, which included the main house, the library, and several outbuildings. The ruins of Noble Jones's tabby house were located within the more than eight hundred acres given to the foundation.[33] The foundation facilitated excavations by archaeologist William Kelso of the tabby house site in 1968–1969.[34]

In the 1970s, after the Georgia Supreme Court revoked the Wormsloe Foundation's tax-exempt status, Elfrida's son, Craig Barrow Jr., contacted the Nature Conservancy about taking the land as an intermediary that could then transfer ownership to the state to create a state historic site. The deal was finalized in December 1972 when the state's Heritage Trust pledged to acquire 750 acres of Wormsloe from the Nature Conservancy for $250,000.[35] Governor Jimmy Carter commended the Barrow family for their "far-sighted and generous recognition of the value of preserving Georgia's cultural and historic heritage for the benefit of present and future generations," adding that the state should continue the "careful stewardship" of the Barrow family estate.[36]

The Department of Natural Resources oversaw the listing of Wormsloe on the National Register of Historic Places in 1973, as they began surveying the property and planning for opening the site to the public. The state proposed a "two-pronged interpretive approach, combining conservation of the property's natural environment with selected interpretation of its cultural past."[37] Complications arose, however, such as the discovery of a pine beetle infestation in 1974 that led to the clear-cutting of twenty-five acres of the pine forest on the property—the largest timbering episode in the plantation's history.[38] The logging operations contributed to a formidable mosquito outbreak on the Isle of Hope.[39] Development of the property as a historic site continued, however, and Wormsloe opened to the public in 1979 following the construction of a museum.

From the arrival of Noble Jones in the 1730s to the present day, the land that is now Wormsloe State Historic Site has been shaped and remade to serve the purposes of its owners. It is a place that has been kept whole by eight generations of one family. Each generation has left its mark, creating a palimpsest in which traces of the past are still visible across this historic landscape.

Touring the Site

A new visitor center, opened in late 2023, is the starting point for visitors to Wormsloe. The visitor center has ample parking and a gift shop. From the visitor center, visitors take a tram or walk along the 1.5-mile drive under the live oaks to the museum. The former entrance to the site, the gate at the concrete archway, erected in 1913, is now closed to automobile traffic.

The museum includes exhibits about the archaeological surveys conducted at the site as well as the history of the family that owned Wormsloe for almost 250 years. The main path from the museum leads to the spectacular tabby ruins of Noble Jones's eighteenth-century fortified house. While much of the tabby was removed and reused by George Jones in the 1820s as the foundation for his main residence, enough remains of the tabby walls to allow visitors to see the impressive scale of Noble Jones's original fortified residence.

A trail leads from the tabby ruins to the original family burial plot (the families' remains were later moved to Colonial Cemetery in Savannah),

Historic 1913 entrance gate to live oak avenue at Wormsloe.

Tabby ruins of Noble Jones's fortified house at Wormsloe.

Wattle-and-daub house in the Colonial Life and Living History area at Wormsloe.

as well as to a view across the marsh toward the river. Another trail leads to the Colonial Life Area, where living history demonstrations are held at the blacksmith shop and wattle-and-daub house. The site hosts several events throughout the year, including the "Colonial Faire and Muster" in February, which highlights aspects of eighteenth-century life, such as music, dancing, crafts, and military drills.[40] The trail continues through the woods to the Confederate earthworks of Battery Wymberly.

While traversing the oak-lined drive, visitors may catch a glimpse of the 1828 family residence situated east of the oak avenue. This remains the family home and is not open to the public, although it is the host site for the University of Georgia's Center for Research and Education at Wormsloe. Several outbuildings, an abandoned silo, and the old dairy complex mark the last major agricultural use of Wormsloe Plantation.[41]

Notes

1. Paul S. Sutter, "Wormsloe as Palimpsest," foreword to Drew A. Swanson, *Remaking Wormsloe: The Environmental History of a Lowcountry Landscape* (Athens: University of Georgia Press, 2012), ix.

2. Marilyn J. Pennington, "Wormsloe Plantation," National Register of Historic Places Nomination Form (Washington, D.C.: U.S. Department of the Interior, National Park Service, 1973), section 8.

3. Edwin L. Jackson, "James Oglethorpe," *New Georgia Encyclopedia*, last modified July 21, 2020, https://www.georgiaencyclopedia.org/articles/government-politics/james-oglethorpe-1696-1785/.

4. William Harris Bragg, *De Renne: Three Generations of a Georgia Family* (1949; rpt., Athens: University of Georgia Press, 1999), xvi.

5. Merton E. Coulter and Albert B. Saye, *A List of the Early Settlers of Georgia* (Athens: University of Georgia Press, 2009), 26.

6. Swanson, *Remaking Wormsloe*, 15.

7. William M. Kelso, *Captain Jones's Wormslow: A Historical, Archaeological, and Architectural Study of an Eighteenth-Century Plantation Site Near Savannah, Georgia* (1979; rpt., Athens: University of Georgia Press, 2008), 88.

8. Kelso, 20–21.

9. Robyn Asleson, "Bethesda Orphan House," History of Early American Landscape Design, National Gallery of Art, accessed September 14, 2023, https://heald.nga.gov/mediawiki/index.php/Bethesda_Orphan_House.

10. Kelso, *Captain Jones's Wormslow*, 11.

11. Swanson, *Remaking Wormsloe*, 42.

12. Pauline Tyson Stephens, "The Silk Industry in Georgia," *Georgia Review* 7, no. 1 (Spring 1953): 47.

13. W. S. Kirkpatrick, "Historic Wormsloe in One Family 223 Years," *Atlanta Journal*, April 19, 1959, 29.

14. Kelso, *Captain Jones's Wormslow*, 12.

15. Archibald Cox, "Sketch of the Northern Frontiers of Georgia," accessed September 14, 2023, https://www.loc.gov/resource/g3922s.ar157000/.

16. William Harris Bragg, "Noble W. Jones," *New Georgia Encyclopedia*, last modified September 16, 2014, https://www.georgiaencyclopedia.org/articles/history-archaeology/noble-w-jones-ca-1723-1805/.

17. Kelso, *Captain Jones's Wormslow*, 13.

18. Kirkpatrick, "Historic Wormsloe," 29.

19. Kelso, *Captain Jones's Wormslow*, 14–15.

20. Swanson, *Remaking Wormsloe*, 59.

21. Robert Preston Brooks, "Wormsloe House and Its Masters," *Georgia Historical Quarterly* 40, no. 2 (June 1956): 147.

22. Brooks, "Wormsloe House and Its Masters," 148.

23. William Harris Bragg, "De Renne Family," *New Georgia Encyclopedia*, last updated September 9, 2014, https://www.georgiaencyclopedia.org/articles/history-archaeology/de-renne-family/.

24. Swanson, *Remaking Wormsloe*, 99.

25. Swanson, 102.

26. Brooks, "Wormsloe House and Its Masters," 148.

27. Kirkpatrick, "Historic Wormsloe," 29.

28. Swanson, *Remaking Wormsloe*, 106–108.

29. Brooks, "Wormsloe House and Its Masters," 149.

30. Bragg, "De Renne Family."

31. Swanson, *Remaking Wormsloe*, 116.

32. Kelso, *Captain Jones's Wormslow*, xi.

33. Jane Roy Brown, "Preservation Hero: Craig Barrow III, Steward of Womsloe," *View*, no. 14 (Summer 2014): 20.

34. Kelso, *Captain Jones's Wormslow*, xi.

35. Swanson, *Remaking Wormsloe*, 166.

36. Barbara Casson, "Conservancy Now Holds Wormsloe for the State," *Atlanta Constitution*, December 31, 1972, 8.

37. Swanson, *Remaking Wormsloe*, 167.

38. Wormsloe—Master Plan Report, C 295992, rcb: 29475, c: 295992. Georgia Archives.

39. Swanson, *Remaking Wormsloe*, 159–160.

40. "Wormsloe Historic Site," Friends of Georgia State Parks & Historic Sites, accessed October 4, 2022, https://friendsofgastateparks.org/wormsloe-historic-site.

41. Wormsloe Information Pamphlet, "1828 Plantation House & Dairy Site (Private)," Georgia Department of Natural Resources, 2012.

Further Reading

Bragg, William Harris. *De Renne: Three Generations of a Georgia Family*. Athens: University of Georgia Press, 1999.

Bragg, William Harris. "De Renne Family." *New Georgia Encyclopedia*, last modified September 9, 2014. https://www.georgiaencyclopedia.org/articles/history-archaeology/de-renne-family/.

Bragg, William Harris. "Noble W. Jones." *New Georgia Encyclopedia*, last modified September 16, 2014. https://www.georgiaencyclopedia.org/articles/history-archaeology/noble-w-jones-ca-1723-1805/.

Bragg, William Harris. "Wormsloe Plantation." *New Georgia Encyclopedia*, last modified September 25, 2014. https://www.georgiaencyclopedia.org/articles/history-archaeology/wormsloe-plantation/.

Coulter, E. Merton. *Wormsloe: Two Centuries of a Georgia Family*. Athens: University of Georgia Press, 1955.

Kelso, William M. *Captain Jones's Wormslow: A Historical, Archaeological, and Architectural Study of an Eighteenth-Century Plantation Site Near Savannah, Georgia*. 1979; rpt., Athens: University of Georgia Press, 2008.
Swanson, Drew A. *Remaking Wormsloe Plantation: The Environmental History of a Lowcountry Landscape*. Athens: University of Georgia Press, 2012.
Wood, Betty. "Slavery in Colonial Georgia." *New Georgia Encyclopedia*, last modified July 27 2021, https://www.georgiaencyclopedia.org/articles/history-archaeology/slavery-in-colonial-georgia/.

CHAPTER 13

Fort McAllister

Jennifer W. Dickey

Basic Information

PERIOD OF SIGNIFICANCE: 1861–1864

DATE ESTABLISHED AS A HISTORIC SITE: 1968

ACREAGE: 30 acres

LOCATION: 3894 Fort McAllister Road, Richmond Hill, Ga. 31324, Bryan County

Located near the mouth of the Great Ogeechee River, Fort McAllister was considered "the key to the city" of Savannah during the Civil War. This earthwork fortress constructed in 1861 on Genesis Point, positioned ten miles from the Atlantic Ocean and fifteen miles from Savannah, guarded an important waterway and was part of the network of Savannah's defenses. The fort, listed in the National Register in 1970, is considered "an outstanding example of Confederate earthwork fortifications" and is significant for demonstrating "that earthen fortifications could withstand the heaviest naval ordnance of that time," and because "its capture by Gen. William T. Sherman in 1864 enabled the Union Army to obtain supplies from its offshore vessels thus ending the 'March to the Sea.'"[1]

Attacked by the U.S. Navy on seven occasions from the river, the fort proved impregnable. Only through a land assault from the rear in December 1864 was Sherman's army able to take the fort. The capture of Fort McAllister by U.S. forces on December 13, 1864, opened the "back door" to Savannah and completed Sherman's March to the Sea.[2]

The earthworks of Fort McAllister.

History of Fort McAllister

Following Georgia's secession from the United States in January 1861 and the bombardment of Fort Sumter in April of that same year, the Confederate high command began surveying its coast to identify vulnerabilities. The city of Savannah, with a population of more than 22,000, including 7,712 enslaved people, was Georgia's largest city and one of the most important ports along the Atlantic coast.[3] The state was a leader in terms of rice and cotton production, and the port of Savannah served as the gateway for exports of these commodities to Europe. Protecting this city was a major concern for the Confederate leadership as well as for Georgia governor Joseph Brown, who had ordered the occupation by the state militia of Fort Pulaski on January 3, 1861, even before Georgia seceded from the Union.[4]

Fort Pulaski, named for the Polish immigrant Count Casimir Pulaski, who fought for the United States in the American Revolution, was a five-sided masonry fort at the mouth of the Savannah River constructed between 1829 and 1847. A recent graduate of the U.S. Military Academy at West Point, Lieutenant Robert E. Lee, oversaw the early years of construction. With its 7.5-foot brick walls and its 146-cannon mounts, the fort was considered impregnable. However, in April 1862, U.S. captain Quincy Gillmore under the command of Brigadier General Thomas W. Sherman employed eleven batteries on the north end of Tybee Island to bombard the fort.[5] Confederate officers in the fort observed the activity on Tybee Island, some two and a half miles away, but were unconcerned because they believed the fort was beyond the range of the U.S. guns. However, the batteries included rifled cannons, a new technology that allowed for greater distance and increased accuracy. After thirty-six hours of constant shelling, the southeast face of the fort had incurred severe damage with two thirty-foot holes, and the Confederates were forced to surrender. Rifled cannons had made masonry forts obsolete, and a key piece of the defensive network that surrounded Savannah was now in U.S. hands.[6]

Even before the fall of Fort Pulaski, Confederate military leaders had begun planning a network of fortifications to protect the cities and waterways along the coast. While the fall of Fort Pulaski was a shock to Confederate leaders, it reinforced the strategy of constructing earthworks at key positions to defend Savannah. Earthen fortifications were relatively inexpensive and could be constructed quickly, both key considerations for the Confederates. Earthen fortifications also proved to be better able to sustain heavy artillery bombardments and could be repaired easily.

The U.S. blockade of southern ports, part of General Winfield Scott's "Anaconda Plan," disrupted international trade, which was vital for the Confederate states. Keeping the waterways accessible to southern ships and protecting its port cities as well as the plantations along the coast was key to the Confederacy, and a series of fortified earthworks was constructed along the major coastal access points beginning in 1861. The southernmost waterway with access to Savannah was the Ogeechee River, a deepwater river that flowed from the Ossabaw Sound to within a dozen miles of the city. Two important bridges, the Atlantic and Gulf Railroad bridge and the King's Bridge, which was on the road between Savannah and Darien, crossed the Ogeechee and provided land access to Savannah. At a place called Genesis Point, a bluff at a bend in the river ten miles from the Atlantic Ocean, Company A of the First Georgia Infantry Regiment, also known as the DeKalb Rifles, began construction of the Genesis Point Battery on the west bank of the river.[7]

Designed by Captain John McCrady and built with the assistance of more than thirty enslaved people, the fort soon became known as Fort McAllister for the family who owned the rice plantation on which the fort was located. Strathy Hall was developed as a 1,400-acre rice plantation in the late 1700s by James McKay and sold to George McAllister in 1840. McAllister expanded the plantation to include more than 2,800 acres with rice as the predominant crop. More than 130 enslaved people worked the fields of the Strathy Hall plantation and produced 620,000 pounds of rice in 1851. Following George McAllister's death in 1846, the plantation transferred to his wife, Charlotte, and then to his son, Joseph, in 1850 following Charlotte's death.[8] Joseph McAllister, who enlisted in the Confederate Army and served with the Hardwicke Rifles, was more than happy to allow the Confederate Army to construct the battery on his land. His friendship with Alfred Hartridge, who would command the DeKalb Riflemen upon completion of the fort, led to the renaming of the fort from Genesis Point Battery to Fort McAllister by January 1862.[9]

Genesis Point was a heavily wooded bluff at a bend in the Ogeechee River that, once it was cleared, afforded an excellent view of the river and marshes that surrounded it, both upstream and downstream. The fort was far enough along by August 1861 to be garrisoned, although construction continued for more than a year. Upon completion of construction in November 1862, the fort, which had five irregular sides, measured 650 feet on the side facing the river and about 750 feet on the side facing the Ossabaw Sound. The landward approach to the fort was along a narrow stretch of land and was protected by a deep, dry ditch, while the right flank looked out over swampland "and so needed no such exterior protection." Because the fort was primarily for defense of the river, the guns were placed in a position to "command the channel" with a focus toward the Ossabaw Sound, which was the direction from which enemy ships would approach.

Within the fort were two large earthen shelters, or bombproofs, in which the troops "ate and slept, and where in times of battle the wounded found shelter."[10] Under instructions from General Robert E. Lee, who commanded the Department of South Carolina, Georgia, and East Florida before being dispatched to Richmond to command the Army of Northern

Cannon overlooking the Ogeechee River at Fort McAllister.

Virginia, "an obstruction on the Ogeechee" was constructed using enslaved workers in March 1862. The obstruction consisted of two rows of wooden pilings driven into the river channel with a chain between the rows, essentially creating a barrier across the river with a narrow channel on the side closest to the fort to allow the passage of "friendly vessels."[11]

Construction on the fort was not quite complete when it saw its first action in July 1862. The USS *Potomska*, a former merchant vessel that had been converted into a U.S. Navy gunboat, steamed up the river in pursuit of a Confederate schooner that had made it through the naval blockade. The commander of the *Potomska*, Lt. Cmdr. Pendleton G. Watmough, had received a report of Fort McAllister from a runaway enslaved person, and he encountered the battery as he rounded the bend. The *Potomska* opened fire on the fort and the schooner, which had sailed beyond the obstruction, and the DeKalb Riflemen returned fire "with considerable accuracy," according to Watmough. The commander "deemed it imprudent to prolong the exposure of the vessel to damage," and he retreated downriver with the ebb tide.[12]

Watmough reported news of his action and the fort to U.S. admiral Samuel DuPont, who recognized that the Ogeechee River offered an attractive route to the blockade runners that were necessary to the economic and military well-being of the Confederacy, and he ordered a reconnaissance mission up the river. However, before the reconnaissance mission could commence, a legendary blockade runner, the *Nashville* (also known as the *Thomas L. Wragg* and the *Rattlesnake*), loaded with arms and ammunition slipped through the blockade and made its way up the Ogeechee. The *Nashville* unloaded its cargo at the Atlantic and Gulf Railroad bridge and took on a cargo of cotton, pitch, and tobacco for the return voyage across the Atlantic.

Getting out proved harder than coming in for the *Nashville*, however, as four U.S. vessels steamed up the river and began shelling Fort McAllister on July 29, 1862. Once again, the men of the DeKalb Rifles returned fire. Commander Charles Steedman, captain of the USS *Paul Jones*, reported that the fort "answered with spirit, most of their shots striking near, and several passing over me." After about two hours of action, Steedman concluded that it would be wise "to withdraw from the contest" and ordered a retreat.[13] The earthen fort had withstood the bombardment, and overnight a group of enslaved workers impressed from nearby plantations repaired much of the damage to the exterior walls. Not long thereafter, the DeKalb Rifles were reassigned to a new post and were replaced by the Emmett Rifles and the Republican Blues, troops formerly stationed at Fort Jackson in Savannah.[14]

The next assault on the fort began on November 19 when three U.S. Navy vessels, led by the USS *Wissahickon*, traveled up the river to within about one hundred yards of the pilings. The troops in the fort opened fire, and the first shot put a hole in the *Wissahickon* below the water line. The ship retreated downstream to make repairs while the other two ships continued firing on the fort. By midafternoon, the ships retreated. Paymaster Robert Pierce on board the USS *Dawn* reported, "Our expedition was partly to find out where the piles were driven and partly what their guns would do." He concluded, "Not many were killed at the Battery for we could see them run for their holes when they saw the flash of our guns." Pierce's assessment was correct, as no one inside the fort was seriously injured during the attack. Repairs to the fort were made quickly by more than one hundred enslaved workers, and additional weapons and ammunition soon arrived from Savannah.[15]

The federal blockade succeeded in keeping the *Nashville* trapped upriver from Fort McAllister, and in September 1863, the ship traveled back upstream to the railroad bridge and unloaded its cargo. The *Nashville* was sold to a new owner, who refitted the ship to serve as a privateer and rechristened it the *Rattlesnake*. The new name and purpose, however, did not change the ship's fate, as it was unable to make its way past the federal blockade of the Ossabaw Sound. DuPont, in an effort to test the capabilities of the new ironclad warships, ordered the USS *Montauk* up the river to test the ship against direct fire from the fort. On January 27, 1863, the *Montauk* steamed up the river and anchored within 150 yards of the river pilings. For five hours the *Montauk* bombarded the fort, and the troops in the fort returned fire, but both sides proved to be largely immune to the barrage of shells thrown their way.

The *Montauk* fired 378 rounds, and the fort fired about half that many. The ironclad was struck twelve times but received only minor damage in the form of several dents in the iron shell. The fort, meanwhile, suffered considerable damage to its outer walls, but the walls were repaired overnight by a workforce of more than 150 enslaved laborers. Lt. Col. Charles Jones Jr. reported that despite the "enormous expenditure of shot and shell on the part of the enemy, the damage done to the fort was repaired before morning, and not a single casualty occurred among the members of the garrison."[16]

The *Montauk* had proven itself in combat, but so too had Fort McAllister. The ironclad ship made another assault on the fort on February 1, 1863, with much the same results, although Fort McAllister's commander, Major John B. Gallie, was killed when he was hit by a piece of shrapnel. The captain of the USS *Seneca*, which accompanied the *Montauk* upriver, noted that since the previous attack only four days prior, "The fort has been enlarged and strengthened with huge traverses . . . and though but an earthwork, is now really colossal of its kind."[17]

The *Montauk* returned on February 28, 1863, following reports that the *Nashville/Rattlesnake* had run aground just north of the fort. As the *Montauk* steamed into range of the *Nashville* and began shelling the ship, the fort unleashed fire on the *Montauk*. The triangular bombardment continued for about an hour before the *Nashville* caught fire and exploded. The *Montauk* retreated downriver, but along the way it struck a Confederate torpedo, which blew a hole in the ship's underside.[18] The captain ran the *Montauk* aground so that temporary repairs could be made, and the ship then made its way downstream to a repair yard.[19] The destruction of the *Nashville* was cause for celebration for Admiral DuPont as well as for the residents of the coast who had come to believe that the presence of the ship on the Ogeechee was the main reason for the repeated attacks on Fort McAllister.[20]

Another assault on Fort McAllister came on March 3, 1863, when DuPont ordered three ironclads up the river to test their guns in live action against the fort. The ironclads *Patapsco*, *Passaic*, and *Nahant* were accompanied by the *Montauk* and eight wooden gunboats loaded with troops that were expected to take command of the fort once it was subdued by the armored fleet. The ensuing bombardment raged for seven hours, during which time the fort inflicted little damage on the ironclads, but the ships left their mark on the fort. A news correspondent aboard the *Montauk* wrote, "The outline of the fort, which early in the morning had presented such regularity, now began to assume an entirely different aspect. Huge holes were clearly discernable, and it did not look like the work we saw in the bright glow of the morning's sun." Despite the destruction, the Confederate troops in the fort continued to man their posts. Remarkably, the only casualty inside the fort was the garrison mascot, a cat named Tom Cat. The ironclads finally retreated, and although the wooden gunboats tried to prevent the Confederates from making repairs by continuing to bombard the fort through the night, around daybreak they too retreated.[21]

The attack on March 3 would be the final effort by the U.S. Navy to take the fort, but it would not be the last attempt to destroy the battery. That would come in the form of a land assault in December 1864 as General William T. Sherman's army arrived at the coast following their march from Atlanta, which began on November 19. Sherman's army, sixty thousand strong, had cut a path through Georgia for four weeks. Cut loose from their supply lines, the army had lived off the land, consuming or destroying almost everything in its path. In the area along the coast, the prospects for foraging were slim, and supplies were running out. Savannah was well defended, so Sherman hatched a plan to capture Fort McAllister, which would open supply and communication lines along the coast.

In his notes about the capture of Fort McAllister, Lt. Col. William E. Strong noted, "In our march through Georgia from Atlanta to Savannah, supplies in great abundance were found. The army never fared better; but this was accomplished by keeping the command constantly in

Marker memorializing the fort mascot, Tom Cat, who was killed in a bombardment at Fort McAllister.

motion. Halt the army for one day and the country was most thoroughly cleaned of provisions and forage for twenty miles in every direction."[22] On December 12, 1864, Lt. William Pittenger of the Thirty-Ninth Ohio Volunteer Infantry wrote in his diary, "Our last issue of bread expired last night which makes it necessary to do our work quickly. Must eat to fight. We must take Savannah or reach a base very soon. Time is precious."[23] The situation for Sherman and his army was getting desperate, and on December 13, 1864, Strong wrote that the fort "lay, in plain view, two and one half miles away, sullen and silent, like a great lion at bay—conscious of its own strength, yet not deigning to speak to us; the key to the city, which we were besieging."[24]

The Confederates knew that Sherman was coming, and they anticipated a land assault. They had reinforced the back side of the fort, expanding the ditch that was filled with palisades and clearing the tree canopy across the approach. The tree branches and brambles were piled up along a line to form an abatis, and the open field was armed with land mines. Now under the command of Major George Anderson, the troops at Fort McAllister were determined to defend their battery. Anderson had stockpiled supplies so that the fort could hold out for up to fifteen days under siege. When the attack came around 5:00 p.m. on December 13, it lasted barely fifteen minutes. The 4,300 U.S. troops under the command of General William B. Hazen, who had led the ill-fated attack on the Confederate lines at Pickett's Mill, overwhelmed the 275 men inside the fort. Strong reported 134 U.S. casualties and 70 Confederate casualties, with 178 captured. Anderson and his men fought "gallantly till the very last moment, and in fact, never surrendered at all. The garrison was captured," wrote Strong, "one man at a time, or in squads, after our troops gained possession of the fort, and the rebel colors (garrison flag) were hauled down by one of our Brigade commanders."[25]

As planned, the capture of Fort McAllister opened the supply and communication lines for Sherman's army. Confederate general William J. Hardee and his army, which had occupied Savannah, slipped out of the city and fled to South Carolina on December 20. Sherman's troops quickly occupied the city, and on December 22 Sherman himself arrived in Savannah. That same day he dispatched to President Lincoln a telegram that read, "I beg to present to you as a Christmas gift the City of Savannah, with one hundred and fifty heavy guns and plenty of ammunition and about twenty-five thousand bales of cotton."[26] Sherman would occupy Savannah for a month before marching north into South Carolina.

In the aftermath of the war, Fort McAllister fell into a state of ruin. The land at Genesis Point, once part of the prosperous McAllister rice plantation, changed hands several times over the following decades, and while the land upon which Hazen's army had marched in their assault on the fort was used for grazing livestock and agriculture, the fort's earthworks eroded and were largely overgrown with trees. In the 1920s, automobile magnate Henry Ford acquired the property as part of an effort to develop a winter resort for his family and friends. A decade later, Ford began restoring the fort after two students from his Greenfield Village School in Dearborn, Michigan, discovered the ruins and encouraged him to do so. Ford spent almost $15,000 restoring the bombproof and magazines, which generated great interest in the fort among local residents. By the mid-1940s, however, Ford's interest had waned, and following his death in 1947, the property was sold to the International Paper Company.[27]

In January 1958, the International Paper Company announced it would give the fort and thirty acres of surrounding land to the state for development by the Georgia Historical Commission into a "War Between the States shrine."[28] The development process moved slowly. In 1961 the state legislature authorized $75,000 for restoration of the fort and construction of a museum at the site.[29] Bids were received in December 1962 for the construction of the museum and facilities building, with a low bid of $40,803.[30] The museum, built to resemble the Confederate barracks located outside the fort, and restoration of the fort itself were "virtually complete" by late 1963, and the Historical Commission held a formal opening on November 14. Although additional work was still to be done at the site, members of the public were "beginning to come in increasing numbers" to the site.[31]

Atlanta Journal columnist Jack Spalding, writing in the aftermath of the opening, declared that "Fort McAllister is as historic a place as can be found in Georgia," citing the use of rifled shell and ironclad ships as technological developments that made the fort significant. On display in the museum were sketches of the fort from the Civil War era as well as a couple of dioramas. Spalding declared the development of the Fort McAllister Historic Site to be "another fine job by the Historical Commission and another significant piece of our past preserved for the pleasure of our own people and the delectation of tourists from over the world."[32] On the one-hundredth anniversary of the capture of the fort by Sherman's army, December 13, 1964, a formal dedication was held.[33]

In February 1969, Historical Commission chair Joseph B. Cumming wrote to Governor Carl Sanders that he was dismayed to hear that the state legislature was recommending that the Fort McAllister Historic Site be moved from the Historical Commission to the State Parks Department. Such an action would be "a tragic mistake," wrote Cumming, who noted that the commission "scrupulously avoid ever having any of our sites used as amusement parks. We feel that such use would impair the integrity and true significance of these historic shrines, and the thousands of visitors to Fort McAllister who praise the work of the Commission there will no longer find it a source of patriotic inspiration and education if it is converted to a recreation area."[34] Despite Cumming's misgivings, the Fort McAllister Historic Site was combined with the Richmond Hill State Park property, donated to the state in 1970, and additional acreage under the auspices of Game Management to create Fort McAllister Historic Park in 1980.

Touring the Site

Upon arrival at the site, visitors will see an outdoor display of machinery from the CSS *Nashville*. A series of panels tells the story of the ship, which was sunk by the USS *Montauk* in 1863. The visitor center, which opened following the consolidation of the historic site with the state park, includes a gift shop and exhibits about the history of the area, from its occupation by the Guale Indians through the Civil War. Visitors can watch a twelve-minute film entitled *Exceptional Valor* (also available online at https://gastateparks.org/FortMcAllister) that recounts the story of the fort and its significance during the Civil War.

Reconstructed noncommissioned-officer huts (left) and barracks (right) at Fort McAllister.

Bridge over the moat at Fort McAllister.

The crown jewel of the site is the restored fort itself, which is located behind the visitor center. Exit out the back door for a short walk along the causeway toward the fort. Along the way, visitors will pass a reconstructed signal tower and reconstructed barracks for noncommissioned and commissioned officers. The commissioned officers' barracks building was the original museum building at the historic site when it first opened to the public in 1963.

The earthworks of the fort have been reconstructed and appear much as they did prior to the final assault in December 1864. Visitors can walk inside the fort and follow a pathway across the parapet to overlook the Ogeechee River and the adjacent marshlands. Interpretive markers, including a marker about Tom Cat, the garrison mascot, are located in and around the fort. The tour is self-guided, but the markers, in conjunction with the site brochure available from the visitor center, allow visitors to understand the events that transpired here.

Located on the edge of a swamp, the site is frequently plagued by swarms of mosquitoes. The gift shop sells mosquito repellant, and visitors are encouraged to use it liberally. Mosquitoes aside, the restored fort is well worth the trip.

Notes

1. William R. Mitchell Jr., "Fort McAllister," National Register of Historic Places Nomination Form (Washington, D.C.: U.S. Department of the Interior, National Park Service, 1970), section 8.

2. Buddy Sullivan, "Fort McAllister," *New Georgia Encyclopedia*, last modified June 6, 2017, https://www.georgiaencyclopedia.org/articles/history-archaeology/fort-mcallister/.

3. Buddy Sullivan, "Savannah," *New Georgia Encyclopedia*, last modified July 9, 2021, https://www.georgiaencyclopedia.org/articles/counties-cities-neighborhoods/savannah/.

4. William Christman, *Undaunted: The History of Fort McAllister, Georgia* (Atlanta: Department of Natural Resources, 1996), 5.

5. David H. McGee, "Fort Pulaski," *New Georgia Encyclopedia*, last modified April 25, 2017, https://www.georgiaencyclopedia.org/articles/history-archaeology/fort-pulaski/.

6. National Park Service, "Rifled Cannon," last modified April 14, 2015, https://www.nps.gov/fopu/learn/historyculture/rifled-cannon.htm.

7. Christman, *Undaunted*, 5–6.

8. Victoria Reeves Gunn, "Strathy Hall," National Register of Historic Places Nomination Form (Washington, D.C.: U.S. Department of the Interior, National Park Service, 1971), section 8.

9. Roger S. Durham, *Guardian of Savannah: Fort McAllister, Georgia, in the Civil War and Beyond* (Columbia: University of South Carolina, 2008), 5–6, 10.

10. R. Jervis Cooke, *Sand and Grit: The Story of Fort McAllister; A Confederate Earthwork on the Great Ogeechee River, Genesis Point, Georgia* (Washington, D.C.: National Park Service, 1938), 8–10.

11. Durham, *Guardian of Savannah*, 10.

12. Durham, 16.

13. Christman, *Undaunted*, 15–16.

14. Durham, *Guardian of Savannah*, 19–20.

15. Durham, 28–29.

16. Durham, 48.

17. Durham, 53–54.

18. Christman, *Undaunted*, 42–43.

19. Durham, *Guardian of Savannah*, 77.

20. Durham, 79–80.

21. Durham, 93–95.

22. William E. Strong, "The Capture of Fort McAllister, December 13, 1864," *Georgia Historical Quarterly* 88, no. 3 (Fall 2004): 410.

23. Durham, *Guardian of Savannah*, 132.

24. Strong, "Capture of Fort McAllister," 406–407.

25. Strong, 419.

26. Burke Davis, *Sherman's March: The First Full-Length Narrative of General William T. Sherman's Devastating March through Georgia and the Carolinas* (New York: Vintage Books, 1988), 118.

27. Durham, *Guardian of Savannah*, 195–197.

28. "Fort McAllister Offered to State for Development," *Newnan (Ga.) Times-Herald*, January 30, 1958, 5.

29. "1865 Fort Outguns Gunboat," *Atlanta Constitution*, February 28, 1961, 8.

30. John C. Le Bey, Preliminary Progress Report, December 15, 1962, Georgia Historical Commission—Director's Office—Administrative Records—1952–1964, RCB-9951 061-01-001, Georgia Archives (hereafter, GHC Director's Office).

31. Joseph B. Cumming to Carl E. Sanders, December 9, 1963, GHC Director's Office.

32. Jack Spalding, "Another Historic Place Has Been Preserved," *Atlanta Journal*, November 21, 1963, 38.

33. Cumming to Sanders.

34. Joseph B. Cumming to All Members of the Legislative Delegation, GHC Director's Office.

Further Reading

American Battlefield Trust. "Fort McAllister." Accessed September 25, 2023. https://www.battlefields.org/learn/civil-war/battles/fort-mcallister.

Bailey, Anne J. "Sherman's March to the Sea." *New Georgia Encyclopedia*, last modified September 30, 2020. https://www.georgiaencyclopedia.org/articles/history-archaeology/shermans-march-to-the-sea/.

Bailey, Anne J. *War and Ruin: William T. Sherman and the Savannah Campaign*. Lanham, Md.: Rowman & Littlefield, 2002.

Christman, William E. *Undaunted: The History of Fort McAllister, Georgia*. Atlanta: Department of Natural Resources, 1996.

Cooke, R. Jervis. *Sand and Grit: The Story of Fort McAllister; A Confederate Earthwork on the Great Ogeechee River, Genesis Point, Georgia*. Washington, D.C.: National Park Service, 1938. https://www.nps.gov/parkhistory/online_books/fopu/McAllister.pdf.

Davis, Burke. *Sherman's March: The First Full-Length Narrative of General William T. Sherman's Devastating March Through Georgia and the Carolinas*. New York: Vintage Books, 1988.

Durham, Roger S. *Guardian of Savannah: Fort McAllister, Georgia, in the Civil War and Beyond*. Columbia: University of South Carolina, 2008.

Fowler, John D. "Civil War in Georgia." *New Georgia Encyclopedia*, last modified August 24, 2020. https://www.georgiaencyclopedia.org/articles/history-archaeology/civil-war-in-georgia-overview/.

Rubin, Anne Sarah. *Through the Heart of Dixie: Sherman's March and American Memory*. Chapel Hill: University of North Carolina Press, 2014.

Sherman, William T. *Memoirs of General William T. Sherman, Written by Himself.* 2 vols. New York: Scribner's Sons, 1875.

Sullivan, Buddy. "Fort McAllister." *New Georgia Encyclopedia*, last modified June 6, 2017. https://www.georgiaencyclopedia.org/articles/history-archaeology/fort-mcallister/.

CHAPTER 14

Fort Morris

Allison Allen and Jennifer W. Dickey

Basic Information

PERIOD OF SIGNIFICANCE: 1776–1865

OPENED TO THE PUBLIC: 1976

ACREAGE: 66 acres

LOCATION: 2559 Fort Morris Road, Midway, Ga. 31320, Liberty County

Fort Morris was established in 1776 to protect the thriving port town of Sunbury on the Midway River, which was second in size and importance only to Savannah at the time. The residents of Sunbury feared an attack from the river by the British, and in 1776 the Continental Congress ordered the construction of a fort to defend the town. A heroic stand by American Patriots in 1778 was followed in early 1779 by the British capture and eventual destruction of Fort Morris. Although Fort Morris was short-lived, another fort, Fort Defiance, was constructed on the same site in 1814 to defend the town during the War of 1812. By the time of the Civil War, the hastily constructed fort was a mere remnant of its former self with nothing but the outer earthworks remaining. Likewise, the former town of Sunbury, which in the 1770s had boasted a population of about 1,000, had only 150 residents by the late 1820s.[1] Nevertheless, Confederate troops encamped at the site during the Civil War until overtaken by U.S. troops in 1864.

What remains today in the former town of Sunbury is a historic cemetery and the earthworks of the fort surrounded by modern-day residences and vacation homes. The fort was listed on the National Register

Visitor center (left) and earthworks (center rear) at Fort Morris.

of Historic Places in 1970 and is considered one of the "best preserved fortifications from the Revolutionary era." It is "a classical example of 18th century military planning."[2] The town of Sunbury no longer exists, but the eight-foot parapet that surrounded the fort during the War of 1812 is a reminder of the importance of the place that was once the second-largest town in the Georgia colony.

History of Fort Morris

In 1877, Dr. James Holmes, a prominent medical doctor in Darien who was born in the town of Sunbury in 1808, wrote: "In its palmy days, Sunbury was a beautiful village with its snow-white houses, green blinds, and a red roof here and there. From the fort to the point was a carpet of luxuriant Bermuda grass shaded with ornamental trees on either side of its wide avenues. Today it is a cotton field with one or two dilapidated buildings."[3]

While it is possible that Holmes was romanticizing the place of his birth, this description captures the essence of this once important town and its adjacent fortification, both of which were mere memories by the second half of the nineteenth century. Although Sunbury is not Georgia's only "dead" town, and Fort Morris is not the only fortification from Georgia's early years to have largely disappeared, both are significant for the roles that they played in the late years of the colonial period and the early years of Georgia statehood.

The town of Sunbury had its beginnings when Mark Carr, an early settler who arrived in the Georgia colony around 1738, was granted a 1000-acre plot of land (500 for himself and 500 for his son, Thomas) along the Midway River (sometimes spelled Medway) in 1748. Ten years later, Carr conveyed 300 of his 500 acres along the Midway River to a group of men "in trust that the same should be laid out as a town by the name of Sunbury."[4] The town was laid out with 496 lots of 70 feet by 130 feet and three town squares—King's Square, Church Square, and Meeting Square. That same year, Georgia governor Henry Ellis proposed that the colony be divided into eight electoral districts, or parishes, and in March 1758, the General Assembly passed an act that created, among others, St. John's Parish, which encompassed the new town of Sunbury.[5]

Carr and others built wharves along the Midway River, and by 1761 Governor James Wright had declared Sunbury to be a port of entry for the colony. Thomas Carr was appointed to serve as the tax collector for the port. Wright noted in 1763 that Sunbury had "eighty dwelling houses in the place; three considerable merchant stores for supplying the town and planters in the neighborhood with all kinds of necessary goods; and around it for about fifteen miles is one of the best settled parts of the country."[6] At the request of the House of Commons in London, this "port of entry" was protected by a battery of cannons and a lookout post on Cedar Hammock. All incoming ships were to be cleared for passage into the port at the battery.[7]

Sunbury continued to grow and flourish and became "a pleasant residence for the families of many planters whose plantations were located in the swamp regions." The majority of the 496 lots were sold and occupied, and the town was second only to Savannah in terms of the number of ships that arrived at the port.[8] When naturalist William Bartram visited Sunbury in 1773, he described it as:

> A sea-port town, beautifully situated on the Main between Medway and Newport rivers, about fifteen miles south of great Ogeechee river. The town and harbour are defended from the fury of the seas by the north and south points of St. Helen and South Catherine's islands, between which is the bar and entrance into the sound. The harbor is capacious and safe, and has water enough for ships of great burthen. . . . There are about one hundred houses in the town neatly built of wood frame having pleasant Piasas [*sic*] around them. The inhabitants are genteel and wealthy, either Merchants or Planters from the Country who resort here in the Summer and Autumn, to partake of the Sallubrious Sea breeze, Bathing & sporting on the Sea Islands. Here is a Custom house and Naval office for the incrouagement [*sic*] of Commerce.[9]

According to historian Charles C. Jones Jr., Sunbury "culminated in prosperity, population, and importance about the beginning of the Revolutionary War, when its inhabitants, black and white, numbered, we should say between eight hundred and a thousand." Commodities such as rice, cattle, and lumber from the inland parts of the colony were transported to Sunbury for export to England. On at least two occasions, ships that had made the Middle Passage from Africa delivered enslaved people to Sunbury. The town had grown "steadily, although slowly," and its residents had "advanced in material wealth," according to Jones, "until the retarding influences of the Revolutionary struggle."[10]

On the eve of the Revolution, 317 of the 496 lots in Sunbury had been sold, and among the most prominent residents was Dr. Lyman Hall, a leading physician in the area. Hall, who would serve as Georgia's governor in 1783–1784, was elected to represent St. John's Parish at the Second Continental Congress in Philadelphia in 1775. A year later he, along with George Walton and Button Gwinnett, who resided across the river from Sunbury on St. Catherine's Island, returned to Philadelphia and, as representatives of Georgia, signed the Declaration of Independence.

Meanwhile, the citizens of St. John's Parish committed themselves to the independence movement and attempted to form an alliance with the city of Charles Town, South Carolina, to support the boycott of imported British goods. Although Charles Town encouraged the citizens of St. John's Parish to continue their nonimportation, they declined the proposed alliance, given that other parts of the Georgia colony were not supporting the cause. When a ship carrying British wine and other goods arrived in June 1775, residents of Sunbury prevented the crew from unloading their cargo. In the aftermath, the residents of Sunbury erected a "Liberty Pole" to celebrate.[11] In 1777, when the state assembly consolidated St. John's, St. Andrew's, and St. James's Parishes, the new county was named Liberty in recognition of the leadership that the citizens of St. John's Parish had shown in supporting early efforts for independence.[12]

By the end of 1775, Governor Wright had fled the Georgia colony, and the Council of Safety, based in Savannah, assumed responsibility for governing the colony. Among the council's top priorities was improving Georgia's military readiness by organizing troops and developing fortifications to protect the towns and cities along the coast. Militia troops and two volunteer companies guarded the town of Sunbury, and after an attack by the British in April 1776 in which two cargo ships were burned, the Council of Safety ordered additional troops to the area and the construction of entrenchments at the town.[13]

Approximately 350 yards south of the town on a bluff that overlooked a bend in the Midway River, work began on a fort to defend Sunbury. The fort was an enclosed earthwork that embraced a parade ground "about an acre in extent" and a two-story, brick barrack for the troops. In addition to the barrack inside the fort, additional troops and commanding officers were housed in the adjacent town. According to Charles C. Jones Jr., the eastern front of the fort along the river was 275 feet long, while the western face was 241 feet. The northern and southern sides of the fort were 191 and 140 feet long, respectively, giving the fort an "irregular" shape. The heaviest guns were mounted on the eastern side of the fort to protect against an attack by the British from the river. The guns were mounted on raised platforms to fire over the ten-foot earthen walls. A ten-foot moat surrounded the fort.[14] Initially under the command of Captain Thomas Morris, the fort, which was completed in 1777, was named in his honor.[15]

By November 1778, the fort was under the command of Colonel John McIntosh, and the state of Georgia was under siege by the British. The Americans had made three unsuccessful attempts to invade British East Florida during 1777 and 1778, all of which were launched from Sunbury. These efforts to secure the coast merely aggravated the British, who in 1778 launched a southern strategy aimed at returning Georgia, the Carolinas, and Virginia to British rule. In November 1778, British troops from East Florida began what was a two-pronged invasion of Georgia. As British troops under the command of Lieutenant Colonel Jacques Marcus Prevost marched overland toward the meetinghouse in Midway, Lieutenant Colonel Lewis Fuser and his five hundred troops sailed up the Midway

Model of Fort Morris as it appeared when completed during the Revolutionary War.

River and dropped anchor a few miles downstream from Sunbury. On the morning of November 25, McIntosh, who had fewer than two hundred men under his command, received a letter from Fuser informing him of the following:

> Four armies are in motion to reduce this province; the one is already under the guns of your fort, and may be joined when I think proper by Col Prevost, who is now at the Meetinghouse. The resistance you can or intend to make, will only bring destruction upon this country. On the contrary, if you deliver me the fort which you command, lay down your arms, and remain neuter until the fate of America is determined, you shall as well as all the inhabitants of this parish, remain in the peaceable possession of your property.[16]

McIntosh's reply to Fuser came quickly, and it would become the stuff of legend. Acknowledging that he was aware of Fuser's army and its intentions to "reduce this state," McIntosh wrote: "We have no property, compared with the object we contend for, that we value a rush, and would rather perish in a vigorous defence than accept of your proposals. We, Sir, are fighting the battle of America, and therefore disdain to remain neuter till its fate is determined—As to surrendering the fort, receive this laconic reply—COME AND TAKE IT."[17]

Although Colonel Prevost had occupied the area around Midway meetinghouse briefly, he received false intelligence that a "large body of American recruits from South Carolina" was headed his way. Fearing that he and his men would be trapped, Prevost ordered a retreat rather than advancing to support Fuser's effort to subdue Sunbury and Fort Morris. Prevost ordered the Midway settlement be burned, and his soldiers complied. Meanwhile, Fuser received word of Prevost's retreat, and he followed suit and returned to Florida.[18]

Sunbury was saved, at least temporarily, but the area around the town was devastated. Many of the residents had fled upon hearing news of the British invasion. The capture of Savannah by the British in December 1778, followed by the fall of Augusta in January 1779, were discouraging developments for the citizens of Georgia who supported independence.

On January 6, 1779, Prevost and his infantry of 900 men marched toward Sunbury, and by the next day, they had taken possession of the town. By January 9, Prevost demanded that the fort, now under the command of Major Joseph Lane of the Continental Army, surrender unconditionally. Although he was under orders from his commanding officer, General Howe, to evacuate Sunbury in the wake of the fall of Savannah, Lane refused to leave. He and his 204 soldiers attempted to defend the fort, which triggered a fierce bombardment from the British. The barracks caught fire, and four men were wounded, but Lane held out for several more hours, affording two American ships that were moored downriver a chance to escape.

Lane was forced to surrender when British troops arrived at the gate of the fort. The British took as prisoners seventeen commissioned officers and 195 noncommissioned officers and privates and seized twenty-four pieces of artillery. Four Americans had been killed in the siege, including a captain and three privates, and seven wounded. British casualties totaled one killed and three wounded.[19] The British undertook repairs of the damaged fort and renamed it Fort George in honor of King George III.

Following the capture of Sunbury by the British, the town became a prisoner-of-war camp for the American Continental Army officers who were captured in Savannah. Among the internees were Colonel Samuel Elbert, later governor of Georgia, and Colonel Commandant George Walton, acting commander-in-chief of the Georgia militia forces.[20] Citizens were offered a chance to take an oath of allegiance to the Crown, and a reward was offered to anyone who apprehended someone "still adhering to the Rebel cause." Strict regulations on trade were implemented, and steep financial penalties were imposed upon merchants caught dealing with anyone who had not pledged their allegiance to the king. All of Liberty County was in a "deplorable condition," and many of the remaining residents fled the area for South Carolina.[21] The depopulation of Liberty County deprived Sunbury of the steady stream of commodities for export. Charles C. Jones Jr. stated, "All who could possibly get away fled the place, and those who remained led lives of disquietude and penury."[22]

The British would occupy Sunbury until April 1782, when they began evacuating Georgia following the surrender of British general Cornwallis in late 1781. The town and the fort, however, were "a picture of complete desolation." British troops burned much of the town as they evacuated, and although some of the town's former residents would return and rebuild, Sunbury would never again be as prosperous as it had been during its "golden age" prior to the war.[23]

There were some bright spots, however. The town was designated as the county seat of Liberty County in 1784, and in 1788 the Sunbury Academy, which became "the most famous institution of learning in Southern Georgia," was established. Renowned educator Reverend William McWhir arrived in Sunbury in 1793 and served as the school's principal for nearly thirty years. McWhir was credited with making the Sunbury Academy "the leading institution in this entire region."[24] The success of the academy notwithstanding, the population and prestige of Sunbury continued to decline throughout the latter part of the eighteenth century. In 1796, the county seat was moved inland to the town of Riceboro.[25] In 1804 and 1824, the town was hit by major hurricanes, which led to further evacuations by its residents. Many did not return.[26]

In spite of its dwindling fortunes, fear of another British invasion arose after the United States declared war on Britain in June 1812. Although the town was no longer a thriving port, following the commencement of the War of 1812, Sunbury was chosen as the staging area for a U.S. naval expedition. As reports came in of British ships capturing American ships off the coast of Georgia, the citizens of Sunbury appealed to the U.S. government for protection. The navy plan was to have small craft "ply the intercoastal waterways between Savannah and St. Mary's" in an effort to disrupt British attacks on American trading ships.[27] Unfortunately, the navy's plans were not communicated to the residents of Sunbury, who were alarmed to see a small fleet of armed barges coming toward the town in late July 1812. The commander of the local militia, John Cuthbert, called out the troops, who mustered on the bluff, while the citizens of the town "hid valuables or left town altogether." Only the raising of an American flag by the crew of one of the barges kept the militia from firing on the fleet.

The town was unprepared to receive the sailors who disembarked. Officer Charles Grandison, who commanded the barges, wrote to his superiors, "No provisions can be procured at Sunbury for the crews of the Barges."[28] Over the next six months, the situation did not improve. Supply problems continued, as did disciplinary issues with the crews, some of whom deserted. The citizens of Sunbury remained hostile toward the undersupplied and undisciplined operation, and they breathed a sigh of relief when the U.S. Navy departed the town in December 1812.[29]

Although the departure of the U.S. Navy was at first welcomed, many of the denizens of Sunbury had living memory of the previous occupation by the British and feared the return of British troops. In an effort to shore up the town's defenses, the residents of Sunbury employed enslaved people to rebuild the fort on the bluff. Slightly smaller and less elaborate than its predecessor, the newly christened Fort Defiance was nearly complete with a parapet, moat, and palisades in place by January 1815. By that time, the war was over, and the fort was never garrisoned.[30]

Over the next decades, the town of Sunbury continued to decline in population and prominence. The post office closed in 1841, and Sunbury was essentially abandoned shortly thereafter. The town was "without trade, destitute of communications, and visited more and more each season with fevers," according to Charles C. Jones Jr., who added that the town had "ceased to exist save in name."[31] Despite its decline, the site of Fort Morris was likely the base for a small group of Confederate troops during the Civil War. Fifty-seven troops from the Savannah Mounted Rifles Company were stationed there in September 1861. Sunbury was captured in late 1864 by General William T. Sherman during his March to the Sea.[32]

Writing in 1878, historian Jones noted:

> Fort Morris is enveloped in a wild growth of cedars and myrtle. . . . only the bold Bermuda covered bluff and the beautiful river with the green island slumbering in its embrace remind us of this lost town. A Stranger pausing here would find no trace of the past once full of life and importance, but now existent only in the skeleton memories which redeem place and name from that oblivion which sooner or later is the common lot of all things human. . . . Strange that a town of such repute, and within the confines of a young and prosperous commonwealth, should have so utterly faded from the face of the earth![33]

The ruins of Sunbury and its fort lay virtually untouched save for occasional pilfering until the 1950s, when archaeologist Lewis Larson visited the site and made surface collections. Although the artifacts collected by Larson were largely from the eighteenth and nineteenth centuries, he reported the site as an Indian village but made no mention of the Revolutionary War or War of 1812 fortification.[34]

In the 1960s, the Georgia Historical Commission acquired Fort Morris to fill the Revolutionary War gap in their collection of historic sites. The commission planned to place Fort Morris in the forefront of its Bicentennial celebration as the only extant Revolutionary War fortification.[35] Gordon Midgette, archaeologist for the Historical Commission, conducted excavations at the site in 1971 and included a full report in his master's thesis five years later, in which he took into account the comments from his predecessor as staff archaeologist, Steven Baker, that the earthworks on the site were in fact those of Fort Defiance rather than of Fort Morris. Midgette concluded that Fort Defiance did occupy the same site as Fort Morris and conceded that "probably some minor alterations and repairs were made during the War of 1812."[36]

The site became increasingly controversial when Historical Commission historian Tom Agnew took issue with Midgette's work and claimed that the site that the Historical Commission had acquired was indeed the War of 1812 fort, but that it was not the site of Fort Morris. The Historical Commission then hired John Sheftall to carry out additional research about the site. Sheftall concluded, as had Midgette, that the site that the Historical Commission acquired in 1968 was the site of both Fort Morris and Fort Defiance, the second of which was built atop the first. After the Historical Commission was disbanded and its functions transferred to the Department of Natural Resources Historic Preservation Section, the DNR conducted additional archaeological investigations at the site, but no significant cultural resources were found. This cleared the way for the construction of the museum, which opened in 1976.

A more extensive archaeological study was conducted by Daniel Elliott in 2002. Elliott used ground-penetrating radar to identify areas worthy of further exploration, and he and his team then carried out extensive excavations that yielded a treasure trove of Revolutionary War–era artifacts.[37] Elliott declared unequivocally that "the earthworks that everyone sees here are definitely the 1812 fortifications of Fort Defiance, . . .but it was built on top of Fort Morris."[38] Elliott determined that Fort Morris was "significantly larger than Fort Defiance on its southern end" and posited that the British would have likely expanded the fort during their brief occupation in 1779.[39]

The results from the 2002 excavations were a great relief to the staff of the Division of State Parks and Historic Sites at the site, who could finally provide a more in-depth interpretation of the site. "Until we did some archaeology, we couldn't say much about what was here ourselves, because we really weren't sure," said site manager Arthur Edgar.[40] Some of the objects uncovered by Elliott were put on display inside the museum, which helped provide a three-dimensional aspect to the exhibition. The site, which was listed on the National Register of Historic Places in 1970, was declared a Heritage Preserve by Governor Zell Miller in 1998.

Touring the Site

Located about seven miles off I-95 in Liberty County, the Fort Morris State Historic Site includes a museum, the earthwork remains of Fort Defiance, which was built on top of the ruins of Fort Morris, a nature trail, and a living history area. The site encompasses sixty-six acres. The museum offers exhibits about Sunbury, the American Revolutionary War, and the War of 1812. Artifacts uncovered during the 2002 excavations are on display, and visitors can also watch a film about the town of Sunbury (available on the website at https://gastateparks.org/FortMorris).

The museum has limited hours, generally Friday through Sunday from 9:00 a.m. to 5:00 p.m., but the outdoor facilities are open seven days a week. Outdoor facilities include a picnic area and the pioneer campground as well as the fort and nature trail. Camping is available year-round at the site. Reservations can be made on the Fort Morris website.

The fort overlooks the Midway River and surrounding marshlands. Visitors can walk inside the eight-foot earthen parapet remains of the

View of Fort Morris earthworks from the visitor center.

fort, which is now covered with trees. At the time of occupation during the Revolutionary War, the War of 1812, and the Civil War, the area would have been cleared of its tree canopy. The fort is surrounded by a moat, which historically was filled with palisades, or sharpened poles, rather than water. Interpretive panels in and around the fort explain its configuration and the archaeological excavations that have taken place at the site.

Benches are available along the nature trail that runs along the northeast edge of the site between the fort and the river. The trail follows along the edge of the marsh to an overlook point, then winds its way back through the woods to the pioneer campground and living history area. Here, staff and volunteers offer blacksmith demonstrations as well as other living history activities. The site also hosts living history activities related to key events that took place during the Revolutionary War, including Colonel John McIntosh's defiant "Come & Take It!" reply to the British demand for surrender in 1778 and the British occupation of the fort in 1779. See the website for details about upcoming events.

After visiting the park, visitors may want to take a one-mile drive up the road to Sunbury Cemetery located in what was once Church Square

View of the marsh and Midway River at Fort Morris.

Blacksmith shop at Fort Morris.

near the heart of the town of Sunbury. The cemetery is the final resting place of several important Sunbury residents. While most grave markers from the eighteenth and nineteenth centuries are long gone, a few remain, including that of Rev. William McWhir, leader of the Sunbury Academy. Most of the markers there are dated after the 1870s. The cemetery is believed to have been the burial site for local soldiers who fought in the Revolutionary War.

Notes

1. Gus Bernd, "Georgia Fort Scene of Rare Courage in 1778," *Macon News*, June 8, 1951, 4.

2. Gordy Moody Midgette, "Fort Morris at Sunbury: Survey and First Excavations" (MA thesis, University of Georgia, 1976), 14.

3. John McKay Sheftall, *Sunbury on the Medway: A Selective History of the Town, Inhabitants, and Fortifications* (Atlanta: Department of Natural Resources, Office of Planning and Research, 1977), iv.

4. Charles C. Jones Jr., *The Dead Towns of Georgia* (Savannah: Morning News Steam Printing House, 1878), 145.

5. Edward J. Cashin, "Royal Georgia, 1752–1776," *New Georgia Encyclopedia*, last modified September 20, 2020, https://www.georgiaencyclopedia.org/articles/history-archaeology/royal-georgia-1752-1776/.

6. Jones, *Dead Towns of Georgia*, 155.

7. Sheftall, *Sunbury on the Medway*, 12–13.

8. Jones, *Dead Towns of Georgia*, 170.

9. William Bartram, "Travels in Georgia and Florida, 1773–74: A Report to Dr. John Fothergill," *Transactions of the American Philosophical Society* 33, no. 2 (November 1943): 134–135.

10. Jones, *Dead Towns of Georgia*, 170–171.

11. Sheftall, *Sunbury on the Medway*, 21.

12. Jones, *Dead Towns of Georgia*, 175–176.

13. Sheftall, *Sunbury on the Medway*, 25–26.

14. Jones, *Dead Towns of Georgia*, 181–182.

15. Sheftall, *Sunbury on the Medway*, 28; "Fort Morris," Georgia Historical Society, accessed September 20, 2023, https://georgiahistory.com/marker-monday-fort-morris-2/.

16. Sheftall, *Sunbury on the Medway*, 36.

17. Sheftall, 37.

18. Sheftall, 38–39.

19. Jones, *Dead Towns of Georgia*, 196.

20. Sheftall, *Sunbury on the Medway*, 47.

21. Jones, *Dead Towns of Georgia*, 198.

22. Jones, 202.

23. Sheftall, *Sunbury on the Medway*, 56–57.

24. Jones, *Dead Towns of Georgia*, 214.

25. Sheftall, *Sunbury on the Medway*, 59.

26. Daniel T. Elliott, *Archaeological Investigations at Fort Morris State Historic Site, Liberty County, Georgia* (Ellerslie, Ga.: Southern Research, Historic Preservation Consultants, 2003), 41.

27. Gerald Judson Smith, "War of 1812 and Georgia," *New Georgia Encyclopedia*, last modified September 25, 2014, https://www.georgiaencyclopedia.org/articles/history-archaeology/war-of-1812-and-georgia/.

28. G. Judson Smith Jr., "'All's Not Well': The U.S. Navy Expedition to Sunbury in 1812," *Georgia Historical Quarterly* 81, no. 4 (Winter 1997): 968.

29. Smith, 973.

30. Sheftall, *Sunbury on the Medway*, 79–80.

31. Jones, *Dead Towns of Georgia*, 221.

32. Elliott, *Archaeological Investigations*, 42.

33. Jones, *Dead Towns of Georgia*, 221–223.

34. Elliott, *Archaeological Investigations*, 46.

35. Midgette, "Fort Morris at Sunbury," 3.

36. Midgette, 7.

37. Elliott, *Archaeological Investigations*, 121.

38. Mike Toner, "Fort under Fort Is Revolutionary Find for Historic Site," *Atlanta Constitution*, October 19, 2002, A1.

39. Elliott, *Archaeological Investigations*, 124.

40. Toner, "Fort under Fort," A12.

Further Reading

Cashin, Edward J. "Revolutionary War in Georgia." *New Georgia Encyclopedia*, last modified September 30, 2020. https://www.georgiaencyclopedia.org/articles/history-archaeology/revolutionary-war-in-georgia/.

Cashin, Edward J. "Royal Georgia, 1752–1776." *New Georgia Encyclopedia*, last modified September 30, 2020. https://www.georgiaencyclopedia.org/articles/history-archaeology/royal-georgia-1752-1776/.

Coleman, Kenneth. *The American Revolution in Georgia, 1763–1789*. Athens: University of Georgia Press, 1958.

Elliott, Daniel T. *Archaeological Investigations at Fort Morris State Historic Site, Liberty County, Georgia*. Ellerslie, Ga.: Southern Research, Historic Preservation Consultants, 2003. https://www.thelamarinstitute.org/index.php?option=com_content&view=article&id=48&Itemid=58.

Jones, Charles C., Jr. *The Dead Towns of Georgia*. Savannah: Morning News Steam Printing House, 1878. https://archive.org/details/deadtownsofgeorgoojonerich.

Jones, Charles C., Jr. *The History of Georgia*. Vol. 2, *Revolutionary Epoch*. Boston: Houghton, Mifflin, 1883. https://dlg.usg.edu/record/dlg_zlgb_gb0159b.

Sheftall, John McKay. *Sunbury on The Medway: A Selective History of the Town, Inhabitants, and Fortifications*. Atlanta: Department of Natural Resources, Office of Planning and Research, 1977.

Smith, Gerald Judson. "War of 1812 and Georgia." *New Georgia Encyclopedia*, last modified September 25, 2014. https://www.georgiaencyclopedia.org/articles/history-archaeology/war-of-1812-and-georgia/.

Walker, Winston E. "Liberty County." *New Georgia Encyclopedia*, last modified July 12, 2022. https://www.georgiaencyclopedia.org/articles/counties-cities-neighborhoods/liberty-county/.

CHAPTER 15

Fort King George

Jennifer W. Dickey

Basic Information

PERIOD OF SIGNIFICANCE: 1721–1727
DATE ESTABLISHED AS A HISTORIC SITE: 1967
ACREAGE: 25 acres
LOCATION: 302 McIntosh Road, Darien, Ga. 31305, McIntosh County

Established in 1721 by the British to protect the Altamaha River from the French, Fort King George was for a dozen years the southernmost outpost of British occupation in North America. The fort, listed in the National Register of Historic Places in 1971, is significant as the site of the "first effort to establish Britain's claim to 'the debatable land' and first step in a chain of events that brought the Southeast under the British flag."[1] The site of the fort had been previously occupied by Guale Indians and, briefly, by the Spanish. Fort King George was fully garrisoned for only six years, and during that time it developed a reputation as an unpleasant and deadly outpost. An estimated 140 soldiers died during those six years, mostly from disease.

Following the establishment of the Georgia colony in the 1730s, the town of Darien was developed adjacent to the fort site. In the nineteenth century, with the fort long gone, the site was redeveloped as a lumber mill. After the lumber industry died out in the area in the early twentieth century, the site lay abandoned until the location of the fort was rediscovered by historian Bessie Lewis in the 1930s.

Following archaeological excavations in the 1950s and acquisition by the Georgia Historical Commission in 1961, the state opened a museum at the

Historic marker and boardwalk at Fort King George.

site in 1970. The fort was reconstructed in the late 1980s. Since that time, the Fort King George State Historic Site has provided a rich interpretation of more than three centuries of occupation of this site, from the Guale Indians to the nineteenth-century sawmill operations, with the story of the brief but important existence of the fort itself as the centerpiece.

History of Fort King George

In the spring of 1720, the residents of Britain's South Carolina colony were uneasy. Having recently endured the Yamassee War, in which more than one hundred colonists were killed by Native tribes enraged by the imbalanced trading relationship imposed by European traders and the intrusion of white settlers, the colonists were now under threat from the French.[2] The French had conjured up a strategy of encirclement that would enable them to push out the British from North America. The leaders of the South Carolina colony expressed great concern that French "emissaries have been viewing the coast between this settlement [Charles Town] and St. Augustine." Already the French had seized control of the Mississippi River, and they were eyeing the Ocmulgee and Altamaha Rivers to access the Atlantic Ocean without having to navigate around Spanish-occupied Florida.[3]

Although Spain loomed large as a threat to the south, a buffer, known as "the debatable land," existed between South Carolina and Florida. This land, which had previously been occupied by Guale Indians and briefly by Spanish missionaries who tried to Christianize the Guale, would in 1733 become the Georgia colony.[4] But in 1720, this area along the coast was largely uninhabited, and the British colonists in South Carolina feared encirclement by the French more than they feared an attack by the Spanish.

The French threat motivated two of the colony's "most persuasive men," Joseph Boone, the English agent for South Carolina, and Colonel John Barnwell, to travel to London in March 1720 to appeal to the Board of Trade for permission and funding to build a series of forts along the Atlantic Coast to protect the waterways from a French incursion. Barnwell was "a highly respected, competent, and energetic Irishman who had settled in South Carolina in 1701 [and] 'passed thro' all the public offices except that of Governor.'"[5] He had settled with his wife and six children in the Port Royal area, where he had become a successful planter. In 1711 Barnwell led an expedition against an uprising of the Tuscarora Indians in North Carolina, earning him the nickname "Tuscarora Jack," and he commanded a "waterborne militia force that patrolled the inland passage between Charleston and St. Augustine" during the Yamassee War. Barnwell's patrols along the coast had familiarized him with the area, and he presented to the Board of Trade the "Barnwell Plan" of settlement, which included a series of forts surrounded by settlements developed through grants of free land.[6] The board agreed that something needed to be done to increase security along the coast and forwarded Barnwell's plan onward. However, the privy council granted permission and funds for the construction of only one fort, which was to be built at the mouth of the Altamaha River.[7]

Barnwell returned to Carolina with plans to construct a blockhouse and attendant structures necessary to house a garrison surrounded by a moat and a palisade. Well aware of the climate and the conditions in which the men under his command would have to work while building the fort, Barnwell requested one hundred "young robust men able to undergo fatigue, and if possible such men as have been abroad on former expeditions." What Barnwell got was one hundred "invalids and older veterans of European campaigns" in an "Independent Company of Foot" rather than the "pioneering stock" he had requested.[8] To make matters worse, by the time the two ships carrying the members of the Forty-First Independent Company arrived in Charles Town in May 1721, the commissioned officers who accompanied them reported that the majority of the soldiers were "dangerously ill of the Scurvy." Instead of embarking immediately for the mouth of the Altamaha River to build the fort, most of the company was hospitalized.

Barnwell determined that those soldiers who were not hospitalized were "too unskilled and unacclimated to construct a fort," so he appealed to the new governor, Francis Nicholson, that he take a team of provincial scouts from Port Royal to the mouth of the Altamaha to build and occupy the fort until such time that the invalid troops were able to report for duty. Nicholson approved the revised plan, and Barnwell embarked from Beaufort for the Altamaha delta on July 6, 1721, with a group of men, "all drunk as beasts," that consisted of twenty-six scouts, a sawyer, four enslaved men, and two Indians who were responsible for hunting.[9]

According to Barnwell, the scouts were "a wild Idle people & Continually Sotting if they can get any Rum. . . . Yet they are greatly useful for Such Expeditions as these if well & Tenderly managed." Even worse, Barnwell himself became ill along the way. He soon recovered, however, and on July 12 he located a "very high Bluff" that he determined would be the site of the fort. By July 15, Barnwell and his crew had unloaded their equipment and guns from the two ships on which they had sailed from Beaufort and had erected tents and built three huts at the site. Two days later, Barnwell reported that the men were "in a Mutiny about their work" once they realized that the nearest supply of cypress trees from which the fort was to be constructed was almost three miles away. Barnwell quickly devised a plan to get the men to work that involved offering to pay the men "15 shillings a piece" if they would go to the swamp and bring back the requisite logs from which to build the fort. Half the men took advantage of the offer for extra pay and by the end of the day had brought seven logs to the site.[10]

After he managed to get the scouts working to supply the lumber for the fort, Barnwell began a reconnaissance mission of the Altamaha delta to scout for additional sites that he felt were suitable for outposts. He identified the island of St. Simons as "the fittest place to built [*sic*] a large fort" to secure the passageway into the river.[11] A large fort and settlement would be built at St. Simons, but not until 1736, by which time "the debatable land" between South Carolina and Florida was part of the new British colony of Georgia.[12] In the meantime, work continued apace at the current site. By late September, the South Carolina governor and legislature had authorized additional compensation to Barnwell, who was serving as the engineer for the project in the absence of an engineer who failed to arrive from England, and had determined that the fort should be called Fort King George in honor of King George I.[13]

Construction of the fort was completed in October 1721. The centerpiece of the triangular-shaped fort was the blockhouse, a three-story, twenty-six-foot-square, timber-framed, gabled building covered with four-inch cypress planks from which the soldiers could defend themselves in case of attack. The ground floor was the magazine where ammunition was stored. The second floor was the gun floor where cannons were emplaced, and the top floor, which jutted out above the floors below, served as both a lookout post and defensive position from which guns could be fired. Both the second and third floors contained loopholes from which the soldiers could fire their muskets, and the third floor also included a lookout window near the top of the gable ends from which a sentry could see across the river and marsh.

The blockhouse was surrounded on the land side by a six-foot-high earthen parapet and a moat with palisades. The marsh side was reinforced with palisades, and the river side was reinforced with a parapet strengthened by bundles of sticks, or fascines. Sentry boxes on the corners provided additional lookout posts. Within the fortified exterior walls was a space of approximately two hundred by three hundred feet. An array of smaller buildings, including the original huts that had been constructed on the first day of Barnwell's and his crew's arrival, offered shelter, but the barracks, which were to be constructed in Beaufort and floated down the river to the fort, would not arrive until 1722. Eventually, the fort included a separate officers' barracks, a baking oven, and a blacksmith shop.[14]

By February 1722, the Spanish had grown concerned about what they considered to be "a flagrant intrusion into ancient Spanish territory." Spain sent an emissary, Don Francisco Menendez Márques, and almost thirty men to Charles Town to meet with Governor Nicholson and negotiate a treaty over the territory, but Nicholson refused to negotiate, claiming he had no authority to do so. Nicholson claimed that the settlement on the Altamaha was not a new territorial claim but merely an effort "for the better Securing of his Majesty's dominions." The Spanish eventually left empty-handed, but they would continue to protest the new fort, both directly to the British government and indirectly by inciting periodic attacks on the fort by their Indian allies, the Yamassee.[15]

Upon completion of initial construction, Barnwell left the fort and returned to his home at Port Royal, where he died following a short illness in 1724. Meanwhile, in February 1722, the Forty-First Independent

Blockhouse at Fort King George.

Company, a regiment in less-than-perfect health, arrived. Life at the fort would prove challenging for the Invalid Company, as it was known, with the men suffering from malnutrition and plagued by bouts of malaria. Periodic skirmishes with the Indians, largely incited by the Spanish, added to the peril. More than 50 percent of the troops would die at the site over the next several years, and the fort developed a reputation as an unpleasant place to be garrisoned.

More difficulties arose in the winter of 1725 when a fire destroyed much of the fort. Strapped for money, the South Carolina Assembly ordered the fort rebuilt, but the reconstruction was done using inferior materials. Discontent among the soldiers, already quite high, escalated further, and the British Board of Trade sent Captain Edward Massey to investigate. Massey reported that conditions at the fort were unacceptable and recommended that the soldiers be restationed at Port Royal. Although Massey's recommendation was poorly received in Charles Town, Governor Nicholson was forced to relocate the Independent Company to Port Royal following an Indian raid on the Altamaha River in which eight English traders were killed in 1727. Following the removal of the Independent Company soldiers, two lookouts were posted at Fort King George. They remained there until 1734, at which time the area had become part of the Georgia colony.[16]

The fort had never been properly reconstructed following the 1725 fire, and it was abandoned following the departure of the two lookouts in 1734. However, in 1736, James Oglethorpe recruited a group of Scottish Highlanders to come to Georgia to help defend the colony. The Scots were given fifty-acre land allotments near the ruins of the fort and developed a settlement that became known as Darien. The Darien Scots also built a fort to replace the abandoned Fort King George.[17] They participated in Oglethorpe's failed siege of St. Augustine in 1740 and in the more successful Battle of Bloody Marsh in 1742, in which Oglethorpe's troops thwarted an attempted invasion of St. Simons by the Spanish.[18]

By the late 1700s, Darien became an important port for the export of rice and cotton, and the settlement was incorporated as a town by the state legislature in 1816. Two years later Darien was designated as the county seat of McIntosh County. By that time, the site of Fort King George was beginning to be redeveloped by the Darien Eastern Sawmill Company, which was organized in 1817. For the next century, a series of sawmills operated at the site of the former fort. Originally a tidal-powered operation, by the mid-1820s a 120-foot-long sawmill building housed a steam-powered sawmill. Logs were floated down the Altamaha River and cut at the sawmill before being shipped farther afield from the port of Darien. During the latter part of the nineteenth century, Darien was the leading port for lumber exports on the southern Atlantic coast.[19] The sawmill operations continued until the 1920s, when the depletion of Georgia's interior forests led to the discontinuation of the business.[20]

The sawmill facilities had encroached on the site of Fort King George by the time history teacher Bessie Lewis arrived in Darien, and there were no above-ground remnants to indicate the fort's location. The fort, it seemed, was lost to history. However, Lewis, who had come to Georgia from Ohio, began researching the British Public Records held in the South Carolina Archives, and she soon identified what she thought was the site of the colonial fort. Excavations conducted by archaeologist Joseph Caldwell in

1940 uncovered the graves of fifteen British soldiers as well as evidence of a Spanish mission site. The Department of Natural Resources (DNR) Division of State Parks, Historic Sites and Monuments installed a marble marker, "To the Soldiers of Fort King George," near the grave sites. The marker recognized the site as "the first English settlement in the land which is now Georgia," noting that "more than 140 British soldiers lost their lives in this first planned effort to hold the old Southeast for English-speaking people."[21]

Further investigations by archaeologist Sheila Caldwell, funded by the Georgia Historical Commission in 1952, uncovered additional evidence of an important Spanish site as well as evidence of Native American settlement.[22] The Caldwells also discovered an additional sixty-five graves that appeared to be those of British soldiers, which seemed to confirm Bessie Lewis's assertion of the location of the fort.[23] Lewis led the organization of a local citizens group, the Fort King George Association, Inc., to spearhead plans to reconstruct the fort on its original site. By March 1953, work was underway on the outer fortifications including the fourteen-foot moat, the parapet, and the banquette. The work was supported by the McIntosh Board of County Commissioners.[24]

The Georgia Historical Commission acquired the site in 1961 and helped facilitate additional improvements. The Daughters of the American Revolution sponsored the installation of headstones on the fifteen graves adjacent to the DNR marker that was erected in 1940. Local citizens began a fundraising effort for a complete reconstruction of the fort while the executive secretary of the Georgia Historical Commission lobbied Governor Carl Sanders for funds to develop the site into a proper state historic site. By 1965, enough money had been raised to pay for the construction of a museum and a superintendent's residence. Additional archaeological excavations conducted in 1969 uncovered more evidence of Native American occupation dating back to the early Woodland Period, and the Native American story was incorporated into the museum, which opened in 1970.[25]

Reconstruction of the fort was put on hold until the 1980s, when the Lower Altamaha Historical Society raised over $50,000 for the project and partnered with the Parks and Historic Sites Division of the DNR to reconstruct the fort according to Barnwell's plans from 1721. The reconstructed twenty-six-foot-square blockhouse was completed in 1988 and opened to the public on October 23 of that year.[26] Over the next several decades, additional buildings and structures were reconstructed to complete the fort as it would have appeared prior to the fire of 1725.

The parade ground at Fort King George.

The reconstructed fort welcomes visitors to what was once the most remote southern outpost of the British Empire in North America. The life of Fort King George was short, but during the brief time that it was occupied, it served its purpose of keeping the French from encircling the British colonies on the Atlantic coast. It also gave the British a toehold in "the debatable land" between the British and Spanish colonies, securing for Britain what would become the Georgia colony.

Touring the Site

Fort King George is located on the outskirts of Darien overlooking the marshes that make up the Altamaha River Delta. The twenty-five-acre site includes the museum, where visitors can view a film (also available on the website at https://gastateparks.org/FortKingGeorge) and exhibits that cover the story of the site from the Guale Indian period through the sawmill era. The museum also contains a small gift shop.

The big draw is the reconstructed fort. Given the many layers of history on the site, the DNR elected to preserve remnants of the sawmill operations

Interior of the barracks at Fort King George.

Monument to the soldiers of Fort King George placed by the Department of Natural Resources.

and to reconstruct a wattle-and-daub Guale roundhouse. Both the Guale roundhouse and the sawmill ruins are located adjacent to the path that runs from the museum to the fort itself.

Within the palisade, visitors can go inside the reconstructed blockhouse, where they can peer out the lookout window on the top floor and look into the barracks and other buildings inside the fort. The fort, which was reconstructed according to the plans drawn by John Barnwell in 1722, is equipped as it would have been during its occupation with an artillery battery that includes nine cannon emplacements and a mortar facing the river.

A nature trail leads from the fort to a marsh overlook. Past the overlook is a reconstructed Highlander Cottage that is representative of the homes that were constructed by the Scottish Highlanders who in 1736 settled what would become the town of Darien. The trail passes by additional ruins from the sawmill operations as it winds its way back to the museum. Additional points of interest include the burial grounds of the British soldiers, located south of the museum, and the tabby ruins of what archaeologists believe was the Spanish mission Santo Domingo de Talaje.

Notes

1. William R. Mitchell Jr., "Fort King George," National Register of Historic Places Nomination Form (Washington, D.C.: U.S. Department of the Interior, National Park Service, 1971), section 8.

2. Michael P. Morris, "Yamassee War," *South Carolina Encyclopedia*, last modified August 22, 2022, https://www.scencyclopedia.org/sce/entries/yamassee-war/.

3. Norman Edwards, "The Old Southeast and Fort King George: Borderlands of Three Empires" (MA thesis, Georgia Southern College, 1980), 52.

4. "Santa Cataline de Guale Mission Site," National Park Service, accessed September 16, 2023, https://www.nps.gov/parkhistory/online_books/explorers/sitee8.htm.

5. Jeannine Cook, *Fort King George: Step One to Statehood* (Darien, Ga.: Darien News, 1990), 5.

6. Lawrence S. Rowland, "John Barnwell," *South Carolina Encyclopedia*, last modified July 15, 2022, https://www.scencyclopedia.org/sce/entries/barnwell-john/.

7. Cook, *Fort King George*, 8.

8. Cook, 15–17.

9. Edwards, "Old Southeast and Fort King George," 56.

10. Joseph Barnwell, "Fort King George: Journal of Col. John Barnwell (Tuscarora) in the Construction of the Fort on the Altamaha in 1721," *South Carolina Historical and Genealogical Magazine* 27, no. 4 (October 1926): 196–198.

11. Barnwell, "Fort King George," 202.

12. Patricia Barefoot, "Fort Frederica," *New Georgia Encyclopedia*, last modified March 10, 2016, https://www.georgiaencyclopedia.org/articles/history-archaeology/fort-frederica/.

13. Cook, *Fort King George*, 33.

14. Cook, 34–38.

15. Cook, 41–45.

16. Bessie Smith, "Fort King George," *Georgia Magazine*, October-November 1967, 24.

17. Buddy Sullivan, "Darien," *New Georgia Encyclopedia*, last modified June 23, 2022, https://www.georgiaencyclopedia.org/articles/counties-cities-neighborhoods/darien/.

18. Julie Anne Sweet, "Battle of Bloody Marsh," *New Georgia Encyclopedia*, last modified October 31, 2018, https://www.georgiaencyclopedia.org/articles/history-archaeology/battle-of-bloody-marsh/.

19. Sullivan, "Darien."

20. Cook, *Fort King George*, xvi.

21. "To the Soldiers of Fort King George," marble marker at the Fort King George State Historic Site, visited December 19, 2021.

22. Joseph Floyd, "Ghosts of Guale: Sugar Houses, Spanish Missions, and the Struggle for Georgia's Colonial Heritage," *Georgia Historical Quarterly* 97, no. 4 (Winter 2013): 408; Mitchell, "Fort King George."

23. Cook, *Fort King George*, xvii.

24. "Fort George Reproduction Work Starts," *Atlanta Constitution*, March 18, 1953, 14.

25. Fort King George—Kelso, William M.—Notes and Report on excavations, 1969, C 331393, rcb: 27612, c: 331393, Georgia Archives.

26. Cook, *Fort King George*, xx.

Further Reading

Barefoot, Patricia. "Fort Frederica." *New Georgia Encyclopedia*, last modified March 10, 2016. https://www.georgiaencyclopedia.org/articles/history-archaeology/fort-frederica/.

Cook, Jeannine. *Fort King George: Step One to Statehood*. Darien, Ga.: *Darien News*, 1990.

Legare, John Girardeau. *The Darien Journal of John Girardeau Legare, Ricegrower*. Edited by Buddy Sullivan. Athens: University of Georgia Press, 2010.

Lewis, Bessie Mary. *A Low Country Diary: Bessie Mary Lewis & McIntosh County, Georgia*. Edited by Buddy Sullivan. Scotts Valley, Calif.: CreateSpace, 2016.

Parker, A. W. *Scottish Highlanders in Colonial Georgia: The Recruitment, Emigration and Settlement of Darien, 1735–1748*. Athens: University of Georgia Press, 1997.

Purcell, Kim. "Fort King George." *New Georgia Encyclopedia*, last modified September 5, 2018. https://www.georgiaencyclopedia.org/articles/history-archaeology/fort-king-george/.

Sullivan, Buddy. "Darien." *New Georgia Encyclopedia*, last modified June 23, 2022. https://www.georgiaencyclopedia.org/articles/counties-cities-neighborhoods/darien/.

Sweet, Julie. "Battle of Bloody Marsh." *New Georgia Encyclopedia*, last modified October 31, 2018. https://www.georgiaencyclopedia.org/articles/history-archaeology/battle-of-bloody-marsh/.

CHAPTER 16

Hofwyl-Broadfield Plantation

Jennifer W. Dickey

Basic Information

PERIOD OF SIGNIFICANCE: 1806–1942
DATE ESTABLISHED AS A HISTORIC SITE: 1974
ACREAGE: 1,268 acres
LOCATION: 5556 U.S. Highway 17 N, Brunswick, Ga. 31525, Glynn County

Hofwyl-Broadfield Plantation, situated on a 1,268-acre landscape covered with live oak trees draped in Spanish moss, provides visitors a glimpse into a version of the rice plantation culture that dominated Georgia's tidewater region from the mid-eighteenth century until the late nineteenth century. The property includes numerous buildings and marshlands that were once part of one of the region's premier rice plantations. From the 1750s until the Civil War, Georgia was the second-largest producer of rice, after South Carolina, in the United States.[1] Commercial rice production in the tidewater region of Georgia enabled a high standard of living for the plantation owners while it proved dangerous and exploitative for the enslaved workforce that carried out the labor in the fields. The site was listed on the National Register of Historic Places in 1976 and is significant for "having been a center for the cultivation of rice in the coastal Georgia rice society of the late eighteenth and nineteenth centuries."[2]

Developed as a rice plantation in the early 1800s, Hofwyl-Broadfield was gifted to the state by Ophelia Dent in 1973 following five generations of ownership by the Brailsford/Troup/Dent family. Dent, the last resident, specified in her will that the property would go to the State Historical

Live oak drive between visitor center and main house at Hofwyl-Broadfield Plantation.

Commission.[3] The State Parks and Historic Sites Division has owned and managed the former rice plantation/dairy farm as a state historic site since 1974. Located on the Altamaha River, Hofwyl-Broadfield is the only former rice plantation along Georgia's coast that has been preserved and interpreted as such.

History of Hofwyl-Broadfield Plantation

While early efforts to grow rice in Georgia were modest at best, the elimination of the prohibition against slavery and changes in limitations on property ownership in the 1750s opened Georgia to large-scale plantation agriculture, and the lands along the tidal rivers proved ideal for growing rice. As historian Julia Floyd Smith noted, the "tidewater experiment in rice planting along the Georgia coast proved to be a productive and profitable enterprise." These plantations, Smith explained, were "unique among the plantations of the Old South—they were limited geographically to suitable areas of swamp land along the Atlantic Coast where fresh river water tides were available for irrigating crops."[4]

Development of what became known as the Hofwyl-Broadfield Plantation began in 1806 when William Brailsford, a planter from Charleston, South Carolina, acquired an uncleared tract of land called Broadface along the Altamaha River. Brailsford, who had married into the "rice-planting dynasty" Heyward family of Charleston, had purchased nearby Broughton Island in 1803 with the intention of operating an existing rice plantation on the island. However, a hurricane in fall 1804, which killed more than seventy enslaved people, destroyed the Broughton Island plantation.[5] According to Brailsford's granddaughter, Ophelia Troup Dent, the debt incurred by Brailsford associated with the Broughton Island plantation was carried by Brailsford's estate for almost fifty years.[6]

Brailsford abandoned the Broughton Island plantation and acquired Broadface, a wooded, unimproved tract across the river, which he renamed Broadfield.[7] Following Brailsford's death in 1810, his wife, Maria, and their daughter, Camilla, inherited the heavily indebted plantation. Maria struggled to pay the debts and relied heavily upon the council of her half brother, William Heyward. Following Heyward's advice, Maria continued growing rice on the marshes and began cultivating cotton on the high ground at Broadfield. Following the Embargo of 1807 and the ensuing War of 1812, shipping commodities was a risky business, but "both rice and cotton commanded high prices" for anyone willing to take the risk.[8]

The family spent the winter months at Broadfield and summer months on Cumberland Island to escape the heat and disease associated with summers on the coastal rice plantations.[9] Camilla was "more than a right hand to her mother," according to Dent, who cited her "high courage and fine judgement" as well as her "devotion" to the enslaved people at Broadfield that fostered "loyalty and contentedness."[10] Whether or not the enslaved people on Broadfield were contented, they were certainly numerous. By the 1850s, more than three hundred enslaved people lived and worked on the plantation. Those workers lived there year-round, while the white property owners moved to safer environs away from the malarial swamps of the rice fields in the spring and returned after the first frost.[11]

Upon Camilla's marriage to Dr. James M. Troup in 1814, Troup assumed management of the plantation. A medical doctor by training, James Troup was the youngest brother of George Troup, who served two terms as governor of Georgia (1823–1827).[12] James trained in the study of medicine under Dr. Benjamin Rush in Philadelphia. Following his graduation from the University of Pennsylvania in 1812, he established a medical practice in Darien.[13] During the final stages of the War of 1812, as the British invaded the sea islands along Georgia's coast, Troup sent the family inland to stay with a friend, and he sent the enslaved people to his brother's plantation in Montgomery County. The main house at Broadfield was vandalized during this time.[14]

Troup expanded the family holdings, acquiring an adjacent property known as New Hope. He also acquired land on Sapelo Creek, where he planted cotton and corn and kept cattle. The 1830 census indicated that James Troup had his primary residence in Darien, five miles from the Broadfield plantation, and that he claimed 66 enslaved people, 34 males and 32 females.[15] Troup hired out many of his workers to assist with construction on the Brunswick Canal, which began in 1837 near the Broadfield property. Over the next three years, Troup received $10,000 a year for his hired-out workers, a sum that he claimed "saved him, for the three canal years were not good rice years." Camilla died in 1847, and James died in 1849. At the time of James's death, his "property" included more than 7,300 acres and 357 enslaved people, each listed by name alongside his or her dollar value. The estate was also encumbered with almost $80,000 (over $3 million in 2023) in debt. The distribution of the estate among his three children who remained in the area was delayed for more than six years while his debts were settled.[16]

James and Camilla's daughter, Ophelia, married George Dent in 1847. The couple inherited part of her father's estate and moved in 1856 to a section of the Broadfield plantation that the couple called Hofwyl after the school in Switzerland where George was educated. According to family legend, the main house on the Broadfield plantation burned in the late 1850s, so when George and Ophelia and their three sons relocated from a site near Darien to the plantation, they moved into a two-story, wood-framed house nearer the rice fields. Although some accounts state that the house was constructed around 1851, other versions indicate that George and Ophelia built the house in the mid-1850s upon inheriting the land.

The two-story house that overlooked the rice fields would serve as the primary residence on the property for the family and their descendants until 1973.[17]

During the Civil War, George served as a captain in the Confederate Army, and their oldest son, James Troup Dent, born in 1848, served as a color bearer and signal corpsman.[18] Ophelia and her three younger children moved inland to Ware County near Waycross, taking most of the enslaved workers with them, for the duration of the war.[19] They returned to the coast in 1865 to find the plantation in a state of ruin.[20] Ophelia's cousin, Georgia Conrad, later wrote that prior to returning to the plantation, Ophelia called the now emancipated workers together and told them that they were free to leave. They began to leave the inland settlement, "in twos and threes, carrying with them their belongings tied in immense bundles," according to Conrad, who added, "When the rice planters returned to the coast, they found that the Negroes had simply preceded them. There they were, settled down in their own quarters again."[21]

Although many of the formerly enslaved people did return to the plantation, the labor dynamics had changed. The rice industry along the coast of Georgia declined precipitously in the second half of the nineteenth century. The devastation wrought by war, the loss of a "captive" labor force, and the development of mechanized rice production techniques in the Old Southwest states of Arkansas, Louisiana, and Texas made rice production along the coast of Georgia and South Carolina unprofitable.[22] Commercial rice production in the tidewater region of Georgia, which had been the region's most important agricultural commodity since the mid-eighteenth century, peaked in 1859 at more than 51 million pounds. By 1879, Georgia's rice production was less than half what it had been twenty years earlier. By 1899, the state produced less than 9 million pounds of rice, and by 1919, Georgia, which had once been second only to South Carolina as a center of rice production, accounted for only 0.2 percent of the rice produced in the United States.[23]

George and Ophelia's son, James, inherited Hofwyl following his father's death in 1884. Although he continued operating Broadfield as a rice plantation throughout the end of the nineteenth century and into the twentieth century, he also began diversifying his farming operations by planting cotton and acquiring dairy cattle.[24]

The salvation of the plantation came with James's marriage in 1880 to Miriam Gratz Cohen, the daughter of Solomon Cohen Jr., a wealthy Savannah lawyer. Cohen was also a real estate developer, banker, and Georgia's first Jewish state senator. Miriam's wealth allowed the family to keep a house in Savannah and to pay off much of the debt accumulated in the postwar years. Following James's death in 1913, Miriam and James's children assumed responsibility for the property. Son Gratz, who lived in Savannah, decided to cease rice production by 1915 and convert the property to a dairy farm, which his sisters Miriam and Ophelia would operate. The two sisters, neither of whom ever married, eschewed the social life of Savannah in favor of staying on the farm at Hofwyl. They operated the Hofwyl Dairy until 1942, with Miriam taking care of the business side of the operation and Ophelia making deliveries.

The Dent sisters had attended Rosemary Hall, a private girls' school in Connecticut, and there they became friends with the Maurice sisters, whose father was one of the charter members of the Jekyll Island Club. The connection to the Maurice family begun in Connecticut continued in Georgia as the sisters, especially Ophelia, were frequent visitors at the Maurice family's home, Hollybourne Cottage, during their winter stays on Jekyll Island. Ophelia was maid-of-honor in Emily Maurice's wedding at Jekyll's Faith Chapel in 1911. The connections that the Dent sisters made at Rosemary Hall provided them access to a social scene to which they would otherwise not have been entitled.[25] Although they were descendants of a once-prosperous family, by the twentieth century the Dents' fortune was meager compared to that of the millionaires who frequented the Georgia Sea Islands during the winter.

Among Ophelia's closest friends was Alice Belin DuPont, wife of Pierre DuPont. This connection proved advantageous for Miriam and Ophelia as Pierre, who owned property near Hofwyl-Broadfield, served as a financial adviser to the sisters. They and their brother Gratz had divested themselves of several family properties—land adjacent to the Hofwyl Dairy as well as family properties in Savannah—to pay off the debt accumulated from the rice plantation in the later nineteenth and early twentieth centuries. With the money left over from their property sales, the sisters developed an investment portfolio, following advice from Pierre DuPont, that would support them for the rest of their lives. While the sisters' dairy operation proved profitable, their investments were what enabled them to continue living at Hofwyl.[26] By 1969, Ophelia had an investment portfolio worth over $700,000 (approximately $5.8 million in 2023), which allowed her to leave the property to the state upon her death and provide an endowment for its preservation.[27]

The Dent sisters closed the Hofwyl Dairy in 1942 but continued to live in the main house on the property. Ophelia survived her sister by twenty years, during which time she lived alone in the house. She did have the support of several workers who helped her maintain the property. The most long-lasting of these was Rudolph Capers, whose grandmother, Fibby, had purportedly worked on the plantation as the cook for fifty years, as both an enslaved and emancipated worker.[28] Capers began working for the Dent sisters in 1933 at age thirty. He cooked and took care of the house and its inhabitants. It was Capers who found Ophelia on the morning of September 5, 1973, after she passed away in her home. In her will, Ophelia Dent left the Hofwyl property, along with an endowment for its upkeep, to the Georgia Historical Commission for "scientific, historical, educational and aesthetic purposes."[29] She also left a stipend for Capers, who would serve for many years as the on-site historian and guide at Hofwyl after the site opened to the public in 1979.[30]

Six months prior to Ophelia Dent's death, Governor Jimmy Carter's reorganization of state government, which transferred the functions of the Georgia Historical Commission to the Department of Natural Resources, temporarily delayed the transfer of Hofwyl-Broadfield to state ownership.[31] The Nature Conservancy stepped in as an intermediary to accept the gift, and less than a year later the conservancy sold the land to the state for the price of one dollar.[32] Since that time, Hofwyl-Broadfield has been under the auspices of the State Parks and Historic Sites Division of the Department of Natural Resources. The state formally accepted the plantation under Georgia's Heritage Trust in the summer of 1974.[33] The property was appraised at approximately $350,000.[34]

The state embarked on a preservation program to prepare the site for visitors, an effort that would take five years. Among the improvements were repairs to the main house and outbuildings and construction of a visitor center. While renovation work to the main house was underway, some of the antique china and crystal that had belonged to the family and had been placed in storage at the nearby Fort King George Historic Site was stolen.[35] Nevertheless, the bulk of the furnishings and family possessions remained safe and have been preserved at the site. The house, outbuildings, and landscape today appear much as they did during Ophelia Dent's final years.

Touring the Site

Visitors enter the site through a gate on the east side of Georgia Highway 17. A winding driveway through the moss-draped live oaks leads to the parking lot in front of the visitor center, which was constructed in the late 1970s. Near the entrance to the visitor center, visitors encounter two interpretive tools that are used throughout the site—an outdoor panel and a solar-powered audio speaker.

Inside the visitor center are a gift shop, well stocked with postcards, books, and souvenirs, a theater, where visitors may watch a seventeen-minute introductory film entitled *The People of Hofwyl-Broadfield* (also available on the website at https://gastateparks.org/HofwylBroadfield Plantation), and an exhibition.

While the museum provides visitors with baseline information about the people and the place, the main attraction at Hofwyl-Broadfield is the collection of buildings that look out over the former rice fields. The centerpiece is the relatively modest two-story 1850s house, which is surrounded by a collection of outbuildings and structures including a silo foundation, pay shed (where workers received their compensation), bottling house, dairy barn, commissary, servant quarters, garage, icehouse, and laundry yard. The once-detached kitchen was connected to the house during the dairy farm years. All of the outbuildings and structures are open to the public for self-guided exploration. Signs in front of each building or structure explain the historic use and, in some cases, how the building evolved over time.

In front of the servant quarters, half of which was converted to a public restroom facility, is an audio speaker with recordings related to "Slavery & Freedom on a Low Country Rice Plantation." Among the two-minute audio clips is an explanation of the Gullah-Geechee dialect, which is presented through a reading of a widely familiar text, the Lord's Prayer, in both English and Gullah-Geechee. Other audio clips provide information about some of the enslaved workers on the plantation whose names are known and the reality of enslaved life on a low-country rice plantation.

Main house at Hofwyl-Broadfield Plantation.

Along the live-oak allée from the visitor center is an outdoor text panel entitled "Enslavement, Resistance, Creativity, and Resilience: Africans and African Americans in Georgia's Low Country." Added to the site within the last few years, the panel provides more detail about the resident labor force on the plantation during the antebellum period. The panel, which features information bubbles for different topics, includes a section titled "Emancipation & the Aftermath" that links to an array of photographs of former enslaved workers and their descendants across the bottom of the panel. Two other recent additions include a panel adjacent to the icehouse and garage and a panel not far from the garage entitled "The Legacy of the Land and the Stewards of Hofwyl-Broadfield." The former traces the evolution of the laundry room from its origins in

The garage and Ophelia Dent's last car at Hofwyl-Broadfield Plantation.

the nineteenth century as a smokehouse to its twentieth-century use as an icehouse and laundry room and describes the construction in 1930 of the attached garage. Ophelia Dent's last car, a 1970 Oldsmobile Cutlass, is parked in the garage.

While tours of the outbuildings and landscape are self-guided, the tour of the main house, which occurs at set times throughout the day, is led by a docent. Visitors assemble on the front porch overlooking the former rice fields, where the tour begins with an explanation of the importance of the marsh for the cultivation of rice. The guided tour concludes on the back porch, where guests are invited to roam freely among the outbuildings and along the nature trail, which winds through the woods along the edge of the marsh to the ruins of the rice mill. A raised path out into the marsh provides access to a wooden platform that allows visitors to look out over the marsh at what were once the rice fields of Hofwyl-Broadfield. The expanse of the marsh is breathtaking, as is the sense of danger, exacerbated by the signs warning visitors, "Be aware, alligators present."

That so much of this former plantation remains intact is a testament to the foresight of Ophelia Trent Dent, who once declared, "I have no other wish but that Hofwyl does not fall into speculators hands and become a trailer camp or a subdivision or worse. It has been beloved by my family over the years. . . . I have been lucky enough to live here happily and keep

Dairy barn and bottling house at Hofwyl-Broadfield Plantation.

The former rice fields of Hofwyl-Broadfield Plantation.

it up to the best of my ability, but always with lurking worry about what would eventually become of it."[36] Dent's gift to the state, along with the endowment that is managed by the Friends of Hofwyl-Broadfield, a nonprofit organization that operates as a chapter of Friends of Georgia State Parks and Historic Sites, has made possible the preservation and interpretation of Hofwyl-Broadfield Plantation, the only site in Georgia where visitors can see the remnants of the rice culture that created a coastal aristocracy while perpetuating a system of forced labor.

Notes

1. Julia Floyd Smith, *Slavery and Rice Culture in Low Country Georgia, 1750–1860* (Knoxville: University of Tennessee Press, 1985), 213–215; Peter A. Coclanis, "Distant Thunder: The Creation of a World Market in Rice and the Transformations It Wrought," *American Historical Review* 98, no. 4 (October 1993): 1056.

2. Victoria Reeves Gunn, "Hofwyl-Broadfield Plantation," National Register of Historic Places Nomination Form (Washington, D.C.: U.S. Department of the Interior, National Park Service, 1976), section 8.

3. Jean Cleveland, "Hofwyl-Broadfield Plantation," *New Georgia Encyclopedia*, last modified September 15, 2014, https://www.georgiaencyclopedia.org/articles/history-archaeology/hofwyl-broadfield-plantation/.

4. Smith, *Slavery and Rice Culture*, 207.

5. Gunn, "Hofwyl-Broadfield Plantation."

6. Ophelia Troup Dent, *Memoirs*, 1902, *Dent family (Glynn County) Hofwyl Plantation Records, 1807–1973*, microfilm, Georgia State Archives, reel 215/21.

7. Dent..

8. Dent.

9. Dent.

10. Dent.

11. Georgia Department of Natural Resources, "Hofwyl-Broadfield Plantation," brochure, 1982.

12. Natalie D. Saba, "George Troup," *New Georgia Encyclopedia*, last modified September 11, 2014, https://www.georgiaencyclopedia.org/articles/government-politics/george-troup-1780-1856/.

13. Dent, *Memoirs*.

14. Dent.

15. 1830 U.S. Census, Darien, McIntosh County, Georgia, "James Troup," *Ancestry.com*.

16. Dent, *Memoirs*.

17. Gunn, "Hofwyl-Broadfield Plantation."

18. Larry Hobbs, "Dent Family Reunion Presents Contrasts in Black and White," *Brunswick (Ga.) News*, October 11, 2019, https://thebrunswicknews.com/news/local

_news/dent-family-reunion-presents-contrasts-in-black-and-white/article_a8ce5549-4f7a-51cb-996d-11164493567b.html.

19. Victoria Reeves Gunn, "Hofwyl Plantation" (unpublished manuscript, Hofwyl-Broadfield Plantation State Historic Site, 1975), 75.

20. Dent, *Memoirs.*

21. Gunn, "Hofwyl Plantation," 75.

22. Peter A. Coclanis, "Rice," *New Georgia Encyclopedia*, last modified September 29, 2020, https://www.georgiaencyclopedia.org/articles/business-economy/rice/.

23. Coclanis.

24. "Cotton Pickers Wanted," *Brunswick (Ga.) News*, October 18, 1910, 4; "For Sale or Exchange for Jersey Cows," *Brunswick (Ga.) News*, November 15, 1912, 4.

25. Mason Stewart, "The Hofwyl Connection & the Jekyll Island Club," lecture at the Jekyll Island Museum, September 23, 2022.

26. Bill Giles, interview by Jennifer Dickey, September 23, 2022, in Brunswick, Georgia, digital recording in possession of the author.

27. Dent Family, Assets of Miss Ophelia T. Dent as of October 31, 1969, Hofwyl Plantation Papers, Hofwyl-Broadfield State Historic Site, Brunswick, Georgia.

28. Amy Hedrick, "I Am Hofwyl: Persons Enslaved by the Troup Family of Hofwyl-Broadfield Plantation," notes from public program held February 9, 2020, at Hofwyl-Broadfield Plantation, accessed October 6, 2022, http://www.glynngen.com/enslavement/IAmHofwyl.html.

29. Cleveland, "Hofwyl-Broadfield Plantation."

30. Brandon D. Cross, "The Legacy of the Land and the Stewards of Hofwyl-Broadfield," Historical Marker Database, accessed October 6, 2022, https://www.hmdb.org/m.asp?m=191394.

31. Jann Haynes Gillmore, "Georgia's Historic Preservation Beginning: The Georgia Historical Commission (1951–1973)," *Georgia Historical Quarterly* 63, no. 1 (1979), 19–20.

32. Bill Giles interview.

33. "Preserving the Past," *Atlanta Constitution*, February 2, 1975, 69.

34. "Recreation Site," *Macon Telegraph*, July 7, 1974, 21.

35. Bob Harrell, "Family Camping," *Atlanta Constitution*, February 12, 1978, 93; "GBI Probing the Loss of Historic Antiques," *Atlanta Constitution*, August 11, 1979, 29.

36. Outdoor text panel, "The Legacy of the Land and the Stewards of Hofwyl-Broadfield," Hofwyl-Broadfield Plantation State Historic Site, Brunswick, Georgia.

Further Reading

Cleveland, Jean. "Hofwyl-Broadfield Plantation." *New Georgia Encyclopedia*, last modified September 15, 2014. https://www.georgiaencyclopedia.org/articles/history-archaeology/hofwyl-broadfield-plantation/.

Coclanis, Peter. "Rice." *New Georgia Encyclopedia*, last modified September 29, 2020. https://www.georgiaencyclopedia.org/articles/business-economy/rice/.

Georgia Humanities Council. *The New Georgia Guide*. Athens: University of Georgia Press, 1996.

Georgia State Parks & Historic Sites Division. "History of the Georgia State Parks and Historic Sites Division." Accessed September 2, 2022. https://gastateparks.org/sites/default/files/parks/pdf/HistoryOfGSPHSD.pdf.

Georgia State Parks & Historic Sites Division. "Hofwyl-Broadfield Plantation." Accessed September 2, 2022. https://gastateparks.org/HofwylBroadfieldPlantation.

Gunn, Victoria Reeves. "Hofwyl Plantation," unpublished manuscript, Hofwyl-Broadfield Plantation State Historic Site, July 1975.

Leavy, Sudy Vance. *Hofwyl-Broadfield Plantation*. Charleston, S.C.: Arcadia, 2008.

Smith, Julia Floyd. *Slavery and Rice Culture in Low Country Georgia, 1750–1860*. Knoxville: University of Tennessee Press, 1985.

Stewart, Mart. *"What Nature Suffers to Groe": Life, Labor, and Landscape on the Georgia Coast, 1680–1920*. Athens: University of Georgia Press, 2002.

Conclusion

Since the creation of the Georgia Historical Commission in 1951, the state's support for a comprehensive system of state-owned and operated historic sites has ebbed and flowed. The first decade of the commission's existence marked a time of great enthusiasm for the development of heritage tourism sites across the state. Fueled by the prosperity of the post–World War II period and the approaching Civil War centennial, the Historical Commission was active in acquiring and developing sites that they expected would draw tourists to the state. Ironically, although Fort McAllister was donated to the state in the 1950s, the development of the Civil War–related sites within the system happened largely in the post–Civil War centennial period (1968–1974). The commission had focused most of its Civil War centennial commemorative efforts on installing historical markers to document the war on Georgia's landscape. By 1959, the commission had erected 739 markers related to the Civil War.[1]

The second major phase of development for the system came in the early 1970s with the creation of the Heritage Trust Program by Governor Jimmy Carter. While the program was short-lived, the influx of cash in 1974 led to the acquisition of several key sites that have broadened the system's coverage of the state's history. Whether the state will maintain the status quo or will try to fill in the gaps in the system going forward by adding a site or sites that tell a more inclusive story remains to be seen. Given recent budget cuts and the ongoing underfunding of the system, an expansion seems unlikely.

From the opening of the Chief Vann House in 1958 to the present, the interpretation of Georgia's history at many of the sites in the state system has evolved and expanded. The Vann House is an excellent example of this change, with the addition of the slavery exhibit and the Moravian Mission site. Notably, the slavery exhibit came about not as part of a system-wide effort to offer a more inclusive history but as the result of the individual effort by a park ranger who was inspired and motivated by the work of historians who made new discoveries about the site's history. New interpretive markers at Hofwyl-Broadfield Plantation and A. H. Stephens Liberty Hall provide information about the enslaved people who once lived at those sites. The Civil War museum and house tour at Liberty Hall, however, seem mired in the 1950s.

External forces have also forced changes at the sites, most notably the prehistoric Native American sites. Etowah Indian Mounds and Kolomoki Mounds have both made significant changes to their museums as the

Slavery exhibit in the reconstructed kitchen at the Chief Vann House.

New interpretive marker at A.H. Stephens Liberty Hall.

New interpretive marker at Hofwyl-Broadfield Plantation.

result of updates to the federal Native American Graves Protection and Repatriation Act. The human remains and funerary objects are being returned to the tribes that are the descendants of the people who built and occupied these sites. Even without these artifacts on display, the mound sites remain compelling because of the mounds themselves and the surrounding landscapes.

Some common denominators can be found among all the current sites in the system. They are underfunded and understaffed. Some of this is the residual of the Great Recession that forced cutbacks in the state's budget beginning in 2008. Opening hours and staffing were reduced across the system, and some of the sites have yet to regain their full funding and staffing.[2] Ironically, cutbacks in hours during the Great Recession led to a spike in visitation because of the publicity surrounding the reduced hours. Among the sites that saw an increase in visitors were Fort King George in Darien, which saw a 40 percent increase, and Hofwyl-Broadfield in Brunswick, which boasted an increase in visitation of 50 percent on the days that it was open.[3] Many of the sites drew on volunteers during the cutbacks to supplement their labor force, a practice that continues today.

Friends of Georgia State Parks and Historic Sites, a nonprofit organization created in 1993 to "partner with, promote and preserve Georgia State Parks and Historic Sites," has played an important role in supplementing funding and staffing for the parks. The organization has more than fifty chapters that help maintain and promote their local sites.[4]

In 2017, the Department of Natural Resources reported that the Georgia State Parks and Historic Sites Division (GSPHSD), with more than 10 million visitors, contributed more than $1 billion to the state's economy. Although the DNR offered no breakdown between parks and historic sites, taken as a whole, the system seems to make a significant contribution to the state's economy. Equally as important, the historic sites provide a glimpse into the past that might otherwise be lost were it not for the intervention of the state to preserve and interpret these resources. GSPHSD's mission is "to protect our state's natural beauty and historic integrity while providing opportunities for public enjoyment and education." The division recognizes that "stewardship of our state's natural, cultural, and historical resources is fundamental to the understanding of our past and the well-being of our future."[5]

Notes

1. Jennifer Dickey, "Cameos of History on the Landscape: The Changes and Challenges of Georgia's Historical Marker Program," *Public Historian* 42 (May 2020): 38.

2. Terry Dickson, "Historic Sites Losing Days to Budget Cuts," *Florida Times Union*, June 21, 2009, B1; Bill Giles, interview by Jennifer Dickey, September 23, 2022, in Brunswick, Georgia, digital recording in possession of the author.

3. Mike Morrison, "Historic Sites Reduce Hours," *Florida Times Union*, November 8, 2009, B1.

4. "Friends of Georgia State Parks & Historic Sites," Georgia State Parks & Historic Sites website, accessed January 20, 2023, https://gastateparks.org/FriendsOf.

5. "About Our Division," Georgia Department of Natural Resources website, accessed January 20, 2023, https://gastateparks.org/AboutParks.

Appendix

Thematic List of State Historic Sites

Below are the state historic sites that are owned and operated by the state listed by category as determined by the Georgia State Parks and Historic Sites Division. More information can be found at gastateparks.org/History.

Unique Homes	Hardman Farm Little White House Traveler's Rest
Plantations	Hofwyl-Broadfield Plantation Jarrell Plantation
Native Americans	Chief Vann House Etowah Indian Mounds Kolomoki Mounds New Echota
Civil War	A. H. Stephens Liberty Hall Fort McAllister Pickett's Mill Battlefield
Coastal Forts & Colonial Georgia	Fort King George Fort Morris State Wormsloe
Gold Rush	Dahlonega Gold Museum

Index

Page numbers in *italics* refer to photographs and illustrations, while page numbers in **bold** refer to maps.